Introduction

Collins Scrabble Hints and Tips is aimed at casual Scrabble enthusiasts or those who like to Scrabble dabble. It deals with each letter of the alphabet in turn, covering brief advantages and disadvantages of each letter, followed by a selection of useful and manageable wordlists of words beginning with that letter.

For the most part the wordlists are not intended to be thorough and complete because that would make them too unwieldy and cluttered with words which may not actually be that useful for Scrabble. They are designed to serve as an introduction to useful words that you might be unfamiliar with and to inspire you to increase your Scrabble vocabulary. For example, the three-letter words lists exclude very common words and those that cannot be formed from two-letter words (unless they are worth 8 points face-value or more). Any words that might be deemed offensive are also excluded. Having said that, because of their importance in the game, the lists of two-letter words are complete, as too are the lists showing how those two-letter words can be extended into three-letter words. There is also a complete dictionary of all the three-letter words and definitions at the end of the book for added interest.

THE BASICS

What is Scrabble?

Scrabble is a game for two to four players or, occasionally, teams. Each player draws seven tiles at the start of the game and takes it in turns to form words on the board. After the first word is played, every word formed must touch or intersect a word already on the board, incorporating the tile at the crossover point in the new word. When letters have been played, they are replaced at each turn by drawing tiles from a bag to make up a full rack of seven. High scores may be achieved by using the rarer, high-value letters, by forming words on premium squares on the board, and by playing all seven letters at once to achieve a 50-point bonus.

The Scrabble set

The full list of letters and their values in the Scrabble C set is as follows:

Letter (Vowel)	Number in set	Value
A	9	1
E	12	1
I	9	1
O	8	1
U	4	1
BLANK	2	0

Letter (Consonant)	Number in set	Value
B	2	3
C	2	3
D	4	2
F	2	4
G	3	2
H	2	4
J	1	8
K	1	5
L	4	1
M	2	3
N	6	1
P	2	3
Q	1	10
R	6	1

Collins

SCRABBLE™
BRAND Crossword Game

HINTS & TIPS

HarperCollins Publishers
Westerhill Road
Bishopbriggs
Glasgow
G64 2QT

This edition 2013

Reprint 10 9 8 7 6 5 4 3 2 1 0

ISBN 978-0-00-793589-5

www.collinslanguage.com

A catalogue record for this book is
available from the British Library

Typeset by Davidson Publishing
Solutions, Glasgow

Printed in Great Britain by Clays Ltd,
St Ives plc

The publishers would like to thank
Allan Simmons, for providing the
basic concept for this book.

CONTRIBUTORS
Barry Grossman
Allan Simmons

FOR THE PUBLISHER
Gerry Breslin
Lucy Cooper
Kerry Ferguson
Elaine Higgleton

S	4	1
T	6	1
V	2	4
W	2	4
X	1	8
Y	2	4
Z	1	10

Origins

Scrabble was invented by an American: Alfred Butts. It was originally called Lexico when it was invented in the 1930s but became successful in its current form in the 1960s.

Gameplay tips

Use a dictionary when you play to check which words are eligible when challenged and to avoid any arguments. We suggest *Collins Scrabble Dictionary*, where you will find the meanings for all the words used in this book.

Shuffle the tiles on your rack: rearrange them, jiggle them around, and place them in alphabetical order. Also try to form prefixes or suffixes, verb inflections (-ED, -ING, etc) as this can help to form words in your mind.

Play longer words early on in a game if you can to get the board open to reach those elusive triple word squares. The more places there are to make plays the more you can make wise choices and avoid getting a clogged up board and be forced just to play one or two letters at a time.

The challenge rule: you may challenge a word your opponent plays. If your challenge is successful, i.e. the disputed word is not in the Official Scrabble Dictionary, or the dictionary you are using, your opponent takes back his or her tiles and loses their turn.

Note on diagrams: Diagrams in this section depicting word plays, for aesthetics, don't necessarily show words covering the centre square. In actual games the first move must cover the centre square.

Forming words

Scrabble words can be formed in several ways other than by simply playing a new word to intersect with a word already on the board through a common letter, or by adding letters to an existing word. The key to successful Scrabble is constant awareness of the various opportunities for forming words on the board.

When words are formed in ways other than simple intersection or expansion, more than one new word is created in the process, potentially giving a higher score. The main ways of doing this are 'hooking' and 'tagging'.

Hooking

This is the term for the act of 'hanging' one word on another – the word already on the board acts as a 'hook' on which the other word can be hung – changing the first word in the process. The player adds a letter to the beginning or end of a word already on the board in the process, transforming it into a longer word, as in the following example:

Player A has played COMET. Player B then plays HOUSE on the end of COMET, forming COMETH and HOUSE, and scoring 13 for COMETH plus 16 for HOUSE. COMET is an 'end-hook'; any word ending in H or S can be 'hung' on it.

S is a particularly useful letter when hooking, as most nouns have a plural formed by adding it to the end of the singular.

The following example shows how to add a 'front hook' to the word OX:

Here the player gets the 17 points for FOX as well as those for FICKLE. Thus hooking is generally a more profitable method of word formation than simply playing a word through, or adjacent to, one that is already on the board. In particular, hooking allows players the chance to benefit from high-scoring power tiles played by an opponent, as with the X in FOX in the above example. It is important to note that, when scoring double words like this, only the face value of tiles already played is counted and if the original word had been played on a premium square its bonus value would not count.

Blocking

Words that cannot form other words by having a letter added to their front or back are known as blockers, as they prevent other players from adding words by hooking.

Blockers are useful for preventing your opponent from capitalizing on words that you have played, and for blocking off sections of the board. If you are ahead on the scoreboard in the latter part of a game, you may wish to play tactically by concentrating on blockers, and thereby prevent your opponent from getting further opportunities to play high-scoring words.

Some examples of blocker words are as follows:

Tagging

Playing a word parallel to one already on the board, so that one or more tiles are in contact, is known as tagging. Tagging is more difficult than hooking because you need to form one additional word for each tile in contact with the word already on the board. These will usually be two-letter words, which is why these short words are so vital to the game. The more two-letter words you know, the greater your opportunities for fitting words onto the board through tagging – and of running up some impressive scores!

Player A has played:

Player B now 'tags' TROLL, also forming ET, AR and NO (all valid two-letter words). This play scores 10 for TROLL, 2 each for ET and AR, and 4 for NO, so a total of 18.

Short words are obviously very handy for tagging, as seen in the following example:

Power Tiles

It is important to use the 'power tiles' (J, Q, X and Z) wisely when they land on your rack. Learning some of the words that contain these letters will help you to employ the power tiles to maximum effect when they appear on your rack. Of special interest are words that use Q but not U, as these allow you to avoid the problem of needing to find a U to play your high-scoring Q tile. In the average two-player Scrabble game, you are likely to have two of the power tiles on your rack at some point during play and learning some words using these letters will help you to manoeuvre them onto premium squares for really high scores.

Two- and three-letter words

Two-letter words are essential for tagging: generally, you need one two-letter word for every point of contact. Three-letter words are also very useful in Scrabble, as a crowded board will often prevent you from playing longer words late in the game. Moreover, some very respectable scores can be generated by tagging with three-letter words – creating more two-letter words in the process. While many two- and three-letter words will be familiar, it's a good idea to learn the less common ones, as knowing whether a given combination of two or three letters is a valid word can be vital when you are trying to get a high-scoring set of tiles onto the board through tagging or hooking.

The Appendix lists all the two- and three-letter words that are valid for Scrabble.

Using the S and Blank tiles

S

The S tile is very useful as it can be placed at the end of many words (nearly every noun and verb, in fact) thus making it the ideal tile for end-hooking. This quality also makes S very handy for bonus words, as the odds of making a bonus word from six tiles plus an S are greatly improved from making a bonus from seven letters. However, a player can often get a good score without trying for a bonus by simply hooking an existing word, and scoring for both. S is also well suited for use as a front hook, particularly alongside words starting with H, L, P, T. Also watch out for hooking an S onto a Q word.

Blank

A blank tile has no value but may be used in the place of any letter, thus making it extremely useful, especially when it comes to forming bonus words. It is very important to use the blank tile wisely and not to waste it on a low-scoring word. Look at the letters on your rack and when considering the blank tile, run through the alphabet in your mind when thinking of the letter value to assign to it. Remember, it is much easier to form a bonus word from six letters plus one which you can choose than by using seven letters over which you have no control, so save the blank for a bonus word if you can. Finally, never ever change a blank tile!

Bonus words

Always remember that no matter how many words you form, you are likely to achieve a higher score by playing all seven of your letters in one go, as this earns you a 50 point bonus. It takes a lot of power tiles or bonus squares to achieve 50 points, so playing a bonus word (bingo in the US) is the most reliable method of getting an impressive score.

A bonus play generally involves a word of seven or eight letters – either by tagging or hooking a complete seven-letter word onto a word already on the board, or by forming an eight-letter word intersecting an existing word by playing all seven tiles.

Scrabble Glossary

BLOCKER a word which cannot have a letter added to its beginning or end to form another valid word.

BONUS SQUARE (also called PREMIUM SQUARE) one of the squares on the board that provides extra points: double letter, double word, triple letter or triple word.

BONUS WORD a word that uses all seven of a player's tiles, earning a 50 point bonus.

FRONT-HOOK a word that can form another valid word by having a letter added to its front.

END-HOOK a word that can form another valid word by having a letter added to its end.

HEAVY WORDS (either VOWEL-HEAVY or CONSONANT-HEAVY) words which have many consonants or vowels.

HOOKING playing a word perpendicular to and in contact with another word, so that the first played word (the hook) has a letter added to it.

POWER TILES (J, Q, X or Z) the tiles that score eight (J and X) or ten (Q and Z) points.

RACK the small plastic shelf that holds a player's tiles; the combination of letters on the tiles currently held.

TAGGING playing a word parallel to, and in contact with, another word so that a valid word is formed at each point of contact.

TILE one of the small plaques bearing letters that are used to form words on the board.

Words Ineligible for Scrabble

There are several categories of ineligible words:
- Hyphenated words
- Multiple-word phrases
- Capitalized words
- Abbreviations
- Words over 15 letters in length

Essential info
Value: 1 point
Number in set: 9

A is a common tile and is very useful for forming short words to squeeze into tight corners, as it can be added easily to the majority of other tiles to form two-letter words. A can even be added to itself (to form AA, a Hawaiian word for rough volcanic rock, 2 points). A is also very helpful for short, high-scoring words such as AXE (10 points, or 9 points with its US variant AX). Some more unusual examples of three-letter words include AAL (an Asian shrub, 3 points), APO (a type of protein, 5 points) and the high-scoring ADZ (a tool for cutting roof tiles, 13 points). A is one of the letters of the RETAIN set and is therefore a good letter to keep if trying to get a bonus word.

Two-letter words beginning with A

AA	AI	AT
AB	AL	AW
AD	AM	AX
AE	AN	AY
AG	AR	
AH	AS	

Some three-letter words beginning with A

AAH	AHI	AMU
AAL	AIA	ANA
ABA	AIN	ANE
ABB	AIT	ANI
ABO	AKA	ANN
ABY	ALA	APO
ACH	ALB	ARB
ADO	ALF	ARD
ADZ	ALP	ARF
AFF	ALT	ARY
AGA	AMA	ASP
AGO	AMI	ASS
AHA	AMP	ATT

AWA	AWN	AYU
AWL	AYE	AZO

HOOKS

Hooking requires a player to look at words already on the board without being distracted by their pronunciation. This can lead to simple hooking solutions being overlooked. Fortunately, A is one of the easier tiles to play as a hook or a tag and it can be front-hooked to many words as their negating form (e.g. MORAL can be changed to AMORAL).

Some front-hooks
Two letters to three

A-AH	A-ID	A-NY
A-AL	A-IN	A-PE
A-AS	A-IS	A-PO
A-BA	A-IT	A-RE
A-BO	A-KA	A-SH
A-BY	A-LA	A-TE
A-CH	A-MA	A-WE
A-DO	A-MI	A-YE
A-GO	A-MU	A-YU
A-HA	A-NA	A-ZO
A-HI	A-NE	

Three letters to four

A-BED	A-IDE	A-NIL
A-BET	A-JAR	A-NON
A-BID	A-KIN	A-NOW
A-BUT	A-LAP	A-PAY
A-BYE	A-LAY	A-POD
A-DRY	A-LEE	A-RED
A-FAR	A-LIT	A-RID
A-GAS	A-LOW	A-ROW
A-GIN	A-MEN	A-RUM
A-HEM	A-MID	A-SEA
A-HIS	A-NAN	A-SHY
A-HOY	A-NEW	A-TAP

A-TOP | A-WED | A-YES
A-VOW | A-WEE
A-WAY | A-WRY

Four letters to five

A-BACK	A-GIST	A-MAZE
A-BAND	A-GLEE	A-MEND
A-BASE	A-GLOW	A-MICE
A-BASH	A-GONE	A-MINE
A-BASK	A-GOOD	A-MISS
A-BEAM	A-GRIN	A-MOLE
A-BEAR	A-HEAD	A-MOVE
A-BIDE	A-HEAP	A-MUCK
A-BLED	A-HIGH	A-MUSE
A-BLOW	A-HIND	A-NEAR
A-BODE	A-HINT	A-NIGH
A-BOIL	A-HOLD	A-NODE
A-BORE	A-HULL	A-PACE
A-BOUT	A-ISLE	A-PAGE
A-BRAY	A-ITCH	A-PAID
A-BRIM	A-KING	A-PART
A-BUZZ	A-LACK	A-PEAK
A-COLD	A-LAND	A-PEEK
A-CORN	A-LANE	A-PERT
A-CUTE	A-LANT	A-PING
A-DOWN	A-LATE	A-PORT
A-DOZE	A-LEFT	A-READ
A-DUST	A-LIEN	A-REAL
A-FEAR	A-LIKE	A-REAR
A-FIRE	A-LINE	A-RISE
A-FOOT	A-LIST	A-ROSE
A-FORE	A-LIVE	A-SCOT
A-FOUL	A-LOFT	A-SHED
A-GAIN	A-LONE	A-SIDE
A-GAPE	A-LONG	A-SKEW
A-GATE	A-LOUD	A-STIR
A-GAVE	A-LURE	A-STUN
A-GAZE	A-MAIN	A-SWAY
A-GENE	A-MASS	A-SWIM
A-GENT	A-MATE	A-TILT

A-TOLL

A-TONE

A-TRIP

A-VAIL

A-VALE

A-VAST

A-VINE

A-VOID

A-WAIT

A-WAKE

A-WARD

A-WARE

A-WARN

A-WASH

A-WAVE

A-WING

A-WOKE

A-WORK

A-YELP

Five letters to six

A-BASED

A-BASER

A-BATED

A-BIDED

A-BIDER

A-BLATE

A-BLAZE

A-BLING

A-BLOOM

A-BLUSH

A-BOARD

A-BODED

A-BORNE

A-BOUND

A-BRAID

A-BROAD

A-BURST

A-BUSED

A-CATER

A-CIDER

A-CRAWL

A-CROSS

A-CUTER

A-DREAD

A-DRIFT

A-DROIT

A-ETHER

A-FIELD

A-FLAME

A-FLOAT

A-FRESH

A-FRONT

A-GAZED

A-GEIST

A-GHAST

A-GLARE

A-GLEAM

A-GOING

A-GREED

A-GUISE

A-HORSE

A-LIGHT

A-LINED

A-LINER

A-MATED

A-MAZED

A-MIDST

A-MORAL

A-MOUNT

A-MOVED

A-MUSED

A-MUSER

A-NEATH

A-NIGHT

A-PIECE

A-RAISE

A-REACH

A-RIDER

A-RIGHT

A-RILED

A-RISEN

A-ROUND

A-ROUSE

A-SCEND

A-SCENT

A-SHAKE

A-SHAME

A-SHIER

A-SHINE

A-SHORE

A-SLAKE

A-SLANT

A-SLEEP

A-SLOPE

A-SLOSH

A-SMEAR

A-SPINE

A-SPIRE

A-SPORT

A-SPOUT

A-SQUAT

A-STARE

A-START

A-STERN

A-STONE

A-STONY

A-STOOP

A-STRAY

A-STRUT

A-SWARM

A-SWING

A-SWIRL

A-SWOON

A-TONAL
A-TONED
A-TONER
A-TONIC
A-TOPIC
A-TRIAL
A-TWAIN
A-TWEEL
A-TWEEN
A-TWIXT
A-TYPIC

A-UNTIE
A-VAUNT
A-VENGE
A-VENUE
A-VERSE
A-VISED
A-VITAL
A-VOUCH
A-VOWED
A-VOWER
A-WAKED

A-WAKEN
A-WATCH
A-WEARY
A-WEIGH
A-WHEEL
A-WHILE
A-WHIRL
A-WOKEN
A-WRACK
A-WRONG
A-ZONAL

Six letters to seven

A-BANDED
A-BASHED
A-BASING
A-BATING
A-BETTED
A-BETTER
A-BIDING
A-BIOTIC
A-BODING
A-BOUGHT
A-BRAYED
A-BRIDGE
A-BROACH
A-BUBBLE
A-BUTTED
A-BUTTER
A-CLINIC
A-CORNED
A-CUTELY
A-CUTEST
A-CYCLIC
A-DEEMED
A-DUSTED
A-FEARED
A-GENTRY
A-GROUND
A-LAYING

A-LENGTH
A-LINING
A-LONELY
A-MASSED
A-MAZING
A-MENDED
A-MENDER
A-MENTAL
A-MOTION
A-MOVING
A-MUSING
A-NEARED
A-NOTHER
A-PAYING
A-PLENTY
A-QUIVER
A-RAISED
A-REALLY
A-RIPPLE
A-RISING
A-SCARED
A-SCONCE
A-SCRIBE
A-SEPTIC
A-SHAMED
A-SHIEST
A-SHIVER

A-SOCIAL
A-SPIRED
A-SPRAWL
A-SPREAD
A-SPROUT
A-SQUINT
A-STABLE
A-STATIC
A-STONED
A-STOUND
A-STRAND
A-STRICT
A-STRIDE
A-SUDDEN
A-SUNDER
A-THIRST
A-THRILL
A-TINGLE
A-TONING
A-TROPHY
A-VAILED
A-VENGED
A-VENGER
A-VERTED
A-VOIDED
A-VOIDER
A-VOWING

| A-WAITED | A-WAKING | A-WARDER |
| A-WAITER | A-WARDED | A-WARNED |

Seven letters to eight

A-BANDING	A-KINESES	A-SEPTATE
A-BASHING	A-KINESIS	A-SHAMING
A-BATABLE	A-KINETIC	A-SHINESS
A-BEARING	A-LEGGING	A-SLAKING
A-BEGGING	A-LIGHTED	A-SOCIALS
A-BETTING	A-LOGICAL	A-SPARKLE
A-BOUNDED	A-MASSING	A-SPERSED
A-BRAIDED	A-MAZEDLY	A-SPHERIC
A-BRAYING	A-MEIOSIS	A-SPIRANT
A-BRIDGED	A-MENAGED	A-SPIRING
A-BROOKED	A-MENDING	A-SPORTED
A-BUTTING	A-MIDMOST	A-STARTED
A-CENTRIC	A-MIDSHIP	A-STERNAL
A-CERATED	A-MISSING	A-STEROID
A-CHROMIC	A-MITOSIS	A-STONIED
A-COSMISM	A-MITOTIC	A-STONING
A-COSMIST	A-MORALLY	A-STONISH
A-DEEMING	A-MORTISE	A-STUNNED
A-DREADED	A-MOUNTED	A-SYNERGY
A-DUSTING	A-NEARING	A-SYSTOLE
A-DYNAMIC	A-NEURISM	A-TECHNIC
A-ESTHETE	A-NODALLY	A-TONALLY
A-ESTIVAL	A-NOINTED	A-TREMBLE
A-ETHERIC	A-NOINTER	A-TROPHIC
A-FEARING	A-PIARIST	A-TROPINE
A-FEBRILE	A-PLASTIC	A-TROPISM
A-FLUTTER	A-PRACTIC	A-TWITTER
A-GENESIS	A-PYRETIC	A-TYPICAL
A-GENETIC	A-PYREXIA	A-VAILING
A-GLIMMER	A-RAISING	A-VAUNTED
A-GLITTER	A-REACHED	A-VENGING
A-GNOSTIC	A-READING	A-VENTURE
A-GRAPHIC	A-RETTING	A-VERSION
A-GREEING	A-SCENDED	A-VERTING
A-GRISING	A-SCRIBED	A-VOIDING
A-GUISING	A-SEISMIC	A-VOUCHED

A-VOUCHER   A-WAKENER   A-WARNING
A-WAITING   A-WANTING   A-WEARIED
A-WAKENED   A-WARDING   A-WEATHER

> **Handy Hint: The Challenge**
>
> Never be afraid to challenge a word which looks unusual, misspelled or which you do not recognise. Many a word has slipped through the net this way, and you have nothing to lose by challenging your opponent. DO NOT BE INTIMIDATED. Gamesmanship occurs in Scrabble too and your opponent may be hoping you will let their mistakes or guesses go unnoticed or unchallenged.

Some end-hooks

Two letters to three

AB-A	ER-A	OR-A
AG-A	ET-A	PE-A
AH-A	FA-A	PI-A
AI-A	GO-A	PO-A
AL-A	HO-A	SH-A
AM-A	IT-A	TE-A
AN-A	KO-A	UT-A
AW-A	MA-A	YE-A
BA-A	MO-A	ZO-A
BO-A	OB-A	
CH-A	OD-A	

Three letters to four

ALB-A	GAL-A	MEG-A
ARE-A	GAM-A	MES-A
BET-A	GIG-A	MON-A
BON-A	HAH-A	NAN-A
COD-A	IDE-A	ORC-A
COL-A	KAT-A	PAP-A
DAD-A	KOR-A	PIC-A
DIV-A	LAM-A	PIN-A
DOP-A	LAV-A	PIT-A
FET-A	MAL-A	PUP-A
FIL-A	MAM-A	RAJ-A
GAG-A	MAY-A	RAT-A

ROM-A
ROT-A
SAG-A
SOD-A
SOM-A

SOY-A
TOG-A
TOR-A
TUB-A
TUN-A

VEG-A
VIN-A
VIS-A
WET-A

Four letters to five

BALS-A
BURK-A
CHIN-A
COCO-A
COMM-A
COST-A
DELT-A
DERM-A
DICT-A
DOON-A
DRAM-A
FAUN-A
FELL-A
FETT-A
FLOR-A
GAMB-A

GUAN-A
HOND-A
HYEN-A
KANG-A
LAIK-A
LOOF-A
MANG-A
MANI-A
MOCH-A
MOOL-A
MULL-A
MURR-A
PAND-A
PARK-A
PASH-A
PAST-A

POLK-A
PRIM-A
PUCK-A
PUNK-A
RAGG-A
RAIT-A
RAST-A
SALS-A
SUNN-A
TAIG-A
TIAR-A
TONK-A
VEST-A
VILL-A
VIOL-A
VOLT-A

Five letters to six

CREST-A
FASCI-A
FAVEL-A
FIEST-A
GRAMP-A
KORUN-A
LORIC-A
MAXIM-A
MIASM-A
MINIM-A

NYMPH-A
ORBIT-A
ORGAN-A
PAGOD-A
PATIN-A
PLASM-A
QUANT-A
RHUMB-A
SATYR-A
SCARP-A

SENOR-A
SHISH-A
SPIRE-A
STELL-A
STERN-A
TALUK-A
TAPET-A
TARSI-A
TUNIC-A
VALET-A

Six letters to seven

ADDEND-A
ALUMIN-A
ANALOG-A
ANONYM-A

ARABIC-A
ASHRAM-A
BUZUKI-A
CANDID-A

CANTAL-A
CEMENT-A
CHIASM-A
CHIMER-A

CHOLER-A
CODEIN-A
CORTIN-A
CURIOS-A
CYATHI-A
DEJECT-A
DEODAR-A
DRACHM-A
EMBLEM-A
EXOTIC-A
FAVELL-A
FORMIC-A
GALLET-A
GALLIC-A
GUNNER-A

INFANT-A
INGEST-A
KHALIF-A
LAVOLT-A
LOCUST-A
MADRAS-A
MOMENT-A
PAISAN-A
PERSON-A
PLACIT-A
POTASS-A
PROPYL-A
QUININ-A
ROBUST-A
ROSACE-A

ROTUND-A
SCHISM-A
SECRET-A
SELECT-A
SEQUEL-A
SERING-A
SHEIKH-A
SIGNOR-A
SULTAN-A
TAMBUR-A
TARTAN-A
TAVERN-A
TEMPER-A

Seven letters to eight

ANGELIC-A
ANTEFIX-A
ARBORET-A
AUTOMAT-A
BASILIC-A
BOTANIC-A
BRONCHI-A
BROUGHT-A
CHAMPAC-A
CHARISM-A
CISTERN-A
CONSULT-A
DEMENTI-A
DIASTEM-A
DULCIAN-A

EPITHEM-A
EXCERPT-A
FASCIST-A
HEPATIC-A
JAVELIN-A
MANDIOC-A
MARCHES-A
MARINER-A
MATADOR-A
MELODIC-A
MOLLUSC-A
MONSTER-A
NYMPHAE-A
PERFECT-A
PIGNOLI-A

QUILLAI-A
RAKSHAS-A
SALICET-A
SARMENT-A
SCIATIC-A
SIGNORI-A
STROBIL-A
SYNTAGM-A
TAMANDU-A
TAMBOUR-A
THERIAC-A
TORMENT-A
TOURIST-A
UNGUENT-A

Handy Hint: say AA

If you have too many vowels on your rack, some useful short words beginning with A and using no consonants are: AA, AE and AI (2 points each). It is also worthwhile remembering common words which feature many vowels such as ADIEU (6 points), EERIE (5 points) and COOKIE (12 points).

BLOCKERS

It is useful to know which words are blockers and can't therefore be extended before or after. You may want to play a blocker that your opponent can't extend, or you may want to avoid playing a blocker because you want to keep the board open.

Three-letter blocker beginning with A

AUE

Some four-letter blockers beginning with A

ABLY	AJEE	AREG
ACHY	ALAE	AREW
ADRY	ALEE	AROW
AESC	ALIT	ASEA
AGLY	ALSO	AWRY
AHEM	ANEW	AXAL
AHOY	ANOW	
AJAR	APEX	

Some five-letter blockers beginning with A (except words ending in '-ED', '-J', '-S', '-X', '-Y' or '-Z')

AARGH	AGLEE	APACE
ABACK	AGLOW	APAGE
ABASH	AGOOD	APAID
ABASK	AHEAD	APART
ABEAM	AHEAP	APIAN
ABLOW	AHIGH	AREAR
ABOIL	ALACK	AROSE
ABORE	ALGAE	ASKEW
ABRIM	ALGAL	ASTIR
ACERB	ALGID	ASWIM
ACHOO	ALIKE	ATILT
ACRID	ALIVE	AURAL
ADOZE	ALOFT	AVAST
AFIRE	ALONE	AWASH
AFOOT	ALOOF	AWAVE
AFORE	ALOUD	AWORK
AFOUL	ALTHO	AXIAL
AGAIN	AMAIN	
AGAST	AMINO	

Some six-letter blockers beginning with A (except words ending in '-ED', '-J', '-S', '-X', '-Y' or '-Z')

ABLAZE	AKIMBO	ASLOPE
ABLEST	ALBEIT	ASTERN
ABLOOM	ALMOST	ASTOOP
ABLUSH	ALUMNI	ASTRUT
ABOARD	AMBUSH	ASWARM
ABORNE	AMEBIC	ASWING
ABURST	AMIDST	ASWIRL
ACETIC	AMMINO	ATONAL
ACHIER	AMORAL	ATOPIC
ACIDER	ANEATH	ATWIXT
ACIDIC	ANEMIC	AUDIAL
ACRAWL	ANOXIC	AVERSE
ACUTER	ANYHOW	AVIDER
ADRIFT	AORTAL	AVITAL
ADROIT	AORTIC	AVOUCH
AFIELD	APEMAN	AWARER
AFLAME	APEMEN	AWATCH
AFLOAT	APIECE	AWEIGH
AFRAID	APTEST	AWEING
AFRESH	APTING	AWHILE
AFRONT	ARCANE	AWHIRL
AGHAST	ARDENT	AWOKEN
AGILER	AREACH	AWRACK
AGLARE	ARISEN	AWRONG
AGLEAM	AROUND	AWSOME
AIDMAN	ASHAKE	AXEMAN
AIDMEN	ASHINE	AXEMEN
AIMFUL	ASHORE	AXONIC
AIRMAN	ASLANT	AZONAL
AIRMEN	ASLEEP	

BONUS WORDS

Bonus words on your rack can be hard to spot, especially for the less experienced player. One way to help find them is by using prefixes and suffixes.

Many longer words include a common prefix or suffix – remembering these and using them where you can is a good way to discover any longer words on your rack, including any potential bonus words. The key prefixes to remember beginning with A are AB-, AD-, AIR- and the key suffixes are -ABLE, -AGE, -ANCE, -ANCY and -ARCH.

Some words beginning with AB-
Seven-letter words

AB-ASHED	AB-REACT	AB-STAIN
AB-ASHES	AB-REAST	AB-SURDS
AB-DUCTS	AB-RIDGE	AB-THANE
AB-JOINT	AB-ROACH	AB-USAGE
AB-LATED	AB-ROADS	AB-USERS
AB-LINGS	AB-SEILS	AB-USING
AB-LUTED	AB-SENTS	AB-UTTER
AB-OUGHT	AB-SOLVE	
AB-RAIDS	AB-SORBS	

Eight-letter words

AB-ASHING	AB-ORALLY	AB-SOLUTE
AB-DUCTED	AB-ORIGIN	AB-SOLVED
AB-EARING	AB-RAIDED	AB-SOLVER
AB-EGGING	AB-RAYING	AB-SOLVES
AB-ERRANT	AB-RIDGED	AB-SONANT
AB-ESSIVE	AB-RIDGER	AB-SORBED
AB-LEGATE	AB-ROOKED	AB-STRICT
AB-NEGATE	AB-SEILED	AB-USABLE
AB-NORMAL	AB-SENTED	

Some words beginning with AD-
Seven-letter words

AD-AGIOS	AD-DUCTS	AD-LANDS
AD-APTED	AD-HERES	AD-MIRED
AD-APTER	AD-JOINS	AD-MIRES
AD-AWING	AD-JOINT	AD-MIXED
AD-DICTS	AD-JUDGE	AD-MIXES
AD-DRESS	AD-JUROR	AD-NOUNS
AD-DUCES	AD-JUSTS	AD-OPTED

AD-OPTER
AD-PRESS
AD-READS
AD-RENAL
AD-SORBS
AD-VENTS

AD-VERBS
AD-VERSE
AD-VERTS
AD-VICES
AD-VISED
AD-VISES

AD-VISOR
AD-WARDS
AD-WARES
AD-WOMAN
AD-WOMEN

Eight-letter words

AD-APTING
AD-DEBTED
AD-DEEMED
AD-DICTED
AD-DOOMED
AD-DUCTED
AD-EQUATE
AD-ESSIVE
AD-JACENT
AD-JOINED

AD-JUDGED
AD-JUSTED
AD-JUSTER
AD-MASSES
AD-MIRING
AD-MIXING
AD-MONISH
AD-NATION
AD-OPTING
AD-OPTION

AD-SCRIPT
AD-SORBED
AD-UMBRAL
AD-UNCATE
AD-VERSER
AD-VERTED
AD-VISING
AD-WARDED

Some words beginning with AIR-

Seven-letter words

AIR-BAGS
AIR-BASE
AIR-BOAT
AIR-CREW
AIR-DATE
AIR-DROP
AIR-FARE
AIR-FLOW
AIR-FOIL
AIR-GAPS
AIR-GLOW
AIR-HEAD

AIR-HOLE
AIR-LESS
AIR-LIFT
AIR-LIKE
AIR-LINE
AIR-LOCK
AIR-MAIL
AIR-PARK
AIR-PLAY
AIR-PORT
AIR-POST
AIR-SHED

AIR-SHIP
AIR-SHOT
AIR-SHOW
AIR-SICK
AIR-SIDE
AIR-STOP
AIR-TIME
AIR-TING
AIR-WARD
AIR-WAVE
AIR-WAYS
AIR-WISE

Eight-letter words

AIR-BASES
AIR-BOATS
AIR-BORNE
AIR-BOUND
AIR-BRICK
AIR-BRUSH

AIR-BURST
AIR-BUSES
AIR-CHECK
AIR-COACH
AIR-CRAFT
AIR-DRAWN

AIR-DROME
AIR-DROPS
AIR-FARES
AIR-FIELD
AIR-FRAME
AIR-GLOWS

AIR-GRAPH	AIR-PROOF	AIR-STRIP
AIR-HOLES	AIR-SCAPE	AIR-THING
AIR-LIFTS	AIR-SCREW	AIR-TIGHT
AIR-LINER	AIR-SHAFT	AIR-WAVES
AIR-PLANE	AIR-SPACE	AIR-WOMAN
AIR-POWER	AIR-SPEED	AIR-WOMEN

Some words ending with -ABLE

Seven-letter words

ACT-ABLE	HAT-ABLE	SAL-ABLE
ADD-ABLE	HEW-ABLE	SAV-ABLE
AFF-ABLE	HID-ABLE	SAY-ABLE
AMI-ABLE	HIR-ABLE	SEE-ABLE
BAT-ABLE	LIK-ABLE	SEW-ABLE
BUY-ABLE	LIN-ABLE	SIZ-ABLE
CAP-ABLE	LIV-ABLE	SKI-ABLE
CIT-ABLE	LOS-ABLE	SOW-ABLE
COD-ABLE	LOV-ABLE	SUE-ABLE
CUR-ABLE	MAK-ABLE	TAK-ABLE
DAT-ABLE	MIN-ABLE	TAM-ABLE
DIS-ABLE	MIR-ABLE	TAX-ABLE
DRY-ABLE	MIX-ABLE	TEN-ABLE
DUP-ABLE	MOV-ABLE	TOT-ABLE
DUR-ABLE	MUT-ABLE	TOW-ABLE
DYE-ABLE	NAM-ABLE	TRI-ABLE
EAT-ABLE	NOT-ABLE	TUN-ABLE
EQU-ABLE	OWN-ABLE	TYP-ABLE
EYE-ABLE	PAR-ABLE	UNH-ABLE
FIX-ABLE	PAY-ABLE	USE-ABLE
FLY-ABLE	PLI-ABLE	VAT-ABLE
FRI-ABLE	POK-ABLE	VOC-ABLE
FRY-ABLE	POS-ABLE	VOL-ABLE
GEL-ABLE	POT-ABLE	VOT-ABLE
GET-ABLE	RAT-ABLE	WAD-ABLE
GIV-ABLE	ROW-ABLE	WAX-ABLE

Eight-letter words

ADOR-ABLE	AMIC-ABLE	BAIL-ABLE
AGIT-ABLE	ARGU-ABLE	BANK-ABLE
AMEN-ABLE	ATON-ABLE	BEAR-ABLE

BEAT-ABLE	HOLD-ABLE	REUS-ABLE
BEND-ABLE	HUNT-ABLE	RINS-ABLE
BILL-ABLE	IMIT-ABLE	RIPP-ABLE
BITE-ABLE	INVI-ABLE	SACK-ABLE
BLAM-ABLE	JOIN-ABLE	SALE-ABLE
BRIB-ABLE	JUMP-ABLE	SAVE-ABLE
CASH-ABLE	KICK-ABLE	SEAL-ABLE
CAUS-ABLE	KILL-ABLE	SEIZ-ABLE
CHEW-ABLE	KISS-ABLE	SELL-ABLE
CITE-ABLE	KNOW-ABLE	SEND-ABLE
CLOS-ABLE	LAUD-ABLE	SERV-ABLE
COIN-ABLE	LEAS-ABLE	SHAK-ABLE
COOK-ABLE	LEND-ABLE	SHAM-ABLE
COPY-ABLE	LIKE-ABLE	SHOW-ABLE
CULP-ABLE	LIVE-ABLE	SING-ABLE
CUTT-ABLE	LOCK-ABLE	SINK-ABLE
DENI-ABLE	LOVE-ABLE	SIZE-ABLE
DRAW-ABLE	MAIL-ABLE	SMOK-ABLE
DRIV-ABLE	MEND-ABLE	SOCI-ABLE
EDIT-ABLE	MISS-ABLE	SOLV-ABLE
EDUC-ABLE	MOVE-ABLE	SORT-ABLE
ENVI-ABLE	NAME-ABLE	SUIT-ABLE
ERAS-ABLE	OPEN-ABLE	SURF-ABLE
EROD-ABLE	OPER-ABLE	SWAY-ABLE
EVAD-ABLE	PALP-ABLE	SYLL-ABLE
FACE-ABLE	PASS-ABLE	TAKE-ABLE
FARM-ABLE	PICK-ABLE	TALK-ABLE
FEED-ABLE	PITI-ABLE	TAME-ABLE
FILE-ABLE	PLAY-ABLE	TEAR-ABLE
FILM-ABLE	PORT-ABLE	TEAS-ABLE
FOLD-ABLE	POSE-ABLE	TRAD-ABLE
FUND-ABLE	POUR-ABLE	TURN-ABLE
GAIN-ABLE	PROB-ABLE	UNST-ABLE
GETT-ABLE	PROV-ABLE	VALU-ABLE
GIVE-ABLE	QUOT-ABLE	VARI-ABLE
GRAD-ABLE	RATE-ABLE	VIEW-ABLE
GROW-ABLE	READ-ABLE	VIOL-ABLE
GUID-ABLE	REAP-ABLE	VOID-ABLE
HEAR-ABLE	RELI-ABLE	VOTE-ABLE
HEAT-ABLE	RENT-ABLE	WALK-ABLE

A

WASH-ABLE WINN-ABLE WRIT-ABLE
WEAR-ABLE WORK-ABLE

Some words ending with -AGE

Seven-letter words

ACRE-AGE HAUL-AGE RIBC-AGE
ASSU-AGE HERB-AGE RIFF-AGE
AVER-AGE HOST-AGE RUMM-AGE
BAGG-AGE LEAK-AGE SALV-AGE
BAND-AGE LINE-AGE SAUS-AGE
BARR-AGE LINK-AGE SEEP-AGE
BEER-AGE LUGG-AGE SIGN-AGE
BREW-AGE MASS-AGE SOIL-AGE
BULK-AGE MESS-AGE STOR-AGE
BUOY-AGE MILE-AGE TEEN-AGE
CABB-AGE MONT-AGE TONN-AGE
CARN-AGE ONST-AGE UMBR-AGE
COIN-AGE OUTR-AGE UPST-AGE
COLL-AGE OVER-AGE VANT-AGE
CORS-AGE PACK-AGE VILL-AGE
COTT-AGE PASS-AGE VINT-AGE
COUR-AGE PEER-AGE VOLT-AGE
FLOW-AGE PLUM-AGE WARP-AGE
FOLI-AGE POST-AGE WAST-AGE
FOOT-AGE POTT-AGE WATT-AGE
FROM-AGE PRES-AGE WEBP-AGE
GARB-AGE RAMP-AGE YARD-AGE

Eight-letter words

AMPER-AGE DRAIN-AGE MARRI-AGE
BARON-AGE DRESS-AGE METER-AGE
BEVER-AGE ENVIS-AGE MISUS-AGE
BIRDC-AGE FRONT-AGE MORTG-AGE
BLOCK-AGE FUSEL-AGE OFFST-AGE
BREAK-AGE GRAIN-AGE OVERP-AGE
CARRI-AGE GROUP-AGE PILOT-AGE
CLEAR-AGE HERIT-AGE PLANT-AGE
COVER-AGE HOMEP-AGE PUPIL-AGE
CREEP-AGE LANGU-AGE ROUGH-AGE
CRIBB-AGE LEVER-AGE SABOT-AGE

16

SEWER-AGE	STEER-AGE	TUTOR-AGE
SHORT-AGE	STOPP-AGE	UNDER-AGE
SLIPP-AGE	SUFFR-AGE	VAUNT-AGE
SPILL-AGE	TRACK-AGE	VERBI-AGE
SPOIL-AGE	TUTEL-AGE	VICAR-AGE

Some words ending with -ANCE

Seven-letter words

ADV-ANCE	DUR-ANCE	ROM-ANCE
AID-ANCE	ENH-ANCE	SON-ANCE
ASK-ANCE	FIN-ANCE	SUR-ANCE
BAL-ANCE	JOY-ANCE	VAC-ANCE
CRE-ANCE	PEN-ANCE	VAL-ANCE

Eight-letter words

ABEY-ANCE	ELEG-ANCE	PAST-ANCE
ABID-ANCE	ENTR-ANCE	PIQU-ANCE
ACUT-ANCE	EXIT-ANCE	PITT-ANCE
ADAM-ANCE	FEAS-ANCE	PORT-ANCE
AFFI-ANCE	GUID-ANCE	RADI-ANCE
ALLI-ANCE	INST-ANCE	RELI-ANCE
AMBI-ANCE	ISSU-ANCE	RESI-ANCE
AMOR-ANCE	ITER-ANCE	RIDD-ANCE
BECH-ANCE	LAIT-ANCE	SORT-ANCE
BRIS-ANCE	NOND-ANCE	TADV-ANCE
BUOY-ANCE	NUIS-ANCE	TEND-ANCE
CREP-ANCE	ORDN-ANCE	VALI-ANCE
DEFI-ANCE	OUTD-ANCE	VARI-ANCE
DEVI-ANCE	OUTR-ANCE	VIBR-ANCE
DIST-ANCE	PARL-ANCE	VOID-ANCE

Some words ending with -ANCY

Seven-letter words

ERR-ANCY	SON-ANCY	UNF-ANCY
INF-ANCY	TEN-ANCY	VAC-ANCY
PLI-ANCY	TRU-ANCY	

Eight-letter words

ABEY-ANCY	BUOY-ANCY	DORM-ANCY
ADAM-ANCY	CLAM-ANCY	ELEG-ANCY
BLAT-ANCY	DEVI-ANCY	GEOM-ANCY

IMIT-ANCY	PERN-ANCY	UNCH-ANCY
INST-ANCY	PIQU-ANCY	VAGR-ANCY
MORD-ANCY	RADI-ANCY	VALI-ANCY
MYOM-ANCY	RAMP-ANCY	VERD-ANCY
PECC-ANCY	REGN-ANCY	VIBR-ANCY

Some words ending with -ARCH

Seven-letter words

AUT-ARCH	MON-ARCH	TRI-ARCH
END-ARCH	NAV-ARCH	XER-ARCH
HEX-ARCH	NOM-ARCH	
MES-ARCH	TOP-ARCH	

Eight-letter words

ETHN-ARCH	OMNI-ARCH	POLY-ARCH
HEPT-ARCH	OUTM-ARCH	RESE-ARCH
HIER-ARCH	OVER-ARCH	TAXI-ARCH
HIPP-ARCH	PENT-ARCH	TETR-ARCH
OLIG-ARCH	PHYL-ARCH	UNST-ARCH

UNUSUAL LETTER COMBINATIONS

If you find you have a preponderance of vowels on your rack, a few words from World English can come in handy. Fortunately, there are many from which to choose.

Australian words

ADJIGO	yam plant
ALF	an uncultivated Australian
ARVO	afternoon
ASPRO	associate professor

Canadian words

AGLOO	breathing hole made in ice by a seal
AMAUT	hood on an Inuit woman's parka for carrying a child
ATIGI	Inuit parka

Hindi words

AKHARA   gymnasium
ALAP   vocal music without words
AMBARY   tropical plant
ANKUS   elephant goad
ANNA   old copper coin
ARTI   Hindu ritual
AYAH   maidservant or nursemaid

New Zealand words

New Zealand English features a great variety of words adopted from the Maori language. Many of these words use two (and sometimes three) As but are often also dependent on a consonant such as K or T.

ATUA   spirit or demon
HAKA   war dance
KAUPAPA   strategy, policy or cause
TAIAHA   ceremonial fighting staff
WAKA   Maori canoe

South African words

South African English is fed into by various different languages, including Afrikaans and Nguni languages such as Zulu and Xhosa. Afrikaans-derived words often feature a double A and Nguni words frequently contain two or three.

AMADODA   grown men
AMANDLA   political slogan calling for power to the Black
              population
BABALAS   drunk or hungover
KRAAL   stockaded village
PLAAS   farm

B
3

Essential info
Value: 3 points
Number in set: 2

B can form a two-letter word with every vowel except for U.
If you have a letter B you can form various short everyday words,
some of which can be high-scoring such as BOX (12 points),
BAY (8 points), BOW (8 points), BUY (8 points) and BYE (also 8).
Some more unusual three-letter words beginning with B are BEY
(an official in the Ottoman Empire, 8 points) and BEZ (the second
spike of a deer's antler, 14 points).

Two-letter words beginning with B

BA	BI	BY
BE	BO	

Some three-letter words beginning with B

BAA	BEY	BOK
BAC	BEZ	BON
BAH	BIO	BOP
BAL	BIZ	BOR
BAM	BOA	BOT
BAP	BOD	BUR
BEL	BOH	
BEN	BOI	

HOOKS

Hooking requires a subtle change in a player's thought process,
in that they must look at words already on the board without
becoming distracted by their pronunciation.

Some front-hooks
Two letters to three

B-AA	B-AH	B-AN
B-AD	B-AL	B-AR
B-AG	B-AM	B-AS

B-AT
B-AY
B-ED
B-EE
B-EL
B-EN
B-ES
B-ET
B-ID
B-IN
B-IO

B-IS
B-IT
B-OB
B-OD
B-OH
B-OI
B-ON
B-OO
B-OP
B-OR
B-OS

B-OW
B-OX
B-OY
B-UG
B-UM
B-UN
B-UR
B-US
B-UT
B-YE

Three letters to four

B-AFT
B-AIL
B-ALE
B-ALL
B-AND
B-ANT
B-ARE
B-ARK
B-ARM
B-ASH
B-ASK
B-ATE
B-AUK
B-AYE
B-EAR
B-EAT
B-EAU
B-EGO
B-END
B-EST
B-HAT
B-HUT
B-ICE

B-IDE
B-ILK
B-ILL
B-INK
B-IRK
B-ISH
B-LAB
B-LAD
B-LAG
B-LAW
B-LAY
B-LED
B-LET
B-LEY
B-LIP
B-LOB
B-LOG
B-LOT
B-LOW
B-OAR
B-OAT
B-ODE
B-OFF

B-OIL
B-OLD
B-ONE
B-OOH
B-ORE
B-OUT
B-OWL
B-OXY
B-RAG
B-RAN
B-RAT
B-RAW
B-RAY
B-RED
B-RIG
B-RIM
B-ROD
B-ROO
B-ROW
B-RUT
B-URN
B-YES

Four letters to five

B-ALAS
B-ALKY
B-ALLY

B-ALMS
B-ARMY
B-EACH

B-EARD
B-EAST
B-EAUX

B-EGAD
B-EVER
B-HAJI
B-HANG
B-HOOT
B-IFFY
B-IGGS
B-IOTA
B-LACK
B-LADE
B-LADY
B-LAME
B-LAND
B-LANK
B-LARE
B-LASH
B-LAST
B-LATE
B-LAUD
B-LAWN
B-LAZE
B-LEAK
B-LEND
B-LENT
B-LESS
B-LEST
B-LIMP

B-LIMY
B-LINK
B-LIST
B-LITE
B-LIVE
B-LOCK
B-LOOM
B-LOOP
B-LORE
B-LUSH
B-OGLE
B-OINK
B-ONCE
B-ONUS
B-OOZE
B-ORAL
B-OWED
B-OWER
B-OXEN
B-RACE
B-RAID
B-RAIL
B-RAIN
B-RAKE
B-RANK
B-RANT
B-RASH

B-RAVE
B-RAZE
B-READ
B-REAM
B-REED
B-RENT
B-RICK
B-RIDE
B-RING
B-RINK
B-RISE
B-RISK
B-ROAD
B-ROCK
B-ROOK
B-ROOM
B-ROSE
B-ROSY
B-RUIN
B-RULE
B-RUNG
B-RUNT
B-RUSH
B-RUSK
B-RUST
B-USED

Five letters to six

B-ACHED
B-ADDER
B-ADMAN
B-AILED
B-ALLOT
B-ALLOW
B-ANGER
B-ANGLE
B-ARROW
B-ASHED
B-ASKED

B-ASSET
B-EAGLE
B-EARED
B-EATEN
B-EATER
B-EGGED
B-ELATE
B-ENDED
B-ENDER
B-IONIC
B-LAMER

B-LANKY
B-LATER
B-LAWED
B-LAZED
B-LEACH
B-LEAKY
B-LEARY
B-LIGHT
B-LIMEY
B-LITHE
B-LOBBY

B-LOTTO
B-LOUSE
B-LOUSY
B-LOWED
B-LOWER
B-LUNGE
B-OAKED
B-OATER
B-OFFED
B-OILED
B-OILER
B-OLDEN
B-OLDER
B-ORATE
B-ORDER
B-OTHER
B-OUGHT
B-OUNCE

B-OVATE
B-OWING
B-OWNED
B-RACED
B-RACER
B-RAGGY
B-RAINY
B-RAISE
B-RAKED
B-RANCH
B-RANDY
B-RATTY
B-RAVED
B-RAVER
B-RAWER
B-RAWLY
B-RAYED
B-RAZED

B-RAZER
B-REACH
B-READY
B-RIDGE
B-RIGHT
B-RISKY
B-ROACH
B-ROGUE
B-ROOMY
B-ROUGH
B-ROWED
B-UDDER
B-UNION
B-URNED
B-USHER
B-UTTER

Six letters to seven

B-ACHING
B-AILING
B-ANGLED
B-ASHING
B-ASKING
B-ASSIST
B-ATONED
B-EAGLED
B-EATING
B-EERIER
B-EERILY
B-EGGING
B-ELATED
B-ENDING
B-INNING
B-LACKED
B-LADDER
B-LADING
B-LAGGED
B-LANDER

B-LASTED
B-LASTER
B-LATEST
B-LATHER
B-LATTER
B-LAUDED
B-LAZING
B-LEAKER
B-LENDER
B-LESSER
B-LETTED
B-LINGER
B-LINKED
B-LINKER
B-LISTER
B-LOBBED
B-LOCKED
B-LOCKER
B-LOGGER
B-LOOMED

B-LOOPED
B-LOOPER
B-LOUSED
B-LOWING
B-LOWSED
B-LUBBER
B-LUNGED
B-LUNGER
B-LUSTER
B-OFFING
B-OILING
B-OINKED
B-OLDEST
B-OOZILY
B-OOZING
B-ORATED
B-OWNING
B-OXLIKE
B-RABBLE
B-RACING

B-RACKET
B-RAGGED
B-RAIDED
B-RAIDER
B-RAILED
B-RAINED
B-RAISED
B-RAKING
B-RAMBLE
B-RANKED

B-RASHER
B-RASHLY
B-RATTLE
B-RAUNCH
B-RAVING
B-RAWEST
B-RAYING
B-RAZING
B-REAMED
B-RIDGED

B-RIDING
B-RINGER
B-RISKED
B-RISKER
B-ROCKED
B-ROCKET
B-ROOKIE
B-ROOMED
B-RUSHED
B-RUSHER

Seven letters to eight

B-AILMENT
B-ARTISAN
B-ASHLESS
B-ATONING
B-EAGLING
B-EARDING
B-EARLIKE
B-EATABLE
B-EERIEST
B-ELATING
B-ENDWISE
B-ESPOUSE
B-LACKING
B-LAGGING
B-LASTING
B-LAUDING
B-LEACHED
B-LEACHER
B-LENDING
B-LETTING
B-LIGHTED
B-LIGHTER
B-LINKING
B-LITHELY
B-LOGGING

B-LOOMING
B-LOOPING
B-LOUSIER
B-LOUSILY
B-LOWDOWN
B-LUNGING
B-OLDNESS
B-ORATING
B-ORDERED
B-ORDERER
B-RABBLER
B-RAGGIER
B-RAGGING
B-RAIDING
B-RAILING
B-RAINIER
B-RAINILY
B-RAINING
B-RAISING
B-RAMBLED
B-RANCHED
B-RANCHER
B-RANDING
B-RANKING
B-RASHEST

B-RATPACK
B-RATTIER
B-RATTISH
B-RATTLED
B-REACHED
B-REACHER
B-REACHES
B-READING
B-REEDING
B-RIDGING
B-RIGHTEN
B-RIGHTER
B-RIGHTLY
B-RIMLESS
B-RINGING
B-RISKING
B-ROACHED
B-ROADWAY
B-ROGUISH
B-ROILING
B-ROOMING
B-RUSHIER
B-RUSHING
B-UTTERED

Handy Hint

The more difficult or uncommon words you remember, the greater your chances of clearing your rack and achieving a high score. You could even be lucky enough to have two power tiles at your disposal to be able to play some rare high-scoring gems. Some excellent examples beginning with B are BANJAX (to ruin something, 22 points) and BEZIQUE (a card game, 27 points).

Some end-hooks
Two letters to three

AB-B	GU-B	NE-B
AL-B	HO-B	NO-B
AR-B	JA-B	NU-B
BI-B	JO-B	OR-B
BO-B	KA-B	RE-B
DA-B	KO-B	SI-B
DE-B	LA-B	SO-B
DI-B	LI-B	TA-B
DO-B	LO-B	UR-B
FA-B	MI-B	WE-B
GI-B	MO-B	YO-B
GO-B	NA-B	

Three letters to four

BAR-B	DIE-B	JAM-B
BIB-B	DOR-B	JIB-B
BOA-B	FEE-B	LAM-B
BUR-B	FLU-B	NIM-B
CAR-B	FOR-B	PRO-B
CHI-B	GAM-B	TOM-B
COB-B	GAR-B	WAR-B
CUR-B	HER-B	

Four letters to five

ACER-B	DEMO-B	THRO-B
BLUR-B	PLUM-B	ZEBU-B
CUBE-B	SLUR-B	

Five letters to six

SCRAM-B	SUPER-B

Six letters to seven

POTHER-B   PROVER-B   REPLUM-B

> ### BLOCKERS
> It is useful to know which words are blockers and can't therefore
> be extended before or after. You may want to play a blocker that
> your opponent can't extend, or you may want to avoid playing a
> blocker because you want to keep the board open.

Three-letter blocker beginning with B

BEZ

Some four-letter blockers beginning with B

BABY	BEVY	BUBO
BADE	BLEW	BURY
BEEN	BODY	BUSY

Some five-letter blockers beginning with B (except words ending in '-ED', '-J', '-S', '-X', '-Y' or '-Z')

BANAL	BELCH	BRUNG
BARER	BIRCH	BUILT
BATCH	BLASÉ	BURNT
BEGAN	BLOWN	BUTCH
BEGAT	BLUER	BUXOM
BEGOT	BOXEN	

Some six-letter blockers beginning with B (except words ending in '-ED', '-J', '-S', '-X', '-Y' or '-Z')

BADDER	BATMAN	BIGGER
BADMAN	BAYMAN	BINMAN
BAGMAN	BEATEN	BITTEN
BALDER	BECAME	BLANCH
BALING	BEFORE	BLEACH
BANISH	BEGONE	BLUEST
BAREST	BEHALF	BLUIER
BARFUL	BEHELD	BLUISH
BARING	BENIGN	BOGMAN
BARISH	BEREFT	BOLDER
BARMAN	BIFOLD	BONIER
BASEST	BIFORM	BONZER

BOOING
BOWMAN
BOXIER
BOYING
BOYISH
BREACH

BREECH
BRICHT
BROKEN
BROOCH
BRUNCH
BRUTAL

BUSIER
BUSMAN
BUYING
BYPAST

BONUS WORDS

Bonus words on your rack can be hard to spot, especially for the less experienced player. One way to help find them is by using prefixes and suffixes.

Many larger words include a common prefix or suffix – remembering these and using them where you can is a good way to discover any longer words on your rack, including any potential bonus words. The key prefixes to remember beginning with B are BE- and BI- and the key suffixes are -BACK, -BALL, -BAND and -BIRD.

Some words beginning with BE-

Seven-letter words

BE-ACHED
BE-ARISH
BE-AVERS
BE-CAUSE
BE-COMES
BE-DECKS
BE-DEVIL
BE-DRAIL
BE-DROLL
BE-ECHES
BE-FALLS
BE-FOULS
BE-GUILE

BE-HAVER
BE-HEADS
BE-HINDS
BE-HOLDS
BE-HOOFS
BE-JEWEL
BE-LATED
BE-LAYED
BE-LIEFS
BE-LONGS
BE-LOVED
BE-MOANS
BE-MUSED

BE-NEATH
BE-QUEST
BE-RATED
BE-REAVE
BE-SIDES
BE-SIEGE
BE-SPOKE
BE-STOWS
BE-TIDES
BE-TRAYS
BE-TWEEN
BE-TWIXT
BE-WITCH

Eight-letter words

BE-ACHING
BE-ARABLE
BE-BOPPED
BE-CALMED

BE-CHANCE
BE-COMING
BE-CURSED
BE-DAUBED

BE-DAZZLE
BE-DECKED
BE-FOULED
BE-FRIEND

BE-FUDDLE
BE-GETTER
BE-GINNER
BE-GOTTEN
BE-GRUDGE
BE-GUILED
BE-HAVING
BE-HAVIOR
BE-HEADED
BE-HEADER
BE-HOLDEN
BE-HOLDER

BE-HOOVED
BE-HOVING
BE-KNIGHT
BE-LAYING
BE-LIEVER
BE-LITTLE
BE-LONGED
BE-LONGER
BE-MUSING
BE-RATING
BE-REAVED
BE-REAVER

BE-SIEGED
BE-SIEGER
BE-SMIRCH
BE-SPOKEN
BE-STOWED
BE-STREWN
BE-SUITED
BE-TIDING
BE-TITLED
BE-WARING
BE-WIGGED
BE-WILDER

Some words beginning with BI-
Seven-letter words

BI-AXIAL
BI-BLESS
BI-BLIST
BI-CARBS
BI-CYCLE
BI-DINGS
BI-FOCAL
BI-KINGS

BI-LEVEL
BI-MODAL
BI-OLOGY
BI-OPTIC
BI-PARTY
BI-PEDAL
BI-PLANE
BI-POLAR

BI-SECTS
BI-SHOPS
BI-TABLE
BI-TINGS
BI-TONAL
BI-VALVE
BI-VINYL
BI-ZONAL

Eight-letter words

BI-ANNUAL
BI-CHROME
BI-COLOUR
BI-CONVEX
BI-CUSPID
BI-CYCLED
BI-CYCLER
BI-CYCLIC

BI-FACIAL
BI-FORMED
BI-HOURLY
BI-LINEAR
BI-MANUAL
BI-METHYL
BI-PARTED
BI-PHASIC

BI-RADIAL
BI-STABLE
BI-TEWING
BI-TINGLY
BI-UNIQUE
BI-VALVED
BI-WEEKLY
BI-YEARLY

Some words ending with -BACK
Seven-letter words

BUY-BACK
CUT-BACK
DIE-BACK

FAT-BACK
FIN-BACK
FLY-BACK

LAY-BACK
OUT-BACK
PAY-BACK

RED-BACK   SUN-BACK
SET-BACK   TIE-BACK

Eight-letter words

BARE-BACK   FEED-BACK   PLAY-BACK
BLOW-BACK   FLAT-BACK   PULL-BACK
BLUE-BACK   FULL-BACK   ROLL-BACK
CALL-BACK   GREY-BACK   SEAT-BACK
CASH-BACK   HALF-BACK   SNAP-BACK
CLAW-BACK   HOLD-BACK   TAIL-BACK
COME-BACK   HUMP-BACK   TALK-BACK
DRAW-BACK   KICK-BACK   TURN-BACK
FALL-BACK   LIFT-BACK   WING-BACK
FAST-BACK   LOAN-BACK

Some words ending with -BALL

Seven-letter words

EYE-BALL   LOW-BALL   ODD-BALL
GUM-BALL   NET-BALL   PIN-BALL

Eight-letter words

BASE-BALL   FOOT-BALL   MEAT-BALL
BLUE-BALL   GOOF-BALL   MOTH-BALL
CORN-BALL   HAIR-BALL   PUFF-BALL
FAST-BALL   HAND-BALL   SNOW-BALL
FIRE-BALL   HARD-BALL   SOFT-BALL
FISH-BALL   HIGH-BALL   SPIT-BALL
FOOS-BALL   KICK-BALL

Some words ending with -BAND

Seven-letter words

ARM-BAND   HAT-BAND
DIS-BAND   HUS-BAND

Eight-letter words

BACK-BAND   HEAD-BAND   SARA-BAND
BASE-BAND   NECK-BAND   SIDE-BAND
BROW-BAND   NOSE-BAND   WAVE-BAND
HAIR-BAND   RAIN-BAND   WIDE-BAND

Some words ending with -BIRD

Seven-letter words

ANT-BIRD	COW-BIRD	OIL-BIRD
AXE-BIRD	FAT-BIRD	RED-BIRD
BOO-BIRD	JAY-BIRD	SEA-BIRD
CAT-BIRD	MAY-BIRD	SUN-BIRD

Eight-letter words

BELL-BIRD	KING-BIRD	REED-BIRD
BLUE-BIRD	LADY-BIRD	RICE-BIRD
CAGE-BIRD	LOVE-BIRD	SNOW-BIRD
FERN-BIRD	LYRE-BIRD	SONG-BIRD
FIRE-BIRD	OVEN-BIRD	SURF-BIRD
GAOL-BIRD	PUFF-BIRD	WHIP-BIRD
HANG-BIRD	RAIL-BIRD	YARD-BIRD
JAIL-BIRD	RAIN-BIRD	

> ### Handy Hint: Blank Tiles
>
> A blank tile is, by its nature, incredibly versatile as it can be substituted for any other letter. Although it scores no points in itself, the blank tile can make forming bonus words that much easier and players should never, ever change a blank tile should they be lucky enough to find one on their rack.

UNUSUAL LETTER COMBINATIONS

If you have an unusual combination of letters on your rack, or want to impress your opponent with an unusual word, a few words from World English can come in handy.

Australian words

BARRO	embarrassing
BAUERA	small evergreen shrub
BEAUT	outstanding person or thing
BELAH	casuarina tree
BERKO	berserk
BIFFO	fighting or aggressive behaviour
BILBY	burrowing marsupial
BIZZO	empty and irrelevant talk

BOAB	baobab tree
BODGIE	unruly or uncouth man
BOGAN	youth who dresses and behaves rebelliously
BOOBOOK	small spotted brown owl
BOOFY	strong but stupid
BORA	native Australian coming-of-age ceremony
BORAK	rubbish or nonsense
BRASCO	lavatory
BROLGA	large grey crane with a trumpeting call
BRUMBY	wild horse
BUNYA	tall dome-shaped coniferous tree
BUNYIP	legendary monster

Canadian words

BABICHE	thongs or lacings of rawhide
BARACHOIS	shallow lagoon formed by a sand bar
BATEAU	light flat-bottomed boat
BEIGNET	deep-fried pastry
BREWIS	bread soaked in broth, gravy, etc
BUTTE	isolated steep-sided flat-topped hill

Hindi words

BABU	Mr
BAEL	spiny tree
BAHADUR	title for distinguished Indian during the Raj
BANDH	general strike
BANYAN	tree whose branches grow down into the soil
BHAJI	deep-fried vegetable savoury
BHANGRA	music combining traditional Punjabi music with Western pop
BHAVAN	large house or building
BHISHTI	water-carrier
BINDI	decorative dot in middle of forehead
BOBBERY	mixed pack of hunting dogs
BUND	embankment

New Zealand word

| BOOHAI | thoroughly lost |

South African words

| BAAS | boss |
| BABALAS | drunk or hungover |

BAKKIE	small truck
BRAAI	grill or roast meat
BRAAIVLEIS	barbecue
BUNDU	wild, remote region

Urdu words

BAGH	garden
BALTI	spicy Indian dish stewed until most liquid has evaporated
BASTI	slum
BEGUM	woman of high rank
BIRYANI	Indian dish of highly flavoured rice mixed with meat or fish

Essential info
Value: 3 points
Number in set: 2

C can be a difficult letter to play (for example, it only forms one two-letter word: CH, an old dialect word for I, 7 points). However, it does form some good three-letter words including CAW, COW and COY (all 8 points) and also CAZ (short form of casual, 14 points). Worth remembering also are the short words which don't use any vowels: CLY (a word for steal, 8 points) and CWM (a Welsh word for valley, 10 points).

Two-letter word beginning with C

CH

Some three-letter words beginning with C

CAA	CHA	COR
CAG	CHE	COS
CAM	CHI	COX
CAW	CID	COZ
CAY	CIS	CUM
CAZ	CIT	CUR
CEE	CLY	CUZ
CEL	COO	CWM

HOOKS

Hooking requires a subtle change in a player's thought process, in that they must look at words already on the board without becoming distracted by their pronunciation.

Some front-hooks
Two letters to three

C-AA	C-AM	C-AW
C-AB	C-AN	C-AY
C-AD	C-AR	C-EE
C-AG	C-AT	C-EL

C-HA	C-OD	C-OX
C-HE	C-ON	C-OY
C-HI	C-OO	C-UM
C-ID	C-OP	C-UP
C-IS	C-OR	C-UR
C-IT	C-OS	C-UT
C-OB	C-OW	

Three letters to four

C-AGE	C-HOG	C-OCA
C-AID	C-HOP	C-OCH
C-AKE	C-HOW	C-ODA
C-ALF	C-HUB	C-ODE
C-ALL	C-HUG	C-OFF
C-ALP	C-HUM	C-OFT
C-AMP	C-HUT	C-OHO
C-ANT	C-IDE	C-OIL
C-ANY	C-ILL	C-OLD
C-APE	C-ION	C-ONE
C-ARE	C-IRE	C-ONS
C-ARK	C-LAD	C-ORE
C-ART	C-LAM	C-OUR
C-ASH	C-LAP	C-OWL
C-ASK	C-LAW	C-RAG
C-ATE	C-LAY	C-RAM
C-HAD	C-LEG	C-RAN
C-HAM	C-LIP	C-RAW
C-HAT	C-LOD	C-RAY
C-HAY	C-LOG	C-RED
C-HER	C-LOP	C-RIB
C-HEW	C-LOT	C-RIM
C-HID	C-LOW	C-ROW
C-HIP	C-LOY	C-RUE
C-HIS	C-OAT	C-URN
C-HIT	C-OBS	C-UTE

Four letters to five

C-ABLE	C-AIRN	C-APER
C-ACHE	C-AKED	C-ARED
C-AGED	C-ANON	C-AULD
C-AGER	C-APED	C-AVER

C-AWED
C-EASE
C-HAFF
C-HAIN
C-HAIR
C-HARM
C-HART
C-HATS
C-HAVE
C-HEAP
C-HEAT
C-HECK
C-HELP
C-HERE
C-HEST
C-HICK
C-HIDE
C-HILD
C-HILI
C-HILL
C-HIVE
C-HOCK
C-HOKE
C-HOOF
C-HOOK
C-HOPS
C-HORE
C-HOSE
C-HOUT
C-HOWK
C-HUCK

C-HUFF
C-HUMP
C-HUNK
C-HURL
C-INCH
C-LACK
C-LAME
C-LAMP
C-LAMS
C-LANG
C-LANK
C-LASH
C-LASS
C-LAST
C-LEAN
C-LEAR
C-LEFT
C-LICK
C-LIMB
C-LING
C-LOCK
C-LONE
C-LOSE
C-LOUD
C-LOUT
C-LOVE
C-LOWN
C-LUCK
C-LUMP
C-LUNG
C-OAST

C-OMER
C-OPED
C-ORAL
C-OUCH
C-OVEN
C-OVER
C-OWED
C-RACK
C-RAFT
C-RAKE
C-RAMP
C-RANK
C-RARE
C-RASH
C-RATE
C-RAVE
C-RAZE
C-REAM
C-REDO
C-REED
C-REEK
C-REEL
C-REST
C-RIPE
C-RISE
C-ROCK
C-ROOK
C-RUCK
C-RUDE
C-RUSH
C-RUST

Five letters to six

C-ABLED
C-ABLER
C-ACHED
C-AGING
C-ALLOW
C-AMBER
C-AMPED

C-AMPLY
C-APING
C-ASKED
C-AUGHT
C-EASED
C-HAPPY
C-HASTE

C-HEWED
C-HIDER
C-HILLY
C-HIPPY
C-HOKEY
C-HOPPY
C-HUBBY

C-HUFFY
C-HUNKY
C-LANKY
C-LEAVE
C-LONER
C-LOSED
C-LOSER
C-LOVER
C-LUCKY
C-LUMPY

C-ODDER
C-OILED
C-OLDER
C-OVERT
C-RAGGY
C-RATED
C-RATER
C-RAVED
C-RAVEN
C-RAYON

C-RAZED
C-ROWED
C-RUDER
C-RUMMY
C-RUSTY
C-UMBER
C-UPPED
C-UPPER
C-UTTER

Six letters to seven

C-ABLING
C-ACHING
C-AMPING
C-ANGLED
C-AROUSE
C-ARTFUL
C-ASHIER
C-ASHING
C-ASKING
C-ASTRAL
C-AULDER
C-EASING
C-ENSURE
C-HACKED
C-HAIRED
C-HAMPER
C-HANGED
C-HANGER
C-HARING
C-HARKED
C-HARMED
C-HARMER
C-HASTEN
C-HATTED
C-HATTER
C-HAWING
C-HEAPER
C-HEATED

C-HEATER
C-HELPED
C-HEWING
C-HIDING
C-HILLED
C-HILLER
C-HIPPED
C-HIPPER
C-HIPPIE
C-HITTER
C-HOPPED
C-HOPPER
C-HUCKLE
C-HUFFED
C-HUFFER
C-HUGGED
C-HUGGER
C-HUMMED
C-HUNTER
C-INCHED
C-LACKED
C-LACKER
C-LAMBER
C-LAMMED
C-LAMMER
C-LAMPED
C-LAMPER
C-LANGER

C-LANKED
C-LAPPED
C-LAPPER
C-LASHED
C-LASHER
C-LATTER
C-LEANED
C-LEANER
C-LEANLY
C-LEARED
C-LEAVED
C-LEAVER
C-LICKED
C-LICKER
C-LIMBED
C-LIMBER
C-LINGER
C-LINKED
C-LINKER
C-LIPPED
C-LIPPER
C-LITTER
C-LOBBER
C-LOCKED
C-LOCKER
C-LOGGED
C-LOGGER
C-LOPPED

C-LOSING	C-RAFTER	C-RINGER
C-LOTTED	C-RAGGED	C-RIPPLE
C-LUBBER	C-RAMMED	C-ROCKED
C-LUCKED	C-RAMPED	C-ROCKET
C-LUMPED	C-RANKED	C-ROOKED
C-LUMPER	C-RASHED	C-ROSIER
C-LUNKER	C-RASHER	C-ROWING
C-LUSTER	C-RAVING	C-RUDELY
C-OILING	C-REAKED	C-RUDEST
C-OLDEST	C-REAMED	C-RUMBLE
C-OLDISH	C-RESTED	C-RUMPLE
C-ORACLE	C-RIBBED	C-RUSHED
C-RACKED	C-RIBBER	C-RUSHER
C-RACKER	C-RICKED	C-RUSTED
C-RAFTED	C-RINGED	C-UPPING

HIGHEST WORD SCORE

The highest-scoring word ever played in a Scrabble game was CAZIQUES, which achieved an enormous total of 392 points. It was played by Karl Khoshnaw of Richmond, Surrey.

Seven letters to eight

C-AMBERED	C-HICKORY	C-LAPPING
C-ANGLING	C-HILDING	C-LASHING
C-ASHLESS	C-HILLIER	C-LATCHED
C-ENSURED	C-HOPPING	C-LAWLESS
C-ENTERED	C-HUFFING	C-LAWLIKE
C-HAIRING	C-HUGGERS	C-LEANEST
C-HANDLER	C-HUGGING	C-LEANING
C-HANGING	C-HUMMING	C-LEARING
C-HANTING	C-HUMPING	C-LEAVING
C-HAPLESS	C-HUNKIER	C-LICKING
C-HAPPIER	C-INCHING	C-LIMBING
C-HARMFUL	C-LACKING	C-LINGIER
C-HARMING	C-LAGGING	C-LINKING
C-HATTING	C-LAMMING	C-LIPPING
C-HEATING	C-LAMPING	C-LOCKING
C-HELPING	C-LANKIER	C-LOGGING
C-HEWABLE	C-LANKING	C-LOPPING

C-LOSABLE	C-OVERALL	C-RIBBING
C-LOTTING	C-OVERTLY	C-RICKING
C-LOUTING	C-RACKING	C-RIMPLED
C-LUCKIER	C-RAFTING	C-RINGING
C-LUCKING	C-RAGGIER	C-RIPPLED
C-LUMPIER	C-RAMMING	C-RIPPLER
C-LUMPING	C-RAMPING	C-ROCKERY
C-LUMPISH	C-RANKING	C-RUMBLED
C-OFFERED	C-RASHING	C-RUMPLED
C-OLDNESS	C-REAMING	C-RUSHING
C-OTTERED	C-REELING	C-RUSTIER
C-OVERAGE	C-RESTING	C-RUSTILY

Some end-hooks
Two letters to three

AR-C	MI-C	RE-C
BA-C	MO-C	SI-C
DO-C	MY-C	SO-C
HI-C	OR-C	TE-C
HO-C	PA-C	TI-C
LA-C	PE-C	TO-C
MA-C	PI-C	

Three letters to four

ABA-C	DIS-C	SYN-C
ALE-C	HUI-C	TOR-C
BAN-C	MAR-C	ZIN-C
CHI-C	SAI-C	

Four letters to five

ANTI-C	ILIA-C	SERA-C
ARTI-C	LOTI-C	TARO-C
CODE-C	MAGI-C	TOPI-C
CONI-C	MALI-C	TORI-C
DURO-C	MANI-C	TRON-C
ILEA-C	RABI-C	YOGI-C

Five letters to six

ACINI-C	CHOLI-C	FILMI-C
AGAMI-C	CULTI-C	FUNDI-C

| FUNGI-C | MANIA-C | PARSE-C |
| LIMBI-C | MYTHI-C | TRAGI-C |

Six letters to seven

ALKALI-C	EMBOLI-C	SCORIA-C
CARDIA-C	NUCLEI-C	THALLI-C
COLONI-C	RHOMBI-C	TROPHI-C

Seven letters to eight

AMMONIA-C	CHIASMI-C	SYLLABI-C
AMNESIA-C	DACTYLI-C	TSUNAMI-C
BULIMIA-C	RHYTHMI-C	TYMPANI-C

BLOCKERS

It is useful to know which words are blockers and can't therefore be extended before or after. You may want to play a blocker that your opponent can't extend, or you may want to avoid playing a blocker because you want to keep the board open.

Some three-letter blockers beginning with C

| CAZ | CLY | CUZ |

Some four-letter blockers beginning with C

CASH	COAX	COZY
CAVY	COPY	CRUX
CHEZ	COSH	CUED
CITY	COSY	CURT

Some five-letter blockers beginning with C (except words ending in '-ED', '-J', '-S', '-X', '-Y' or '-Z')

CACTI	CLASH	CREPT
CAJUN	CLUNG	CRUSH
CINCH	COULD	CUING
CIVIL	CRASH	CYBER

Some six-letter blockers beginning with C (except words ending in '-ED', '-J', '-S', '-X', '-Y' or '-Z')

CAGIER	CANIER	CARMEN
CAGING	CANNOT	CATTLE
CALCIC	CARDIO	CAUGHT
CALMER	CARMAN	CAUSEN

CEDING	CLOVEN	CROUCH
CHEVAL	CLUING	CRUDER
CHOSEN	COGENT	CRUTCH
CISTIC	COITAL	CURING
CITING	COMETH	CURTER
CITRIC	CONING	CYANIC
CLENCH	COSMIC	CYSTIC
CLINCH	COXING	
CLONAL	COYEST	

BONUS WORDS

Bonus words on your rack can be hard to spot, especially for the less experienced player. One way to help find them is by using prefixes and suffixes.

Many larger words include a common prefix or suffix – remembering these and using them where you can is a good way to discover any longer words on your rack, including any potential bonus words. The key prefixes to remember beginning with C are COM- and CON-.

Some words beginning with COM-

Seven-letter words

COM-BATS	COM-MENT	COM-PERE
COM-BINE	COM-MODE	COM-PILE
COM-BING	COM-MONS	COM-PLEX
COM-BUST	COM-MUTE	COM-PORT
COM-FIER	COM-PACT	COM-POSE
COM-FORT	COM-PARE	COM-POST
COM-MAND	COM-PASS	COM-POTE
COM-MEND	COM-PEND	COM-RADE

Eight-letter words

COM-BATED	COM-PADRE	COM-PLIER
COM-BINER	COM-PARED	COM-POSED
COM-BINES	COM-PILED	COM-POSER
COM-FIEST	COM-PILER	COM-POUND
COM-MONER	COM-PLAIN	COM-PRESS
COM-MUTED	COM-PLEAT	COM-PRISE
COM-MUTER	COM-PLIED	

Some words beginning with CON-
Seven-letter words

CON-CAVE	CON-FIRM	CON-SOLE
CON-CEDE	CON-FORM	CON-SORT
CON-CERT	CON-FUSE	CON-TACT
CON-CORD	CON-GEAL	CON-TAIN
CON-CUSS	CON-GEST	CON-TEND
CON-DOLE	CON-JOIN	CON-TENT
CON-DONE	CON-JURE	CON-TEST
CON-DUCE	CON-JURY	CON-TEXT
CON-DUCT	CON-NOTE	CON-TORT
CON-DUIT	CON-SENT	CON-TOUR
CON-FESS	CON-SIGN	CON-VENT
CON-FINE	CON-SIST	CON-VERT

Eight-letter words

CON-CAVED	CON-FRONT	CON-SOLED
CON-CEDED	CON-FUSED	CON-SOLER
CON-CEDER	CON-GENIC	CON-SPIRE
CON-CLAVE	CON-JOINT	CON-TEMPT
CON-DENSE	CON-JUGAL	CON-TRACT
CON-DOLED	CON-JUROR	CON-TRITE
CON-DONER	CON-QUEST	CON-VERGE
CON-FINED	CON-SERVE	CON-VERSE
CON-FOUND	CON-SIDER	CON-VEXED

UNUSUAL LETTER COMBINATIONS

If you have an unusual combination of letters on your rack, or want to impress your opponent with an unusual word, a few words from World English can come in handy.

Australian words

CADAGI	tropical eucalyptus tree
CARBY	carburettor
CHEWI	chewing gum
CHIACK	tease or banter
CHOOK	hen or chicken
CHOOM	Englishman
COMPO	compensation
CORREA	evergreen shrub

C

COUCAL	long-legged bird
COUGAN	rowdy person
CRONK	unfit or unsound
CROOL	spoil
CROWEA	pink-flowered shrub

Canadian words

CABOOSE	mobile bunkhouse used by lumbermen
CANOLA	cooking oil extracted from a variety of rapeseed developed in Canada
CAYUSE	small Native American pony used by cowboys
CUSK	gadoid food fish

Hindi words

CHAI	tea, especially with added spices
CHAMPAC	tree with fragrant yellow flowers
CHAPATI	flat coarse unleavened bread
CHAPPAL	sandal
CHARKHA	spinning wheel
CHEETAH	large swift feline mammal
CHELA	disciple of a religious teacher
CHINTZ	printed cotton with glazed finish
CHITAL	type of deer
CHOKEY	prison
CHOLI	short-sleeved bodice
CHOWK	marketplace
CHUDDAR	large shawl or veil
CHUDDIES	underpants
CHUKAR	Indian partridge
CHUKKA	period of play in polo
COWAGE	tropical climbing plant with stinging pods
CRORE	ten million
CUSHY	comfortable

New Zealand word

| COOTIE | body louse |

Urdu words

| CHARPAI | bedstead of woven webbing on a wooden frame |

D
2

Essential info
Value: 2 points
Number in set: 4

D can begin a two-letter word alongside every vowel except for U. It also forms many three-letter words, especially in combination with W or Y: DAY, DYE and DEW are all worth 7 points.

Two-letter words beginning with D

DA	DI
DE	DO

Some three-letter words beginning with D

DAE	DEV	DOM
DAG	DEX	DOO
DAH	DEY	DOP
DAK	DIB	DOR
DAL	DIF	DOW
DAN	DIS	DOY
DAP	DIT	DSO
DAW	DIV	DUH
DEB	DOB	DUN
DEE	DOC	DUP
DEF	DOD	DUX
DEG	DOF	DZO
DEI	DOH	
DEL	DOL	

HOOKS

Hooking requires a subtle change in a player's thought process, in that they must look at words already on the board without becoming distracted by their pronunciation. D benefits from the past participle form of many words, providing many options when it comes to end-hooking.

Some front-hooks

Two letters to three

D-AB	D-EN	D-OO
D-AD	D-EX	D-OP
D-AE	D-ID	D-OR
D-AG	D-IF	D-OS
D-AH	D-IN	D-OW
D-AL	D-IS	D-OY
D-AM	D-IT	D-SO
D-AN	D-OB	D-UG
D-AS	D-OD	D-UH
D-AW	D-OE	D-UN
D-AY	D-OF	D-UP
D-EE	D-OH	D-YE
D-EF	D-OM	D-ZO
D-EL	D-ON	

Three letters to four

D-AFT	D-EMO	D-OWL
D-ALE	D-HOW	D-OWN
D-AMP	D-ICE	D-RAG
D-ARE	D-ILL	D-RAM
D-ARK	D-IRE	D-RAT
D-ART	D-IRK	D-RAW
D-ASH	D-ISH	D-RAY
D-ATE	D-OFF	D-REW
D-AWN	D-OLE	D-RIP
D-EAN	D-ONE	D-ROW
D-EAR	D-OOR	D-RUB
D-ECO	D-OPE	D-RUG
D-EFT	D-OSE	D-RUM
D-ELL	D-OUR	D-ZHO

Four letters to five

D-AIRY	D-ICKY	D-ONER
D-ALLY	D-INKY	D-OOZY
D-AUNT	D-ITCH	D-RAFT
D-EVIL	D-JINN	D-RAIN
D-ICED	D-OILY	D-RAKE

D-RANK   D-RIFT   D-WELL
D-RAWN   D-RILL   D-WELT
D-READ   D-RINK
D-REAM   D-ROLL

Five letters to six

D-AFTER   D-EJECT   D-OFFER
D-AMPLY   D-ELUDE   D-OWNED
D-ANGER   D-EMOTE   D-OWNER
D-ANGLE   D-ICIER   D-RAYED
D-APPLE   D-ICING   D-RIVEN
D-ASHED   D-IMPLY   D-ROGUE
D-AWNED   D-INNER   D-ROVER
D-EARLY   D-OCKER   D-UMBER
D-EARTH   D-OFFED

Six letters to seven

D-ALLIED   D-INKIER   D-RILLED
D-AMPING   D-ITCHED   D-RIPPED
D-ANGLED   D-OFFING   D-RIPPER
D-ANGLER   D-OWNING   D-ROLLER
D-ASHING   D-RAFTED   D-RUBBED
D-AWNING   D-RAGGED   D-RUBBER
D-ELATED   D-RAINED   D-RUGGED
D-ELUDED   D-RAWING   D-RUMMER
D-EMOTED   D-REAMED   D-WELLED
D-EVOLVE   D-REAMER
D-ICIEST   D-RIFTED

Seven letters to eight

D-ALLYING   D-EMOTION   D-READING
D-ANGERED   D-ENOUNCE   D-REAMING
D-ANGLING   D-EVOLVED   D-RIFTING
D-EJECTED   D-INKIEST   D-RUBBING
D-ELUDING   D-ITCHING   D-RUGGING
D-ELUSION   D-RAFTING   D-WELLING
D-EMERGED   D-RAGGING   D-WINDLED
D-EMOTING   D-RAINING

Some end-hooks
Two letters to three

AD-D	GO-D	OR-D
AI-D	HA-D	OU-D
AN-D	HI-D	PA-D
AR-D	HO-D	PE-D
BA-D	KI-D	PO-D
BE-D	LA-D	RE-D
BI-D	LI-D	SO-D
BO-D	LO-D	TA-D
DA-D	MA-D	TE-D
DI-D	ME-D	TI-D
DO-D	MI-D	TO-D
EL-D	MO-D	UR-D
EN-D	MU-D	WE-D
FA-D	NE-D	YA-D
FE-D	NO-D	YO-D
GI-D	OD-D	

Three letters to four

ACE-D	CHI-D	FEU-D
AGE-D	COL-D	FIN-D
AKE-D	CON-D	FON-D
AMI-D	COR-D	FOR-D
APE-D	CRU-D	FOU-D
ARE-D	CUE-D	FUN-D
AWE-D	CUR-D	GAE-D
AXE-D	DIE-D	GAU-D
BAL-D	DOW-D	GEE-D
BAN-D	DUE-D	GEL-D
BAR-D	DYE-D	GIE-D
BEN-D	EAR-D	GOA-D
BIN-D	ECO-D	GOO-D
BON-D	EKE-D	HAE-D
BOR-D	ERE-D	HAN-D
BRO-D	EYE-D	HEN-D
BUN-D	FAN-D	HER-D
BUR-D	FAR-D	HIE-D
CAR-D	FEE-D	HIN-D
CHA-D	FEN-D	HOE-D

HOO-D	PAN-D	SOL-D
HUE-D	PAR-D	SUD-D
ICE-D	PEN-D	SUE-D
IRE-D	PIE-D	SUR-D
KIN-D	PRO-D	TAE-D
KON-D	QUA-D	TEA-D
LAR-D	RAI-D	TEE-D
LEA-D	RAN-D	TEL-D
LEE-D	RED-D	TEN-D
LEU-D	REE-D	TIE-D
LEW-D	REN-D	TIN-D
LIE-D	RIN-D	TOE-D
LIN-D	ROE-D	TYE-D
LOR-D	RUE-D	USE-D
LOU-D	RUN-D	VIE-D
MAN-D	SAI-D	WAI-D
MEL-D	SAN-D	WAN-D
MEN-D	SAR-D	WAR-D
MIL-D	SEE-D	WEE-D
MOL-D	SEL-D	WEN-D
MOO-D	SEN-D	WIN-D
NEE-D	SHE-D	WOO-D
OPE-D	SIN-D	WYN-D
OWE-D	SKI-D	YAR-D

D

Four letters to five

ABLE-D	BLUE-D	CITE-D
ACHE-D	BOAR-D	CLUE-D
ACNE-D	BODE-D	CODE-D
ACRE-D	BONE-D	COKE-D
AIDE-D	BORE-D	CONE-D
AMEN-D	BRAN-D	COPE-D
AXLE-D	CAGE-D	CORE-D
BAKE-D	CAKE-D	COVE-D
BALE-D	CANE-D	COZE-D
BARE-D	CAPE-D	CROW-D
BASE-D	CARE-D	CUBE-D
BEAR-D	CASE-D	CURE-D
BIDE-D	CAVE-D	DARE-D
BIKE-D	CEDE-D	DATE-D

DAZE-D	HAZE-D	MUSE-D
DICE-D	HEAR-D	MUTE-D
DINE-D	HIKE-D	NAME-D
DIVE-D	HIRE-D	NOSE-D
DOLE-D	HOLE-D	NOTE-D
DOME-D	HOME-D	NUKE-D
DOPE-D	HONE-D	OGLE-D
DOSE-D	HOPE-D	OOZE-D
DOTE-D	HOSE-D	PACE-D
DOZE-D	HYPE-D	PAGE-D
DUKE-D	IDLE-D	PALE-D
DUPE-D	JADE-D	PARE-D
EASE-D	JAPE-D	PAVE-D
EDGE-D	JIBE-D	PIKE-D
FACE-D	JIVE-D	PILE-D
FADE-D	JOKE-D	PINE-D
FAKE-D	KNEE-D	PIPE-D
FAME-D	LACE-D	PLEA-D
FARE-D	LAIR-D	PLIE-D
FATE-D	LAZE-D	POKE-D
FAZE-D	LIKE-D	PORE-D
FETE-D	LIME-D	POSE-D
FILE-D	LINE-D	RABI-D
FINE-D	LIVE-D	RACE-D
FIRE-D	LOPE-D	RAGE-D
FRAU-D	LOVE-D	RAKE-D
FREE-D	LOWE-D	RARE-D
FUME-D	LUGE-D	RATE-D
FUSE-D	LURE-D	RAVE-D
GAME-D	LUTE-D	RAZE-D
GAPE-D	MACE-D	RILE-D
GATE-D	MATE-D	ROBE-D
GAZE-D	MAZE-D	ROPE-D
GLUE-D	METE-D	ROSE-D
GORE-D	MIKE-D	ROVE-D
GRAN-D	MIME-D	RULE-D
GRIN-D	MINE-D	RUNE-D
GUAR-D	MIRE-D	SATE-D
HARE-D	MOPE-D	SAVE-D
HATE-D	MOVE-D	SHOE-D

SIDE-D	TIRE-D	WANE-D
SIRE-D	TONE-D	WAVE-D
SITE-D	TREE-D	WEIR-D
SIZE-D	TRIE-D	WINE-D
SPIE-D	TUNE-D	WIPE-D
SURE-D	TWEE-D	WIRE-D
TAME-D	TYPE-D	YOKE-D
TAPE-D	URGE-D	ZONE-D
TILE-D	VOTE-D	
TIME-D	WADE-D	

Five letters to six

ABASE-D	BULGE-D	ELUDE-D
ABATE-D	CABLE-D	EMOTE-D
ABIDE-D	CACHE-D	ENSUE-D
ABUSE-D	CARTE-D	ERASE-D
ADDLE-D	CARVE-D	ERODE-D
ADORE-D	CAUSE-D	EVADE-D
AGREE-D	CEASE-D	EVOKE-D
AMAZE-D	CHASE-D	EXILE-D
AMBLE-D	CHIME-D	FABLE-D
AMUSE-D	CHOKE-D	FENCE-D
ANGLE-D	CLONE-D	FLAKE-D
ANKLE-D	CLOSE-D	FLAME-D
ARGUE-D	CRANE-D	FLARE-D
ATONE-D	CRAVE-D	FLUKE-D
BARGE-D	CRAZE-D	FORCE-D
BASTE-D	CURSE-D	FORGE-D
BELIE-D	CURVE-D	FRAME-D
BINGE-D	CYCLE-D	GAUGE-D
BLAME-D	DANCE-D	GLARE-D
BLARE-D	DELVE-D	GLAZE-D
BLAZE-D	DEUCE-D	GLIDE-D
BOOZE-D	DODGE-D	GLOVE-D
BRACE-D	DOUSE-D	GORGE-D
BRAKE-D	DOWSE-D	GOUGE-D
BRAVE-D	DRAPE-D	GRACE-D
BRIBE-D	DRONE-D	GRADE-D
BUDGE-D	ELATE-D	GRAPE-D
BUGLE-D	ELOPE-D	GRATE-D

GRAVE-D	PRIME-D	SKATE-D
GRAZE-D	PRISE-D	SLATE-D
GRIPE-D	PROBE-D	SLAVE-D
GROPE-D	PROVE-D	SLICE-D
GROVE-D	PRUNE-D	SLIME-D
GUIDE-D	PULSE-D	SLOPE-D
HASTE-D	PURGE-D	SMILE-D
HEAVE-D	QUAKE-D	SMOKE-D
HEDGE-D	QUEUE-D	SNAKE-D
HINGE-D	QUOTE-D	SNARE-D
HORSE-D	RAISE-D	SNIPE-D
HOUSE-D	RANGE-D	SNORE-D
IMAGE-D	REAVE-D	SOLVE-D
ISSUE-D	RETRO-D	SPACE-D
JUDGE-D	RHYME-D	SPARE-D
JUICE-D	RIDGE-D	SPICE-D
KNIFE-D	RIFLE-D	SPIKE-D
LADLE-D	RINSE-D	STAGE-D
LANCE-D	ROGUE-D	STAKE-D
LAPSE-D	ROUTE-D	STALE-D
LEASE-D	SALVE-D	STARE-D
LEAVE-D	SAUTE-D	STATE-D
LEDGE-D	SCALE-D	STOKE-D
LODGE-D	SCARE-D	STONE-D
LOOSE-D	SCOPE-D	STORE-D
LUNGE-D	SCORE-D	STYLE-D
MERGE-D	SEIZE-D	SURGE-D
MINCE-D	SENSE-D	SWIPE-D
NUDGE-D	SHADE-D	TABLE-D
NURSE-D	SHAKE-D	TASTE-D
PASTE-D	SHAPE-D	TEASE-D
PAUSE-D	SHAVE-D	TENSE-D
PHASE-D	SHINE-D	THEME-D
PHONE-D	SHORE-D	TINGE-D
PIECE-D	SHOVE-D	TITLE-D
PLACE-D	SHREW-D	TRACE-D
PLANE-D	SIDLE-D	TRADE-D
POISE-D	SIEGE-D	TRUCE-D
PRICE-D	SIEVE-D	TWINE-D
PRIDE-D	SINGE-D	UNITE-D

UNTIE-D VALUE-D VERGE-D VERSE-D VOICE-D

WAIVE-D WASTE-D WEAVE-D WEDGE-D WHALE-D

WHINE-D WHITE-D WINCE-D

Six letters to seven

ACCRUE-D
ACCUSE-D
ADHERE-D
ADMIRE-D
ADVISE-D
ALLUDE-D
ALLURE-D
ARRIVE-D
ASHAME-D
ASSUME-D
ASSURE-D
AVENGE-D
BABBLE-D
BAFFLE-D
BATTLE-D
BEETLE-D
BEHAVE-D
BELATE-D
BELOVE-D
BEMUSE-D
BERATE-D
BOGGLE-D
BOTTLE-D
BOUNCE-D
BREEZE-D
BRIDGE-D
BRIDLE-D
BRONZE-D
BROWSE-D
BRUISE-D
BUCKLE-D
BUNDLE-D
BUNGLE-D

BURBLE-D
BURGLE-D
BUSTLE-D
CACKLE-D
CASTLE-D
CENTRE-D
CHANCE-D
CHANGE-D
CHARGE-D
CHEESE-D
CIRCLE-D
CLEAVE-D
CLICHE-D
COERCE-D
CORPSE-D
COUPLE-D
COURSE-D
CRADLE-D
CREASE-D
CREATE-D
CRINGE-D
CRUISE-D
CUDDLE-D
CURDLE-D
DAMAGE-D
DANGLE-D
DAPPLE-D
DAWDLE-D
DAZZLE-D
DEBASE-D
DEBATE-D
DECIDE-D
DECODE-D

DECREE-D
DEDUCE-D
DEFACE-D
DEFAME-D
DEFILE-D
DEFINE-D
DEFUSE-D
DEGREE-D
DELATE-D
DELETE-D
DELUDE-D
DELUGE-D
DEMISE-D
DEMODE-D
DEMOTE-D
DEMURE-D
DENOTE-D
DENUDE-D
DEPOSE-D
DERIDE-D
DERIVE-D
DESIRE-D
DETUNE-D
DEVISE-D
DEVOTE-D
DILATE-D
DILUTE-D
DISUSE-D
DIVIDE-D
DIVINE-D
DONATE-D
DOODLE-D
DOUBLE-D

DREDGE-D	GLANCE-D	LOCATE-D
DRUDGE-D	GOBBLE-D	LOUNGE-D
ELAPSE-D	GREASE-D	MANAGE-D
EMERGE-D	GRIEVE-D	MANGLE-D
ENABLE-D	GROOVE-D	MANURE-D
ENCASE-D	GRUDGE-D	MARBLE-D
ENCODE-D	GUZZLE-D	MATURE-D
ENCORE-D	GYRATE-D	MENACE-D
ENDURE-D	HANDLE-D	MINGLE-D
ENGAGE-D	HECKLE-D	MINUTE-D
ENGINE-D	HOMAGE-D	MISUSE-D
ENRAGE-D	HUDDLE-D	MUDDLE-D
ENSURE-D	HUMBLE-D	MUFFLE-D
ENTICE-D	HURDLE-D	MUMBLE-D
EQUATE-D	HURTLE-D	MUSCLE-D
ESCAPE-D	HUSTLE-D	MUTATE-D
ESTATE-D	ICICLE-D	MUZZLE-D
EVOLVE-D	IGNITE-D	NEEDLE-D
EXCISE-D	IGNORE-D	NEGATE-D
EXCITE-D	IMPALE-D	NESTLE-D
EXCUSE-D	IMPEDE-D	NIBBLE-D
EXHALE-D	IMPOSE-D	NOTICE-D
EXHUME-D	INCITE-D	NUANCE-D
EXPIRE-D	INDUCE-D	OBLIGE-D
EXPOSE-D	INFAME-D	OPPOSE-D
FETTLE-D	INFUSE-D	PADDLE-D
FIDDLE-D	INHALE-D	PALACE-D
FIGURE-D	INJURE-D	PARADE-D
FISSLE-D	INVADE-D	PAROLE-D
FIZZLE-D	INVITE-D	PEDDLE-D
FLEDGE-D	INVOKE-D	PEOPLE-D
FLEECE-D	IONISE-D	PERUSE-D
FONDLE-D	JANGLE-D	PHRASE-D
FORAGE-D	JIGGLE-D	PICKLE-D
FRIDGE-D	JINGLE-D	PIERCE-D
FUMBLE-D	JOSTLE-D	PIRATE-D
GARBLE-D	JUGGLE-D	PLAGUE-D
GARGLE-D	JUMBLE-D	PLEASE-D
GENTLE-D	LIAISE-D	PLEDGE-D
GIGGLE-D	LOATHE-D	PLUNGE-D

POLICE-D	REVIVE-D	SUCKLE-D
POOTLE-D	REVOKE-D	SUPPLE-D
POUNCE-D	RIDDLE-D	SWATHE-D
PRAISE-D	ROTATE-D	SWERVE-D
PRANCE-D	RUBBLE-D	TACKLE-D
PSYCHE-D	RUFFLE-D	TICKLE-D
PUDDLE-D	RUMBLE-D	TINGLE-D
PUPATE-D	RUSTLE-D	TIPTOE-D
PURSUE-D	SADDLE-D	TITTLE-D
PUZZLE-D	SALUTE-D	TONGUE-D
RAFFLE-D	SAMPLE-D	TOPPLE-D
RAMBLE-D	SAVAGE-D	TORQUE-D
RATTLE-D	SCHEME-D	TOUCHE-D
RAVAGE-D	SCRAPE-D	TOUSLE-D
REBUKE-D	SCYTHE-D	TRANCE-D
RECEDE-D	SECEDE-D	TREBLE-D
RECITE-D	SECURE-D	TRIFLE-D
REDUCE-D	SEDATE-D	TRIPLE-D
REFINE-D	SEDUCE-D	TRUDGE-D
REFUSE-D	SEETHE-D	TUMBLE-D
REGALE-D	SEVERE-D	TUSSLE-D
REHIRE-D	SNOOZE-D	UMPIRE-D
RELATE-D	SOMBRE-D	UNDATE-D
RELINE-D	SOURCE-D	UNLIKE-D
REMOVE-D	SPONGE-D	UNLOVE-D
RENEGE-D	SQUIRE-D	UNSURE-D
REPUTE-D	STABLE-D	UPDATE-D
RESCUE-D	STAPLE-D	VOYAGE-D
RESIDE-D	STARVE-D	WABBLE-D
RESIZE-D	STATUE-D	WHINGE-D
RESUME-D	STRIPE-D	WIGGLE-D
RETIRE-D	STRIVE-D	WINKLE-D
REVERE-D	STROBE-D	WOBBLE-D
REVILE-D	STROKE-D	
REVISE-D	SUBDUE-D	

Seven letters to eight

ABRIDGE-D	ACHIEVE-D	AGITATE-D
ABSOLVE-D	ACQUIRE-D	AGONISE-D
ACCURSE-D	ADVANCE-D	ALLEDGE-D

53

ANALYSE-D	CRACKLE-D	ENLARGE-D
ANIMATE-D	CREMATE-D	ENTHUSE-D
APPROVE-D	CRINKLE-D	ENTITLE-D
ARCHIVE-D	CRIPPLE-D	EXAMINE-D
ARRANGE-D	CRUMBLE-D	EXCLUDE-D
ARTICLE-D	CRUMPLE-D	EXECUTE-D
ATOMISE-D	CRUSADE-D	EXPLODE-D
ATTACHE-D	CULTURE-D	EXPLORE-D
AVERAGE-D	DECEASE-D	FATIGUE-D
BALANCE-D	DECEIVE-D	FEATURE-D
BANDAGE-D	DECLARE-D	FINANCE-D
BEGUILE-D	DECLINE-D	FLOUNCE-D
BELIEVE-D	DEGRADE-D	GESTATE-D
BEREAVE-D	DEPRAVE-D	GESTURE-D
BRIGADE-D	DEPRIVE-D	GRUNTLE-D
CAPSIZE-D	DESERVE-D	HYDRATE-D
CAPTURE-D	DESPISE-D	IDOLISE-D
CHORTLE-D	DESTINE-D	IMAGINE-D
CHUCKLE-D	DEVALUE-D	IMITATE-D
COLLATE-D	DEVIATE-D	IMMERSE-D
COLLIDE-D	DICTATE-D	IMPLODE-D
COLLUDE-D	DIFFUSE-D	IMPLORE-D
COMBINE-D	DISABLE-D	IMPROVE-D
COMMUTE-D	DISEASE-D	INCLUDE-D
COMPARE-D	DISLIKE-D	INDULGE-D
COMPERE-D	DISPOSE-D	INFLAME-D
COMPETE-D	DISPUTE-D	INFLATE-D
COMPILE-D	DIVERGE-D	INSPIRE-D
COMPOSE-D	DIVORCE-D	INVOLVE-D
COMPUTE-D	DRIBBLE-D	LICENCE-D
CONCEDE-D	EDUCATE-D	LICENSE-D
CONCISE-D	ELEVATE-D	MANACLE-D
CONFIDE-D	EMANATE-D	MANDATE-D
CONFUSE-D	EMBRACE-D	MASSAGE-D
CONJURE-D	EMULATE-D	MEASURE-D
CONSOLE-D	ENCLOSE-D	MESSAGE-D
CONSUME-D	ENDORSE-D	MIGRATE-D
CONVENE-D	ENFORCE-D	MISTIME-D
CORRODE-D	ENGRAVE-D	OBSCURE-D
COSTUME-D	ENHANCE-D	OBSERVE-D

OPERATE-D	REALIZE-D	STUMBLE-D
OUTLINE-D	RECEIVE-D	SUBSIDE-D
OUTRAGE-D	RECYCLE-D	SUFFICE-D
OUTSIZE-D	REJOICE-D	SUPPOSE-D
OVERUSE-D	RELAPSE-D	SURFACE-D
OZONIZE-D	RELEASE-D	SURVIVE-D
PACKAGE-D	RELIEVE-D	SUSPIRE-D
PICTURE-D	REPLACE-D	TEXTURE-D
PILLAGE-D	REPULSE-D	TRAMPLE-D
PLACATE-D	REQUIRE-D	TROUBLE-D
POLLUTE-D	RESERVE-D	UNHINGE-D
PRECEDE-D	REVENGE-D	UNNERVE-D
PREFACE-D	REVERSE-D	UPGRADE-D
PREPARE-D	REVOLVE-D	UPSTAGE-D
PRESUME-D	SALVAGE-D	VENTURE-D
PRODUCE-D	SCUFFLE-D	VIBRATE-D
PROFILE-D	SERVICE-D	VIOLATE-D
PROMISE-D	SHUFFLE-D	WELCOME-D
PROMOTE-D	SILENCE-D	WHISTLE-D
PROPOSE-D	SMUGGLE-D	WHITTLE-D
PROVIDE-D	SPARKLE-D	WREATHE-D
RAMPAGE-D	SQUEEZE-D	WRESTLE-D
REALISE-D	STUBBLE-D	WRIGGLE-D

D

Handy Hint

Some unusual short words it is worth remembering are
DA (a Burmese knife, 3 points), DAW (a shortened form of
jackdaw, 7 points), DEY (an Ottoman governor, 7 points) and
DOW (an Arab ship, also 7).

BLOCKERS

It is useful to know which words are blockers and can't therefore
be extended before or after. You may want to play a blocker that
your opponent can't extend, or you may want to avoid playing
a blocker because you want to keep the board open.

Some three-letter blockers beginning with D

DUH   DUX

Some four-letter blockers beginning with D

DAFT	DIEL	DOTH
DAVY	DIPT	DOTY
DEAF	DISS	DOUN
DEFT	DIXY	DOUX
DEFY	DOBY	DOWF
DEMY	DOEN	DOXY
DENY	DOGY	DOZY
DESI	DOMY	DREW
DEUS	DOPY	DUED
DEWY	DORY	DULY
DEXY	DOSH	DUSH
DIDY	DOSS	DUTY
DIED	DOST	DYED

Some five-letter blockers beginning with D (except words ending in '-ED', '-J', '-S', '-X', '-Y' or '-Z')

DEALT	DOEST	DRIPT
DIACT	DONER	DUNNO
DICTA	DORIC	DURST
DINGO	DRACO	DUTCH
DINNA	DRANK	DWELT
DIRER	DRAWN	
DITCH	DREST	

Some six-letter blockers beginning with D (except words ending in '-ED', '-J', '-S', '-X', '-Y' or '-Z')

DAFTER	DELISH	DINING
DANISH	DELUXE	DIREST
DANKER	DENSER	DOABLE
DARKER	DERMAL	DOGMAN
DAYLIT	DETACH	DOLING
DAZING	DEVOID	DOMING
DEAFER	DEVOUT	DOPIER
DEARER	DEWIER	DOSING
DECENT	DEWING	DOURER
DEEPER	DEXTRO	DOVING
DEFTER	DICIER	DOZIER

DREAMT	DROLER	DULLER
DREICH	DRYEST	DUMBER
DRENCH	DRYISH	DUPING
DRIEST	DUEFUL	DURING
DRIVEN	DUKING	DYABLE

BONUS WORDS

Bonus words on your rack can be hard to spot, especially for the less experienced player. One way to help find them is by using prefixes and suffixes.

Many larger words include a common prefix or suffix – remembering these and using them where you can is a good way to discover any longer words on your rack, including any potential bonus words. The key prefixes to remember beginning with D are DE- and DIS- and the key suffix is -DOM.

Some words beginning with DE-
Seven-letter words

DE-ADMAN	DE-FORMS	DE-POSIT
DE-BASED	DE-FRAUD	DE-PRESS
DE-BASER	DE-FROST	DE-RAILS
DE-BATED	DE-FUSED	DE-RIDER
DE-BONED	DE-GRADE	DE-SCENT
DE-BRIEF	DE-ICING	DE-SIGNS
DE-CADES	DE-LAYED	DE-SIRED
DE-CODED	DE-LIGHT	DE-SPITE
DE-COYED	DE-LIVER	DE-TAILS
DE-CREED	DE-LUGED	DE-TESTS
DE-CRIED	DE-MEANS	DE-TOURS
DE-CRYPT	DE-MERIT	DE-TRACT
DE-FACED	DE-NOTED	DE-VALUE
DE-FAULT	DE-PARTS	DE-VICES
DE-FENCE	DE-PLOYS	DE-VOTED
DE-FILED	DE-PORTS	
DE-FINED	DE-POSED	

Eight-letter words

DE-AERATE
DE-BASING
DE-BUGGED
DE-BUNKED
DE-CANTER
DE-CEASED
DE-CIPHER
DE-CODING
DE-CRYING
DE-DUCTED
DE-FACING

DE-FINITE
DE-FOREST
DE-FORMED
DE-GRADED
DE-LAYING
DE-MISTED
DE-MOTION
DE-NOTING
DE-PARTED
DE-PENDED
DE-PORTED

DE-RAILED
DE-RANGED
DE-RIDING
DE-SCRIBE
DE-SELECT
DE-SERVED
DE-SIGNED
DE-TAILED
DE-VOLVED

Some words beginning with DIS-

Seven-letter words

DIS-ABLE
DIS-ARMS
DIS-BAND
DIS-CARD
DIS-CUSS
DIS-EASE

DIS-GUST
DIS-LIKE
DIS-MISS
DIS-OBEY
DIS-OWNS
DIS-PLAY

DIS-POSE
DIS-SECT
DIS-SENT
DIS-TILL
DIS-TORT
DIS-USED

Eight-letter words

DIS-AGREE
DIS-ALLOW
DIS-APPLY
DIS-ARRAY
DIS-CLOSE
DIS-COLOR
DIS-COVER
DIS-GORGE
DIS-GRACE

DIS-GUISE
DIS-HONOR
DIS-JOINT
DIS-LOYAL
DIS-MOUNT
DIS-ORDER
DIS-OWNED
DIS-PATCH
DIS-PERSE

DIS-PLACE
DIS-PROVE
DIS-QUIET
DIS-SOLVE
DIS-TASTE
DIS-TRACT
DIS-TRUST
DIS-UNITY

Some words ending with -DOM

Seven-letter words

BORE-DOM
DUKE-DOM
EARL-DOM

FIEF-DOM
FREE-DOM
KING-DOM

PAPA-DOM
SERF-DOM
STAR-DOM

Eight-letter words

CHIEF-DOM	LIEGE-DOM	SHEIK-DOM
CLERK-DOM	PAPPA-DOM	THANE-DOM
DEVIL-DOM	POPPA-DOM	THRAL-DOM
DUNCE-DOM	QUEEN-DOM	UNWIS-DOM
HOTEL-DOM	SAINT-DOM	

UNUSUAL LETTER COMBINATIONS

If you have an unusual combination of letters on your rack, or want to impress your opponent with an unusual word, a few words from World English can come in handy.

Australian words

DASYURE	small carnivorous marsupial
DELO	delegate
DERRO	vagrant
DINGO	wild dog
DINKUM	genuine or right
DOCO	documentary
DONGA	steep-sided gully
DORBA	stupid, inept, or clumsy person
DRACK	unattractive
DRONGO	slow-witted person
DROOB	pathetic person
DUBBO	stupid
DUGITE	venomous snake
DURRY	cigarette

Canadian word

DEKE	act or instance of feinting in ice hockey

Hindi words

DACOIT	member of a gang of armed robbers
DACOITY	robbery by an armed gang
DAK	system of mail delivery
DAL	split grain
DATURA	plant with trumpet-shaped flowers
DEKKO	look or glance
DEODAR	Himalayan cedar
DEWAN	chief minister of an Indian princedom
DHAK	tropical tree with red flowers

D

DHAL	curry made from lentils
DHARNA	method of obtaining justice by fasting
DHOBI	washerman
DHOTI	loincloth
DUPATTA	scarf
DURRIE	cotton carpet
DURZI	Indian tailor

South African word

DWAAL	state of befuddlement

Urdu words

DAROGHA	manager
DHANSAK	Indian dish of meat or vegetables braised with lentils

Essential info
Value: 1 point
Number in set: 12

E may be worth only one point, but it is extremely useful as it is the most common letter in the Scrabble set. Many words contain more than one E and it is worthwhile keeping these in mind, as there is a good chance you will find yourself with more than one E on your rack. Three-letter words formed by E on either side of a consonant include EYE, EWE, EVE (6 points) and EKE (7 points). E and K combine well to form a selection of other three-letter words, including ELK, EEK (7 points) and EWK (a dialect word for itch, 10 points). E is also helpful for getting rid of double consonants with words such as EGG (5 points) or EBB (7 points). E is one of the letters of the RETAIN set and is therefore a good letter to keep if trying to get a bonus word.

Two-letter words beginning with E

EA	EH	ER
ED	EL	ES
EE	EM	ET
EF	EN	EX

Some three-letter words beginning with E

EAN	ELL	ERG
EAU	ELT	ERK
ECH	EME	ERN
EDH	EMO	ESS
EEK	EMU	EST
EEN	ENE	ETA
EFF	ENG	ETH
EFT	EON	EWK
EGO	ERE	EXO
ELD	ERF	

HOOKS

Hooking requires a subtle change in a player's thought process, in that they must look at words already on the board without becoming distracted by their pronunciation.

Some front-hooks

Two letters to three

E-AN	E-EN	E-ON
E-AR	E-GO	E-RE
E-AS	E-ME	E-ST
E-AT	E-MO	E-TA
E-CH	E-MU	E-WE
E-EL	E-NE	E-YE

Three letters to four

E-ACH	E-NOW	E-THE
E-ARD	E-PIC	E-TIC
E-AVE	E-RED	E-TUI
E-DIT	E-RES	E-UGH
E-GAD	E-REV	E-VET
E-GAL	E-SKY	E-VOE
E-KED	E-SPY	E-YEN
E-MIR	E-TAT	
E-NEW	E-TEN	

Four letters to five

E-AGER	E-LITE	E-NORM
E-ARED	E-LOGE	E-PACT
E-BONY	E-LOGY	E-POXY
E-BOOK	E-LOIN	E-PROM
E-DICT	E-LOPE	E-QUID
E-DUCE	E-LUDE	E-QUIP
E-GEST	E-LUTE	E-RODE
E-HING	E-MAIL	E-STOP
E-IKON	E-MEER	E-TAPE
E-KING	E-MEND	E-VADE
E-LAIN	E-MOTE	E-VENT
E-LAND	E-MOVE	E-VERY
E-LATE	E-MULE	
E-LINT	E-NEWS	

Five letters to six

E-ASTER
E-CARTE
E-CHARD
E-DITED
E-GALLY
E-ITHER
E-LAPSE
E-LATED
E-LATER
E-LEGIT
E-LICIT

E-LOPED
E-LOPER
E-MERGE
E-METIC
E-MOTED
E-NERVE
E-NEWED
E-PRISE
E-QUATE
E-QUINE
E-RASED

E-RASER
E-SCAPE
E-SCARP
E-SCROW
E-SPIED
E-SPIER
E-SPRIT
E-STATE
E-VADED
E-VILER
E-VOLVE

Six letters to seven

E-ASTERN
E-BAYING
E-BONIST
E-CLOSED
E-COTYPE
E-DITING
E-LANCED
E-LAPSED
E-LECTOR
E-LEGIST
E-LOPING

E-MAILED
E-MERGED
E-MOTION
E-MOTIVE
E-MOVING
E-NERVED
E-RASING
E-RASURE
E-RODING
E-SCAPED
E-SPOUSE

E-SPYING
E-SQUIRE
E-STATED
E-TERNAL
E-VADING
E-VENTER
E-VILEST
E-VOLUTE
E-VOLVED

Seven letters to eight

E-LAPSING
E-LECTION
E-LEVATOR
E-MAILING
E-MENDING
E-MERGING
E-MERSION
E-MIGRANT
E-MIGRATE
E-MISSION
E-MISSIVE

E-NERVATE
E-NERVING
E-QUALITY
E-QUIPPED
E-QUIPPER
E-RADIATE
E-SCALADE
E-SCAPING
E-SCARPED
E-SCRIBED
E-SPECIAL

E-SPOUSAL
E-SQUIRED
E-STATING
E-STOPPED
E-STRANGE
E-TYPICAL
E-VACUATE
E-VALUATE
E-VENTING
E-VERSION
E-VOLVING

E

> **Handy Hint**
>
> If you find yourself with a vowel-heavy rack, handy short words to remember which use no consonants are EA and EE (both 2 points) or EAU (3 points). And there's always EUOUAE (a mnemonic used in Gregorian chant, 6 points) and EUOI (an interjection of Bacchic frenzy, 4 points).

Some end-hooks
Two letters to three

AG-E	GI-E	OP-E
AL-E	GO-E	OR-E
AN-E	GU-E	OS-E
AR-E	HA-E	OW-E
AT-E	HI-E	OY-E
AW-E	HO-E	PE-E
AX-E	ID-E	PI-E
AY-E	JO-E	RE-E
BE-E	KA-E	SH-E
BY-E	KY-E	TA-E
CH-E	LI-E	TE-E
DA-E	MA-E	TI-E
DE-E	ME-E	TO-E
DI-E	MO-E	UR-E
DO-E	NA-E	US-E
EM-E	NE-E	UT-E
EN-E	NY-E	WE-E
ER-E	OB-E	WO-E
FA-E	OD-E	YA-E
FE-E	ON-E	

Three letters to four

ACH-E	BAT-E	CAN-E
ADZ-E	BID-E	CAP-E
AID-E	BIT-E	CAR-E
ANT-E	BON-E	CIT-E
BAL-E	BOR-E	CON-E
BAN-E	BRA-E	COP-E
BAR-E	CAG-E	COR-E
BAS-E	CAM-E	COS-E

CUB-E	HOM-E	MUT-E
CUR-E	HOP-E	NAM-E
CUT-E	HOS-E	NAP-E
DAL-E	HUG-E	NIT-E
DAM-E	HYP-E	NOD-E
DIM-E	JAP-E	NON-E
DIN-E	JIB-E	NOS-E
DIV-E	JUT-E	NOT-E
DOL-E	KIT-E	OBO-E
DOM-E	LAC-E	PAC-E
DON-E	LAM-E	PAL-E
DOP-E	LAT-E	PAN-E
DOS-E	LIN-E	PAR-E
DOT-E	LIT-E	PAT-E
DUD-E	LOB-E	PAV-E
DUN-E	LOD-E	PIN-E
DUP-E	LOP-E	PIP-E
EAS-E	LOR-E	POL-E
ELS-E	LOS-E	POP-E
FAD-E	LUD-E	POS-E
FAR-E	LUG-E	PUR-E
FAT-E	LUR-E	RAG-E
FET-E	MAC-E	RAT-E
FIL-E	MAD-E	RID-E
FIN-E	MAG-E	RIF-E
FIR-E	MAK-E	RIP-E
FLU-E	MAL-E	ROB-E
FOR-E	MAN-E	ROD-E
FUM-E	MAR-E	ROT-E
GAL-E	MAT-E	RUD-E
GAM-E	MEM-E	RUN-E
GAP-E	MIC-E	SAG-E
GAT-E	MIL-E	SAL-E
GEN-E	MIM-E	SAM-E
GIB-E	MIR-E	SAN-E
GON-E	MOD-E	SAT-E
GOR-E	MOL-E	SAV-E
HAT-E	MOP-E	SIN-E
HER-E	MOR-E	SIR-E
HID-E	MUS-E	SIT-E

E

SOL-E TOM-E VIS-E
SOM-E TON-E VOL-E
SUR-E TOP-E WAD-E
TAK-E TOT-E WAG-E
TAM-E TUB-E WAN-E
TAP-E TUN-E WAR-E
THE-E VAN-E WIN-E
TID-E VAR-E WIS-E
TIL-E VAS-E WOK-E
TIN-E VIN-E YOK-E

Four letters to five

AMID-E GRIM-E SLAT-E
BATH-E GRIP-E SLID-E
BING-E HAST-E SLIM-E
BLAM-E HING-E SLOP-E
BOMB-E HIRE-E SNIP-E
BOOS-E LAPS-E SPAR-E
BRUT-E LENS-E SPAT-E
CART-E LOOS-E SPIN-E
CAST-E MANS-E SPIT-E
CHIV-E PASS-E STAG-E
COPS-E PAST-E STAR-E
COUP-E PEAS-E STAT-E
CREW-E PLAN-E SUED-E
CRIM-E PLAT-E SUIT-E
CURS-E PLUM-E TEAS-E
DOWS-E PRIM-E TENS-E
ERAS-E PROS-E THEM-E
FLAK-E PURE-E TRAD-E
FLIT-E QUIT-E TRIP-E
FORT-E RANG-E TWIN-E
GEES-E SCAR-E UNIT-E
GLAD-E SHAM-E WHIN-E
GLOB-E SHIN-E WHIT-E
GRAD-E SING-E WRIT-E

Five letters to six

BLOND-E FINAL-E HUMAN-E
CLOTH-E GRAND-E IMPED-E
EQUIP-E HEARS-E LOATH-E

LOCAL-E REGAL-E SPRIT-E
LUPIN-E REPOS-E STRIP-E
MADAM-E RESIT-E SWATH-E
MORAL-E SCRAP-E TOUCH-E
PETIT-E SOOTH-E URBAN-E
PLEAS-E SPARS-E

Six letters to seven

ADVISE-E ESCAPE-E REFUGE-E
ARTIST-E FIANCE-E RETIRE-E
ATTACH-E FLAMBE-E REVERS-E
AUGUST-E GERMAN-E SECRET-E
BREATH-E HEROIN-E TARTAR-E
CORNEA-E IMPING-E WREATH-E
DEVOTE-E IMPROV-E
DIVERS-E OBLIGE-E

Seven letters to eight

ABSINTH-E EMPLOYE-E LICENCE-E
ALKALIS-E ENDORSE-E LICENSE-E
AMPHORA-E ENVELOP-E NOCTURN-E
BACKBIT-E ESCALOP-E OUTWRIT-E
DECLASS-E GELATIN-E PROTEGE-E
DIVORCE-E INHUMAN-E SILICON-E
DOMICIL-E INTERNE-E

Handy Hint

A good short word which uses the X and a couple of vowels is
EXO (informal Australian term meaning excellent, 10 points).
Note that the word could enable you to make a play that involves
hooking your O onto an existing EX.

BLOCKERS

It is useful to know which words are blockers and can't therefore
be extended before or after. You may want to play a blocker that
your opponent can't extend, or you may want to avoid playing a
blocker because you want to keep the board open.

Some four-letter blockers beginning with E

EASY	ESPY
ELSE	EYRY

Five-letter blocker beginning with E (except words ending in '-ED', '-J', '-S', '-X', '-Y' or '-Z')

ENLIT

Some six-letter blockers beginning with E (except words ending in '-ED', '-J', '-S', '-X', '-Y' or '-Z')

EASIER	EMDASH	ENRAPT
EFFETE	ENCASH	ENRICH
ELDEST	ENDASH	EYEING
ELVISH	ENMESH	

BONUS WORDS

Bonus words on your rack can be hard to spot, especially for the less experienced player. One way to help find them is by using prefixes and suffixes.

Many larger words include a common prefix or suffix – remembering these and using them where you can is a good way to discover any longer words on your rack, including any potential bonus words. The key prefixes to remember beginning with E are EM-, EN- and EX- and the key suffixes are -EAUX, -ENCE, -ENCY, -EST, -ETTE and -EUR.

Some words beginning with EM-
Seven-letter words

EM-AILED	EM-IRATE	EM-PLOYS
EM-BARKS	EM-PANEL	EM-POWER
EM-BRACE	EM-PARTS	EM-PRESS
EM-BROIL	EM-PEACH	

Eight-letter words

EM-AILING	EM-BEDDED	EM-BOLDEN
EM-BALMED	EM-BITTER	EM-BOSSED
EM-BARKED	EM-BLAZED	EM-BRACED
EM-BATTLE	EM-BODIED	EM-PALING

EM-PARTED   EM-PHATIC
EM-PATHIC   EM-PLOYED

Some words beginning with EN-
Seven-letter words

EN-ABLED   EN-DEARS   EN-TAILS
EN-ACTED   EN-FORCE   EN-TIRES
EN-CAGED   EN-GORGE   EN-TITLE
EN-CASED   EN-RAGED   EN-TRAIL
EN-CLOSE   EN-SLAVE   EN-TREES
EN-CODED   EN-SNARE   EN-TRIES
EN-CORED   EN-SUING   EN-VYING
EN-CRYPT   EN-SURED   EN-ZYMES

Eight-letter words

EN-ABLING   EN-DURING   EN-ROLLED
EN-CAMPED   EN-FOLDED   EN-SHRINE
EN-CASING   EN-GENDER   EN-SIGNED
EN-CHANTS   EN-GORGED   EN-SNARED
EN-CIPHER   EN-GRAVED   EN-SURING
EN-CIRCLE   EN-GULFED   EN-TAILED
EN-CLOSED   EN-JOYING   EN-TITLED
EN-CORING   EN-LISTED   EN-TRENCH
EN-DANGER   EN-QUIRED   EN-VIABLE
EN-DEARED   EN-RICHED

Some words beginning with EX-
Seven-letter words

EX-ACTED   EX-PENDS   EX-PRESS
EX-AMINE   EX-PLAIN   EX-TENDS
EX-CITED   EX-PORTS   EX-TOLLS
EX-CLAIM   EX-POSED   EX-TRACT

Eight-letter words

EX-ACTING   EX-CITING   EX-PLAINS
EX-CELLED   EX-PANDER   EX-PORTED
EX-CESSES   EX-PERTLY

E

Some words ending with -EAUX
Seven-letter words

BAT-EAUX
BUR-EAUX

CAD-EAUX
GAT-EAUX

Eight-letter words

BAND-EAUX
BATT-EAUX
BORD-EAUX

CHAP-EAUX
CHAT-EAUX
MORC-EAUX

PLAT-EAUX
TABL-EAUX

Some words ending with -ENCE
Seven-letter words

ABS-ENCE
CAD-ENCE
COG-ENCE
DEF-ENCE
ESS-ENCE

FLU-ENCE
LIC-ENCE
OFF-ENCE
POT-ENCE
SCI-ENCE

SIL-ENCE
URG-ENCE
VAL-ENCE

Eight-letter words

AMBI-ENCE
AUDI-ENCE
COMM-ENCE
CRED-ENCE
DISP-ENCE
EMIN-ENCE
EVID-ENCE
LENI-ENCE

NASC-ENCE
OPUL-ENCE
PATI-ENCE
PRES-ENCE
PRET-ENCE
PRUD-ENCE
SALI-ENCE
SAPI-ENCE

SENT-ENCE
SEQU-ENCE
SIXP-ENCE
TEND-ENCE
TENP-ENCE
TUPP-ENCE
VIOL-ENCE

Some words ending with -ENCY
Seven-letter words

COG-ENCY
DEC-ENCY
FLU-ENCY

POT-ENCY
REC-ENCY
REG-ENCY

URG-ENCY
VAL-ENCY

Eight-letter words

CLEM-ENCY
CURR-ENCY
FERV-ENCY

LENI-ENCY
PUNG-ENCY
SOLV-ENCY

TEND-ENCY

Some words ending with -EST

Seven-letter words

AIRI-EST	HARD-EST	SUBT-EST
BALD-EST	KIND-EST	TALL-EST
BOLD-EST	LONG-EST	TEMP-EST
DAMP-EST	MEEK-EST	TENS-EST
DARK-EST	POOR-EST	WARM-EST
EARN-EST	PRET-EST	WILD-EST
FULL-EST	PROT-EST	
FUNF-EST	REQU-EST	

Eight-letter words

ACRID-EST	FLASH-EST	REDIG-EST
BLACK-EST	GAUDI-EST	SIMPL-EST
BLOND-EST	GRAND-EST	SUNNI-EST
BRIEF-EST	INERT-EST	TALKF-EST
CLEAN-EST	LOVEF-EST	TOUGH-EST
CLEAR-EST	MINUT-EST	URBAN-EST
DIVIN-EST	ORANG-EST	WASPN-EST
EAGER-EST	PEPPI-EST	WRONG-EST
EXACT-EST	QUICK-EST	

Some words ending with -ETTE

Seven-letter words

BLU-ETTE	GAZ-ETTE	PAL-ETTE
CAS-ETTE	LAD-ETTE	PIP-ETTE
DIN-ETTE	MIN-ETTE	POP-ETTE
FUM-ETTE	OCT-ETTE	ROS-ETTE

Eight-letter words

AMUS-ETTE	DISK-ETTE	ROQU-ETTE
BAGU-ETTE	JEAN-ETTE	ROUL-ETTE
BRUN-ETTE	MAQU-ETTE	SEPT-ETTE
CASS-ETTE	NOIS-ETTE	VIGN-ETTE
COQU-ETTE	PALL-ETTE	
CORV-ETTE	ROOM-ETTE	

E

Some words ending with -EUR
Seven-letter words

AMAT-EUR	PRIM-EUR	TRAC-EUR
LIQU-EUR	SABR-EUR	
MASS-EUR	SIGN-EUR	

Eight-letter words

CHASS-EUR	LONGU-EUR	SEIGN-EUR
COIFF-EUR	MONSI-EUR	VOYAG-EUR
GRAND-EUR	SABOT-EUR	
JONGL-EUR	SECAT-EUR	

UNUSUAL LETTER COMBINATIONS

If you have an unusual combination of letters on your rack, or want to impress your opponent with an unusual word, a few words from World English can come in handy.

Australian words

EARBASH	talk incessantly
EMU	large flightless bird
EUMUNG	type of acacia
EVO	evening
EXO	excellent

Essential info
Value: 4 points
Number in set: 2

F can be a useful letter for scoring with short words on premium squares. Although there are only three two-letter words beginning with F (FA and FE, 5 points each, and FY, 8 points), these are complemented with IF and OF. There are also quite a few short, high-scoring words beginning with F which use X (FAX, FIX, FOX, 13 points each), Y (FEY, FLY, FRY, 9 points each) or Z (FEZ, 15 points).

Two-letter words beginning with F

FA	FE	FY

Some three-letter words beginning with F

FAA	FEM	FOB
FAE	FEN	FOH
FAH	FER	FON
FAP	FET	FOP
FAW	FEU	FOU
FAX	FEY	FOY
FAY	FEZ	FUB
FEG	FID	FUG
FEH	FIZ	FUM

HOOKS

Hooking requires a subtle change in a player's thought process, in that they must look at words already on the board without becoming distracted by their pronunciation.

Some front-hooks
Two letters to three

F-AA	F-AE	F-AN
F-AB	F-AG	F-AR
F-AD	F-AH	F-AS

F-AT	F-ES	F-OP
F-AW	F-ET	F-OR
F-AX	F-ID	F-OU
F-AY	F-IN	F-OX
F-ED	F-IT	F-OY
F-EE	F-OB	F-UG
F-EH	F-OE	F-UM
F-EM	F-OG	F-UN
F-EN	F-OH	F-UR
F-ER	F-ON	

Three letters to four

F-ACE	F-EST	F-LOW
F-ACT	F-ETA	F-LUX
F-AFF	F-ILL	F-OIL
F-AIL	F-INK	F-OLD
F-AIR	F-IRE	F-OOT
F-AKE	F-ISH	F-ORD
F-ALL	F-LAB	F-ORE
F-ARE	F-LAG	F-ORT
F-ARM	F-LAP	F-OUR
F-ASH	F-LAT	F-OWL
F-ATE	F-LAW	F-OXY
F-AVA	F-LAX	F-RAG
F-AVE	F-LAY	F-RAT
F-AWN	F-LEA	F-RAY
F-EAR	F-LED	F-REE
F-EAT	F-LEE	F-RET
F-EEL	F-LEW	F-RIZ
F-ELL	F-LEX	F-ROM
F-ELT	F-LIP	F-RUG
F-END	F-LIT	F-USE
F-ERN	F-LOG	
F-ESS	F-LOP	

Four letters to five

F-ABLE	F-AKED	F-ETCH
F-ACED	F-ARED	F-EVER
F-ACER	F-AXED	F-EWER
F-AERY	F-AYRE	F-ILLY
F-AIRY	F-EAST	F-INCH

F-ITCH
F-LACK
F-LAIR
F-LAKE
F-LAKY
F-LAME
F-LANK
F-LARE
F-LASH
F-LEER
F-LEET
F-LICK
F-LIER
F-LING
F-LINT
F-LITE
F-LOCK
F-LOOR
F-LOSS
F-LOUR
F-LOUT
F-LOWN
F-LUFF
F-LUKE
F-LUNG
F-LUNK
F-LUSH
F-LUTE
F-OLIO
F-OYER
F-RAIL
F-RANK
F-REED
F-RILL
F-RISK
F-RITZ
F-ROCK
F-RUMP
F-USED

Five letters to six

F-ABLED
F-ACING
F-ACTOR
F-AILED
F-ALLOW
F-ALTER
F-AMINE
F-ARMED
F-ARMER
F-ARROW
F-AXING
F-EARED
F-ENDED
F-ENDER
F-ESTER
F-ICKLE
F-INNER
F-LAKED
F-LAKER
F-LAMED
F-LAMER
F-LAWED
F-LAYED
F-LAYER
F-LEDGE
F-LETCH
F-LIGHT
F-LINCH
F-LINTY
F-LOWED
F-LOWER
F-LUTED
F-LUTER
F-LYING
F-ODDER
F-OILED
F-OLDER
F-OUGHT
F-RIDGE
F-RIGHT
F-RIGID
F-RISKY
F-USING
F-UTILE

Six letters to seven

F-ABLING
F-ACTION
F-ACTUAL
F-ADDLED
F-AILING
F-AIRILY
F-AIRING
F-AIRWAY
F-ANGLED
F-ARMING
F-ATTEST
F-AWNING
F-EARFUL
F-EARING
F-EASTER
F-EATING
F-ENDING
F-ETCHED
F-ETCHER
F-ICKLER
F-INCHED
F-INNING
F-LACKED
F-LACKER
F-LAGGED
F-LAGGER
F-LAKING

75

F-LAMING
F-LANKER
F-LAPPED
F-LAPPER
F-LASHED
F-LASHER
F-LASKET
F-LATTER
F-LAYING
F-LEDGED
F-LEERED
F-LEGGED
F-LENSED
F-LICKED
F-LICKER
F-LIMPED
F-LINGER

F-LIPPED
F-LIPPER
F-LITTER
F-LOCKED
F-LOGGED
F-LOGGER
F-LOPPED
F-LOPPER
F-LOWING
F-LUBBER
F-LUMMOX
F-LUMPED
F-LUSHED
F-LUSTER
F-LUTING
F-LUTIST
F-OILING

F-OXLIKE
F-OXTAIL
F-RAGGED
F-RAILER
F-RANKED
F-RANKER
F-RANKLY
F-RAPPED
F-RAZZLE
F-RIDGED
F-RINGED
F-RIPPER
F-RISKED
F-RISKER
F-ROCKED
F-RUSHED
F-UNFAIR

Seven letters to eight

F-ALLOWED
F-ALTERED
F-ALTERER
F-EARLESS
F-EASTING
F-ETCHING
F-ICKLEST
F-IRELESS
F-LACKING
F-LAGGING
F-LAKIEST
F-LANKING
F-LAPPING
F-LASHING

F-LAWLESS
F-LETCHED
F-LICKING
F-LIGHTED
F-LINTING
F-LIPPING
F-LOCKING
F-LOGGING
F-LOPPING
F-LOUTING
F-LOWERED
F-LUSHEST
F-RAGGING
F-RANKEST

F-RANKING
F-RAPPING
F-RIDGING
F-RIGHTEN
F-RIGIDER
F-RIGIDLY
F-RINGING
F-RISKIER
F-RISKILY
F-RISKING
F-ROCKING
F-UNCTION
F-USELESS
F-UTILITY

Some end-hooks
Two letters to three

AL-F
AR-F
DE-F
DI-F

DO-F
EF-F
EL-F
ER-F

GI-F
IF-F
KA-F
KI-F

NE-F   OR-F   TE-F
OF-F   RE-F   WO-F
OO-F   SI-F

Three letters to four

BAR-F   GUL-F   RIF-F
BEE-F   HOO-F   ROO-F
CHE-F   HOW-F   SEL-F
CON-F   HUM-F   SER-F
CUR-F   LEA-F   SOW-F
DIF-F   LIE-F   SUR-F
DOF-F   LOO-F   WAI-F
FIE-F   PRO-F   WOO-F
GOO-F   REE-F

F

Four letters to five

BRIE-F   KALI-F   SCUR-F
GANE-F   MOTI-F   SHEA-F
GONE-F   PILA-F   SKEE-F
HOUF-F   PROO-F   SNAR-F
HOWF-F   SCAR-F   SPIF-F

Five letters to six

BELIE-F   GONIF-F   RELIE-F
DECAF-F   PILAF-F

Six letters to seven

SHERIF-F

BLOCKERS

It is useful to know which words are blockers and can't therefore
be extended before or after. You may want to play a blocker that
your opponent can't extend, or you may want to avoid playing a
blocker because you want to keep the board open.

Two-letter blocker beginning with F

FY

Some three-letter blockers beginning with F

FAE	FEW	FRY
FAP	FEZ	
FAX	FLY	

Some four-letter blockers beginning with F

FASH	FIXT	FOXY
FAUX	FLED	FROM
FEET	FLIX	FUMY
FIFI	FLUX	FURY
FILS	FOGY	

Some five-letter blockers beginning with F (except words ending in '-ED', '-J', '-S', '-X', '-Y' or '-Z')

FATAL	FEWER	FOCAL
FETAL	FINCH	FOLIC
FETCH	FLOWN	FUNGO
FETID	FLUNG	

Some six-letter blockers beginning with F (except words ending in '-ED', '-J', '-S', '-X', '-Y' or '-Z')

FACEUP	FEWEST	FLYMEN
FACILE	FEYEST	FOETAL
FAIRER	FILIAL	FOETID
FAKING	FILMIC	FONDER
FALLEN	FINEST	FOREGO
FAMING	FINISH	FORGOT
FAMISH	FINITO	FOULER
FARING	FITFUL	FOXIER
FATTER	FLAXEN	FREEST
FAXING	FLETCH	FRIGID
FAZING	FLIEST	FROZEN
FECUND	FLINCH	FRUGAL
FEEING	FLORID	FUMING
FERRIC	FLUIER	FUNGIC
FERVID	FLUISH	FUNNER
FETISH	FLYEST	FUSILE
FEUDAL	FLYMAN	FUSING

BONUS WORDS

Bonus words on your rack can be hard to spot, especially for the less experienced player. One way to help find them is by using prefixes and suffixes.

Many larger words include a common prefix or suffix – remembering these and using them where you can is a good way to discover any longer words on your rack, including any potential bonus words. The key prefixes to remember beginning with F are FOOT- and FOR- and the key suffixes are -FISH, -FORM and -FUL.

Some words beginning with FOOT-

Seven-letter words

FOOT-AGE	FOOT-ERS	FOOT-MEN
FOOT-BAG	FOOT-LED	FOOT-PAD
FOOT-BAR	FOOT-LES	FOOT-ROT
FOOT-BOY	FOOT-MAN	FOOT-WAY

Eight-letter words

FOOT-BALL	FOOT-LIKE	FOOT-SIES
FOOT-BATH	FOOT-LING	FOOT-SORE
FOOT-ERED	FOOT-MARK	FOOT-STEP
FOOT-FALL	FOOT-NOTE	FOOT-WALL
FOOT-HILL	FOOT-PATH	FOOT-WEAR
FOOT-HOLD	FOOT-RACE	FOOT-WORK
FOOT-LESS	FOOT-REST	FOOT-WORN

Some words beginning with FOR-

Seven-letter words

FOR-AGED	FOR-DING	FOR-GIVE
FOR-AGER	FOR-DONE	FOR-GOER
FOR-AGES	FOR-ESTS	FOR-GOES
FOR-BADE	FOR-EVER	FOR-GONE
FOR-BEAR	FOR-FEND	FOR-KIER
FOR-BIDS	FOR-GAVE	FOR-KING
FOR-BODE	FOR-GETS	FOR-LORN
FOR-CEPS	FOR-GING	FOR-MATS

FOR-MICA
FOR-MING
FOR-RAYS
FOR-SAID

FOR-SAKE
FOR-SOOK
FOR-TING
FOR-WARD

FOR-WARN
FOR-WENT
FOR-WORN

Eight-letter words

FOR-AGING
FOR-BODED
FOR-ESTER
FOR-GIVEN
FOR-GIVER

FOR-GOING
FOR-MATED
FOR-SOOTH
FOR-SPEAK
FOR-SPEND

FOR-SPOKE
FOR-SWEAR
FOR-SWORN
FOR-TRESS
FOR-TUNED

Some words ending with -FISH

Seven-letter words

BAT-FISH
BOX-FISH
CAT-FISH
COD-FISH
COW-FISH
DEA-FISH
DOG-FISH
FIN-FISH
FOX-FISH
GAR-FISH

GEM-FISH
HAG-FISH
HOG-FISH
HUF-FISH
MUD-FISH
OAR-FISH
OUT-FISH
PAN-FISH
PIG-FISH
PIN-FISH

PUP-FISH
RAF-FISH
RAT-FISH
RED-FISH
SAW-FISH
SEL-FISH
SER-FISH
SUN-FISH

Eight-letter words

BAIT-FISH
BLOW-FISH
BLUE-FISH
BONE-FISH
CAVE-FISH
CRAW-FISH
CRAY-FISH
DEAL-FISH
DWAR-FISH
FLAT-FISH
FOOL-FISH
FROG-FISH

GOLD-FISH
GRAY-FISH
GRUF-FISH
KING-FISH
LION-FISH
LUNG-FISH
MONK-FISH
MOON-FISH
OVER-FISH
PIPE-FISH
ROCK-FISH
SAIL-FISH

SALT-FISH
SAND-FISH
SCAR-FISH
SNIF-FISH
STAR-FISH
STIF-FISH
SUCK-FISH
SURF-FISH
TOAD-FISH
WOLF-FISH

Some words ending with -FORM
Seven-letter words

ACI-FORM
ALI-FORM
AUS-FORM
AVI-FORM
CON-FORM

DEI-FORM
DIF-FORM
DIS-FORM
ISO-FORM
MIS-FORM

OVI-FORM
PER-FORM
PRE-FORM
TRI-FORM
UNI-FORM

Eight-letter words

AERI-FORM
CONI-FORM
CUBI-FORM
FREE-FORM
FUSI-FORM
LAND-FORM
LYRI-FORM

MANI-FORM
OMNI-FORM
PALI-FORM
PARA-FORM
PLAN-FORM
PLAT-FORM
POST-FORM

PYRI-FORM
ROTI-FORM
SLIP-FORM
TUBI-FORM
URSI-FORM
VARI-FORM
WAVE-FORM

Some words ending with -FUL
Seven-letter words

ARMS-FUL
BALE-FUL
BANE-FUL
BASH-FUL
BOAT-FUL
BOWL-FUL
BRIM-FUL
CARE-FUL
DARE-FUL
DEED-FUL
DIRE-FUL
DOLE-FUL
DUTI-FUL
FACT-FUL
FATE-FUL
FEAR-FUL
FIST-FUL

FORK-FUL
FRET-FUL
GAIN-FUL
GLEE-FUL
GUTS-FUL
HAND-FUL
HARM-FUL
HATE-FUL
HEED-FUL
HELP-FUL
HOPE-FUL
HURT-FUL
LUNG-FUL
LUST-FUL
MIND-FUL
NEED-FUL
PAIL-FUL

PAIN-FUL
PALM-FUL
PITI-FUL
PLAY-FUL
RAGE-FUL
REST-FUL
RISK-FUL
SACK-FUL
SKIL-FUL
SKIN-FUL
SOUL-FUL
TACT-FUL
TANK-FUL
TEAR-FUL
TUNE-FUL
WAKE-FUL
WILL-FUL

Eight-letter words

BELLY-FUL
BLAME-FUL
BLISS-FUL
BOAST-FUL
CHEER-FUL
COLOR-FUL
DIRGE-FUL
DOUBT-FUL
DREAD-FUL
EVENT-FUL
FAITH-FUL
FANCI-FUL
FORCE-FUL
FRUIT-FUL
GHAST-FUL

GLASS-FUL
GRACE-FUL
GRATE-FUL
GUILE-FUL
HASTE-FUL
MERCI-FUL
MIRTH-FUL
MOURN-FUL
MOUTH-FUL
PEACE-FUL
PLATE-FUL
POWER-FUL
RIGHT-FUL
SCORN-FUL
SHAME-FUL

SKILL-FUL
SPITE-FUL
SPOON-FUL
TASTE-FUL
THANK-FUL
TRUST-FUL
TRUTH-FUL
UNLAW-FUL
VENGE-FUL
WASTE-FUL
WATCH-FUL
WRATH-FUL
WRONG-FUL
YOUTH-FUL

Handy Hint

A useful way to visualise your options is to SHUFFLE (16 points)
the tiles on your rack. If you rearrange tiles, place them in
alphabetical order or try to form prefixes, suffixes or verb inflections
you stand a better chance of thinking up good words to play.

UNUSUAL LETTER COMBINATIONS

If you have an unusual combination of letters on your rack, or
want to impress your opponent with an unusual word, a few
words from World English can come in handy. Here are some
beginning with F.

Australian words

FASTIE	deceitful act
FESTY	dirty or smelly
FIGJAM	very conceited person
FIZGIG	frivolous or flirtatious girl
FOULIE	bad mood
FRIB	short heavy-conditioned piece of wool
FURPHY	rumour or fictitious story

Essential info
Value: 2 points
Number in set: 3

G begins only three two-letter words in Scrabble: GI (a suit worn by martial arts practitioners, 3 points), GO and GU (a kind of violin from Shetland, 3 points). G also combines well with Y to form quite a few short words including GAY, GEY (a Scots word for very, 7 points), GOY (a Yiddish word for a person who is not Jewish, 7 points), GUY and also GYM and GYP (9 points each).

Two-letter words beginning with G

GI	GO	GU

Some three-letter words beginning with G

GAB	GIB	GOR
GAD	GID	GOV
GAE	GIE	GOX
GAL	GIF	GOY
GAM	GIO	GUB
GAN	GIP	GUE
GAR	GIT	GUL
GAT	GJU	GUP
GED	GNU	GUR
GEE	GOA	GUV
GEL	GOE	GYM
GEN	GON	GYP
GHI	GOO	

HOOKS

Hooking requires a subtle change in a player's thought process, in that they must look at words already on the board without becoming distracted by their pronunciation.

Some front-hooks
Two letters to three

G-AB	G-EM	G-ON
G-AD	G-EN	G-OO
G-AE	G-ET	G-OR
G-AG	G-HI	G-OS
G-AL	G-ID	G-OX
G-AM	G-IF	G-OY
G-AN	G-IN	G-UM
G-AR	G-IO	G-UN
G-AS	G-IS	G-UP
G-AT	G-IT	G-UR
G-AY	G-NU	G-US
G-ED	G-OB	G-UT
G-EE	G-OD	
G-EL	G-OE	

Three letters to four

G-AFF	G-ILL	G-OUT
G-AGA	G-LAD	G-OWN
G-AGE	G-LAM	G-RAD
G-AIN	G-LEE	G-RAM
G-AIT	G-LIB	G-RAN
G-ALA	G-LID	G-RAY
G-ALE	G-LOB	G-REW
G-ALL	G-LOW	G-RID
G-APE	G-LUG	G-RIM
G-ARB	G-LUM	G-RIN
G-ASH	G-NAT	G-RIP
G-ASP	G-NAW	G-RIT
G-ATE	G-OAT	G-ROT
G-AVE	G-OES	G-ROW
G-EAR	G-OLD	G-RUB
G-EEK	G-ONE	G-RUE
G-ELD	G-OOF	G-URN
G-ELT	G-OON	
G-ENE	G-ORE	

Four letters to five

G-ABLE	G-AGER	G-APED
G-AGED	G-ALLY	G-APER

G-AUNT
G-AVEL
G-EMMY
G-HAST
G-HOST
G-ILLS
G-ILLY
G-IRON
G-LACE
G-LADE
G-LADY
G-LAND
G-LARE
G-LASS
G-LAZE
G-LAZY
G-LEAM

G-LEAN
G-LINT
G-LOAM
G-LOBE
G-LODE
G-LOOM
G-LOOP
G-LORY
G-LOSS
G-LOST
G-LOUT
G-LOVE
G-LUTE
G-NOME
G-OLDY
G-ONER
G-OOFY

G-OOSE
G-OOSY
G-RACE
G-RADE
G-RAFT
G-RAIL
G-RAIN
G-RAND
G-RANT
G-RASP
G-RATE
G-RAVE
G-RAZE
G-REED
G-REEK
G-REEN

G

Five letters to six

G-ABLED
G-ABOON
G-ADDED
G-ADDER
G-AGGER
G-AGING
G-ALLEY
G-ALLOW
G-AMBIT
G-AMBLE
G-AMINE
G-AMMON
G-APING
G-ARGLE
G-ASHED
G-ASPER
G-ASTER
G-AUGER
G-EARED
G-ELATE
G-ELDER

G-ENDER
G-ENTRY
G-INNER
G-LANCE
G-LAZED
G-LOBED
G-LOOPY
G-LOSSY
G-LOVED
G-LOWER
G-NOMIC
G-OLDEN
G-OLDER
G-RACED
G-RAINY
G-RANGE
G-RATED
G-RATER
G-RAVED
G-RAVEL
G-RAVEN

G-RAVER
G-RAYED
G-RAZED
G-REAVE
G-REEDY
G-RIMED
G-RIPED
G-ROPED
G-ROUND
G-ROUSE
G-ROVED
G-ROWER
G-RUBBY
G-RUING
G-RUMPY
G-UNMAN
G-URNED
G-USHER
G-UTTER

Six letters to seven

G-ABLING
G-ADDING
G-ALLIED
G-AMBLED
G-AMBLER
G-ASHING
G-AUNTLY
G-EARING
G-ELATED
G-ELDING
G-ESTATE
G-HOSTED
G-HOSTLY
G-IGGING
G-IZZARD
G-LACIER
G-LADDER
G-LANCED
G-LANCER
G-LAZIER
G-LAZILY
G-LAZING
G-LEAMED
G-LEANED
G-LEANER
G-LEEING
G-LIBBED
G-LIBBER
G-LIMMER

G-LINTED
G-LISTEN
G-LISTER
G-LITTER
G-LOOMED
G-LOOPED
G-LOVING
G-LOWING
G-OLDEST
G-OLDISH
G-OWNING
G-RACING
G-RAFTED
G-RAFTER
G-RAINED
G-RANGER
G-RANTED
G-RANTER
G-RAPIER
G-RAPING
G-RASPED
G-RASPER
G-RATIFY
G-RATING
G-RAVING
G-RAYING
G-RAZING
G-REAVED
G-REEKED

G-RIDDED
G-RIDDER
G-RIDDLE
G-RIFTED
G-RILLED
G-RIMMER
G-RINDED
G-RIPING
G-RIPPED
G-RIPPER
G-ROOMED
G-ROOMER
G-ROPING
G-ROUSED
G-ROUSER
G-ROUTED
G-ROUTER
G-ROWING
G-RUBBED
G-RUBBER
G-RUFFED
G-RUFFLY
G-RUMBLE
G-RUMMER
G-RUMPED
G-RUNTED
G-UNLESS
G-UNSHOT

Seven letters to eight

G-ALLOWED
G-AMBLING
G-ANGLING
G-ARGLING
G-EARLESS
G-ELASTIC
G-ELATING
G-ESTATED

G-HASTING
G-HOSTING
G-LANCING
G-LAZIEST
G-LEAMING
G-LEANERS
G-LEANING
G-LIBBING

G-LINTIER
G-LINTING
G-LITTERY
G-LOAMING
G-LOOMING
G-LOOPIER
G-LOOPING
G-LOWERED

G-LUGGING	G-RANULAR	G-ROOMING
G-NATTIER	G-RASPING	G-ROUNDED
G-OATLIKE	G-RAVELLY	G-ROUNDER
G-OFFERED	G-REEDIER	G-ROUSING
G-OLDENED	G-REEDILY	G-ROUTING
G-ONENESS	G-RIDDLED	G-ROWABLE
G-RAFTING	G-RIEVING	G-RUMBLED
G-RAINIER	G-RIFTING	G-UNMAKER
G-RAINING	G-RILLING	G-UNSTOCK
G-RANTING	G-RIPPING	G-UTTERED

Handy Hint

Some unusual and high-scoring words beginning with G are GJU (a variant spelling of GU, 11 points), GOX (form of gaseous oxygen, 11 points), GUANXI (Chinese social concept based on the exchange of favours, 14 points) and GYOZA (Japanese fried dumplings, 18 points).

Some end-hooks
Two letters to three

BA-G	HO-G	PE-G
BE-G	JA-G	PI-G
BI-G	JO-G	RE-G
BO-G	LA-G	SO-G
DA-G	LI-G	TA-G
DE-G	LO-G	TE-G
DI-G	MA-G	TI-G
DO-G	ME-G	TO-G
EN-G	MI-G	WO-G
ER-G	MO-G	YA-G
FA-G	MU-G	YU-G
FE-G	NA-G	ZA-G
GI-G	NE-G	
HA-G	NO-G	

Three letters to four

AGO-G	BIO-G	BUN-G
BAN-G	BON-G	BUR-G
BIN-G	BRA-G	DAN-G

DIN-G	LIN-G	SAN-G
DON-G	MAR-G	SIN-G
DUN-G	MUN-G	SON-G
FAN-G	PAN-G	SUN-G
FRA-G	PIN-G	TAN-G
FRO-G	PLU-G	TIN-G
GAN-G	PRO-G	TON-G
GON-G	QUA-G	WIN-G
HAN-G	RAN-G	ZIN-G
HUN-G	RIN-G	
KIN-G	RUN-G	

Four letters to five

AGIN-G	GULA-G	THIN-G
BEIN-G	RUIN-G	THON-G
BLIN-G	SPAN-G	TYIN-G
BRIN-G	STUN-G	
CLAN-G	SWAN-G	

Five letters to six

ACTIN-G	LAWIN-G	RAVIN-G
BASIN-G	LAYIN-G	RICIN-G
BELON-G	LIKIN-G	ROBIN-G
CONIN-G	LININ-G	ROSIN-G
COVIN-G	MATIN-G	SAVIN-G
ELFIN-G	MIRIN-G	SEWIN-G
GAMIN-G	PAVIN-G	TAKIN-G
LAKIN-G	PURIN-G	TAMIN-G

Six letters to seven

BOBBIN-G	HOGGIN-G	OUTWIN-G
BUGGIN-G	JERKIN-G	OVERDO-G
BUSKIN-G	MERLIN-G	PARKIN-G
COPPIN-G	MUFFIN-G	PIPPIN-G
CUFFIN-G	MUNTIN-G	PUFFIN-G
CYCLIN-G	MURLIN-G	RAISIN-G
DENTIN-G	NOGGIN-G	RENNIN-G
DUBBIN-G	OUTRAN-G	ROBBIN-G
GRADIN-G	OUTRUN-G	TANNIN-G
GRATIN-G	OUTSIN-G	TIFFIN-G

G

Seven letters to eight

ASPIRIN-G

CHITLIN-G

CREATIN-G

CRISPIN-G

GELATIN-G

LITTLIN-G

MAHJONG-G

MORPHIN-G

PUMPKIN-G

RATTLIN-G

RAVELIN-G

RELAXIN-G

RESILIN-G

SCULPIN-G

SPELDIN-G

SPONGIN-G

UNDERDO-G

BLOCKERS

It is useful to know which words are blockers and can't therefore be extended before or after. You may want to play a blocker that your opponent can't extend, or you may want to avoid playing a blocker because you want to keep the board open.

Some three-letter blockers beginning with G

GEY · GOX

Some four-letter blockers beginning with G

GAGA	GAZY	GIZZ
GAMY	GEED	GORY
GASH	GEEZ	

Some five-letter blockers beginning with G (except words ending in '-ED', '-J', '-S', '-X', '-Y' or '-Z')

GEESE	GLIAL	GOYIM
GELID	GNASH	GREEK
GENAL	GNAWN	GROWN
GEYER	GONNA	GULCH
GHEST	GONZO	GURSH
GINZO	GOTTA	GYRAL

Some six-letter blockers beginning with G (except words ending in '-ED', '-J', '-S', '-X', '-Y' or '-Z')

GAMEST	GAYEST	GLUIER
GAMIER	GEDDIT	GLUING
GARDAI	GEEING	GNOMIC
GARISH	GEMINI	GOLDER
GASHER	GENIAL	GOOIER
GASLIT	GIBING	GORIER
GASMAN	GIDDUP	GOTTEN
GASMEN	GLOBAL	GRAVEN

| GRAYER | GREYER | GUNMAN |
| GREEBO | GRINCH | GUNMEN |

BONUS WORDS

Bonus words on your rack can be hard to spot, especially for the less experienced player. One way to help finding them is by using prefixes and suffixes.

Many larger words include a common prefix or suffix – remembering these and using them where you can is a good way to discover any longer words on your rack, including any potential bonus words. The key suffixes to remember ending with G are -GEN and -GRAM.

Some words ending with -GEN

Seven-letter words

ANTI-GEN	INDI-GEN	PYRO-GEN
CRYO-GEN	LOXY-GEN	SMID-GEN
ENDO-GEN	MUTA-GEN	TRUD-GEN
HALO-GEN	ONCO-GEN	TWIG-GEN

Eight-letter words

ABORI-GEN	ENLAR-GEN	NITRO-GEN
ALLER-GEN	ESTRO-GEN	PATHO-GEN
ANDRO-GEN	HISTO-GEN	PHOTO-GEN
COLLA-GEN	HYDRO-GEN	
CYANO-GEN	MISCE-GEN	

Some words ending with -GRAM

Seven-letter words

ANA-GRAM	ISO-GRAM	TAN-GRAM
DIA-GRAM	MYO-GRAM	TRI-GRAM
EPI-GRAM	PAN-GRAM	
GRO-GRAM	PRO-GRAM	

Eight-letter words

AERO-GRAM	HEXA-GRAM	LEXI-GRAM
DECA-GRAM	HOLO-GRAM	MONO-GRAM
DECI-GRAM	IDEO-GRAM	NANO-GRAM
ETHO-GRAM	IDIO-GRAM	SONO-GRAM
GENO-GRAM	KILO-GRAM	TELE-GRAM

UNUSUAL LETTER COMBINATIONS

If you have an unusual combination of letters on your rack, or want to impress your opponent with an unusual word, a few words from World English can come in handy.

Australian words

GALAH	grey-and-pink cockatoo
GARBO	dustman
GEEBUNG	tree with edible but tasteless fruit
GIDGEE	small acacia tree that sometimes emits an unpleasant smell
GILGAI	natural water hole
GING	child's catapult
GNOW	ground-dwelling bird
GOANNA	monitor lizard
GOOG	egg
GUNYAH	bush hut or shelter
GYMPIE	tall tree with stinging hairs on its leaves

Canadian word

GROWLER	small iceberg that has broken off from a larger iceberg or glacier

Hindi words

GAUR	large wild cow
GARIAL	fish-eating crocodilian with long slender snout
GHARRI	horse-drawn vehicle for hire
GHAT	stairs or passage leading down to a river
GHEE	clarified butter
GHERAO	industrial action in which workers imprison their employers
GINGILI	oil obtained from sesame seeds
GORAL	small goat antelope
GUAR	plant that produces gum
GUNNY	coarse fabric used for sacks

New Zealand word

GRAUNCH	crush or destroy

South African word

GEELBEK	yellow-jawed fish

G

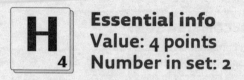

Essential info
Value: 4 points
Number in set: 2

H begins a two-letter word with every vowel except for U (although it can form UH, a sound that people make when they are unsure about something, 5 points), making it very useful for forming short words in different directions. As H is worth 4 points, these words can return very high scores in conjunction with premium squares despite their brevity: HA, HE, HI and HO are all worth 5 points.

Two-letter words beginning with H

HA	HI	HO
HE	HM	

Some three-letter words beginning with H

HAE	HEY	HON
HAH	HIC	HOO
HAJ	HIE	HOX
HAN	HIN	HOY
HAO	HIS	HUB
HAP	HMM	HUH
HAW	HOA	HUN
HEH	HOC	HUP
HEP	HOD	HYE
HET	HOH	HYP
HEW	HOI	
HEX	HOM	

HOOKS

Hooking requires a subtle change in a player's thought process, in that they must look at words already on the board without becoming distracted by their pronunciation.

Some front-hooks
Two letters to three

H-AD	H-ES	H-ON
H-AE	H-ET	H-OO
H-AG	H-EX	H-OP
H-AH	H-ID	H-OS
H-AM	H-IN	H-OW
H-AN	H-IS	H-OX
H-AS	H-IT	H-OY
H-AT	H-MM	H-UG
H-AW	H-OB	H-UH
H-AY	H-OD	H-UM
H-EH	H-OE	H-UN
H-EM	H-OH	H-UP
H-EN	H-OI	H-UT
H-ER	H-OM	H-YE

Three letters to four

H-AFT	H-ARM	H-IRE
H-AHA	H-ART	H-ISH
H-AIL	H-ASP	H-OAR
H-AIN	H-ATE	H-OBO
H-AIR	H-AVE	H-OLD
H-AKA	H-EAR	H-OLE
H-AKE	H-EAT	H-ONE
H-ALE	H-EEL	H-OOF
H-ALF	H-EFT	H-OOP
H-ALL	H-ELL	H-OOT
H-ALT	H-ELM	H-OPE
H-AND	H-ERE	H-OSE
H-ARD	H-ICK	H-OUR
H-ARE	H-IDE	H-OWL
H-ARK	H-ILL	H-UMP

Four letters to five

H-AIRY	H-AUNT	H-EATH
H-ARDS	H-AVER	H-EAVE
H-ARED	H-AWED	H-ECHT
H-ASHY	H-EARD	H-EDGE
H-AULD	H-EAST	H-EDGY

H-EXED H-IRED H-ONER
H-EXES H-ITCH H-OVEN
H-EYED H-OARY H-OVER
H-INKY H-OAST

Five letters to six

H-ACKER H-ASHED H-ILLER
H-AILED H-AUGHT H-INTER
H-AIRED H-AWING H-IRING
H-ALLOW H-EARTH H-ITCHY
H-ALTER H-EATER H-OLDEN
H-ANGER H-EAVED H-OLDER
H-ARBOR H-EDGED H-OTTER
H-ARMED H-EDGER H-OWLED
H-ARMER H-EIGHT H-OWLER
H-ARROW H-EXING H-USHER

Six letters to seven

H-AILING H-ASHIER H-EDGING
H-AIRIER H-ASHING H-EIGHTH
H-AIRING H-AUNTER H-ERRING
H-AMBLED H-AUTEUR H-INKIER
H-ARBOUR H-EARING H-ITCHED
H-ARKING H-EATING H-OVERED
H-ARMFUL H-EAVING H-OWLING
H-ARMING H-EDGIER H-UPPING

Seven letters to eight

H-AIRIEST H-ARBORED H-ITCHILY
H-AIRLESS H-ARMLESS H-ITCHING
H-AIRLIKE H-ARROWED H-OVERFLY
H-AIRLINE H-EATABLE H-OVERING
H-AIRLOCK H-EDGIEST H-USHERED
H-ALLOWED H-INKIEST
H-ALTERED H-ITCHIER

Some end-hooks
Two letters to three

AA-H BO-H ED-H
AS-H DA-H ET-H
BA-H DO-H FA-H

FE-H	NA-H	RE-H
HA-H	NO-H	SH-H
HE-H	OO-H	SO-H
HO-H	PA-H	UG-H
IS-H	PE-H	YA-H
LA-H	PO-H	YE-H

Three letters to four

ARC-H	HAT-H	PAT-H
BAC-H	HET-H	PEC-H
BAS-H	HIS-H	PIT-H
BAT-H	HOG-H	POO-H
BOO-H	KIT-H	POS-H
BOT-H	LAS-H	PUS-H
BUS-H	LAT-H	RAS-H
COS-H	MAC-H	SHA-H
DAS-H	MAS-H	SIT-H
DIS-H	MAT-H	SUK-H
DOS-H	MES-H	TAS-H
DOT-H	MET-H	TEC-H
EAT-H	MOS-H	UMP-H
FAS-H	MOT-H	WAS-H
GAS-H	MUS-H	WIS-H
GOS-H	NIS-H	WIT-H
GOT-H	NOS-H	YEA-H
GUS-H	OAT-H	
HAS-H	PAS-H	

Four letters to five

BOOT-H	HUMP-H	SOUT-H
BRAS-H	LEAS-H	SWAT-H
BRUS-H	MARC-H	SYNC-H
BUMP-H	MARS-H	TENT-H
BURG-H	MERC-H	THIG-H
CLOT-H	MYNA-H	TOOT-H
CRUS-H	NEAT-H	TORA-H
FLUS-H	PLUS-H	TORC-H
FORT-H	SCAT-H	WOOS-H
FRIT-H	SLOT-H	WORT-H
GIRT-H	SMIT-H	
HEAT-H	SOOT-H	

Five letters to six

COMET-H	HOOKA-H	POLIS-H
DELIS-H	HURRA-H	PUNKA-H
EIGHT-H	HUZZA-H	SHEIK-H
FATWA-H	LOOFA-H	SHIVA-H
FELLA-H	MULLA-H	SUNNA-H
FINIS-H	PARIS-H	WALLA-H
HEART-H	PERIS-H	

Six letters to seven

AARRGH-H	OUTWIT-H	SABBAT-H
HAGGIS-H	QABALA-H	

Seven letters to eight

BEGORRA-H	MADRASA-H	PEISHWA-H
HOSANNA-H	MESHUGA-H	SAVANNA-H
HYDRANT-H	NARGILE-H	SCAMPIS-H
KHALIFA-H	OCTOPUS-H	VERANDA-H

BLOCKERS

It is useful to know which words are blockers and can't therefore be extended before or after. You may want to play a blocker that your opponent can't extend, or you may want to avoid playing a blocker because you want to keep the board open.

Some three-letter blockers beginning with H

HEX	HMM	HOX

Some four-letter blockers beginning with H

HAZY	HOAX	HUNG
HELD	HOLY	
HIYA	HUED	

Some five-letter blockers beginning with H (except words ending in '-ED', '-J', '-S', '-X', '-Y' or '-Z')

HARSH	HOOCH	HUNCH
HAULT	HOVEN	HUTCH
HAUTE	HUGER	
HOING	HUMID	

Some six-letter blockers beginning with H (except words ending in '-ED', '-J', '-S', '-X', '-Y' or '-Z')

HABILE	HITMEN	HOSING
HARDER	HOLDEN	HOWZAT
HATING	HOLIER	HUGEST
HAUNCH	HOOTCH	HYENIC
HAZIER	HOOVEN	HYMNIC
HIKING	HOPING	
HITMAN	HORRID	

BONUS WORDS

Bonus words on your rack can be hard to spot, especially for the less experienced player. One way to help find them is by using prefixes and suffixes.

Many larger words include a common prefix or suffix – remembering these and using them where you can is a good way to discover any longer words on your rack, including any potential bonus words. The key suffixes to remember ending with H are -HOLE, -HOOD and -HORN.

Some words ending with -HOLE
Seven-letter words

AIR-HOLE	KEY-HOLE	PIN-HOLE
ARM-HOLE	LUG-HOLE	POT-HOLE
EYE-HOLE	MAN-HOLE	SPY-HOLE
FOX-HOLE	PIE-HOLE	

Eight-letter words

BLOW-HOLE	HELL-HOLE	PORT-HOLE
BOLT-HOLE	KNOT-HOLE	SINK-HOLE
BORE-HOLE	LOOP-HOLE	WELL-HOLE
BUNG-HOLE	PEEP-HOLE	WOOD-HOLE
FEED-HOLE	PLUG-HOLE	WORM-HOLE

Some words ending with -HOOD
Seven-letter words

BOY-HOOD	LAD-HOOD	SON-HOOD
GOD-HOOD	MAN-HOOD	

Eight-letter words

AUNT-HOOD
BABY-HOOD
DOLL-HOOD
GIRL-HOOD
IDLE-HOOD
KING-HOOD

LADY-HOOD
MAID-HOOD
MISS-HOOD
MONK-HOOD
PAGE-HOOD
POPE-HOOD

PUMP-HOOD
SELF-HOOD
SERF-HOOD
WIFE-HOOD
WIVE-HOOD

Some words ending with -HORN

Seven-letter words

ALP-HORN
BET-HORN
BIG-HORN
DIS-HORN

FOG-HORN
INK-HORN
LEG-HORN
SAX-HORN

TIN-HORN
UNS-HORN

Eight-letter words

BOXT-HORN
BUCK-HORN
BULL-HORN

DEER-HORN
HAWT-HORN
LONG-HORN

RAMS-HORN
SHOE-HORN
STAG-HORN

UNUSUAL LETTER COMBINATIONS

If you have an unusual combination of letters on your rack,
or want to impress your opponent with an unusual word,
a few words from World English can come in handy.

Australian words

HAKEA   type of shrub or tree
HOVEA   plant with purple flowers
HUTCHIE   groundsheet draped over an upright stick as a
            shelter

Canadian word

HONKER   Canada goose

Hindi words

HARTAL   act of closing shop or stopping work as a political
            protest
HOWDAH   seat for riding on an elephant's back

New Zealand words

Many Maori words start with the letter H, and if you have an H alongside a selection of vowels you may be able to play some of the following:

HAKA	war dance
HANGI	open-air cooking pit
HAPU	subtribe
HAPUKA	large fish
HEITIKI	neck ornament
HIKOI	protest march
HOKONUI	illicit whisky
HONGI	nose-touching greeting
HUHU	hairy beetle
HUI	conference or meeting
HUIA	extinct New Zealand bird

H

Handy Hint

Some short, useful words starting with H and using power tiles are HAJ (Muslim pilgrimage to Mecca, 13 points, also its variant forms HAJJ and HADJ), HAZE (16 points), HAZY (19 points), HEX (a curse or spell, 13 points) and HOX (a Shakespearean word meaning to cut a horse's hamstring, also 13).

Essential info
Value: 1 point
Number in set: 9

I can be a tricky letter to use in multiples so you need to try and use an I as soon as you can to avoid getting two of them. There are plenty of two-letter words beginning with I to help you make good-scoring parallel plays as shown below. The higher-scoring three letter words beginning with I are worth making note of, such as ICY (8 points), IVY (9 points) and IMP (7 points). The I can also be vital for reaping points with a Q or X with QI or XI. The I is also one of the letters of the RETAIN set and is therefore a good letter to keep if trying to get a bonus word.

Two-letter words beginning with I

ID	IN	IS
IF	IO	IT

Some three-letter words beginning with I

ICH	ION	ISO
ICK	IRE	ITA
IDE	ISH	
IFF	ISM	

HOOKS

Hooking requires a subtle change in a player's thought process, in that they must look at words already on the board without becoming distracted by their pronunciation.

Some front-hooks
Two letters to three

I-CH	I-OS	I-SO
I-DE	I-RE	I-TA
I-ON	I-SH	

Three letters to four

I-BIS	I-KON	I-RES
I-CON	I-LEA	I-RID
I-DEE	I-LEX	I-SIT
I-DOL	I-MAM	I-SOS
I-GAD	I-MID	I-TAS
I-KAT	I-RED	I-URE

Four letters to five

I-DANT	I-MAGE	I-RATE
I-DEAL	I-MINE	I-RING
I-DEES	I-MINO	I-RONE
I-DENT	I-NANE	I-SLED
I-GAPO	I-ODIC	I-VIED
I-LEAL	I-RADE	

Five letters to six

I-CONIC	I-ODISM	I-SATIN
I-GUANA	I-ONIUM	I-SLING
I-LEXES	I-RATER	I-TEMED
I-NYALA	I-RISES	

Six letters to seven

I-MAGISM	I-RISING	I-SOLATE

Seven letters to eight

I-CONICAL	I-SLANDER
I-SABELLA	I-SOLATED

> ### Handy Hint
>
> If you have enough letters to form the suffix -ING, you could be well on the way to scoring a bonus word for 50 points. Look at the other letters on your rack and try to form a word ending in -ING (there are thousands!). But don't hang on to -ING at all costs, as by doing so you are restricting yourself to playing with just four letters, with the consequent likelihood of low scores.

Some end-hooks
Two letters to three

AH-I	HO-I	PO-I
AM-I	JA-I	RE-I
AN-I	KA-I	TA-I
BO-I	KO-I	UN-I
CH-I	MO-I	
DE-I	OB-I	

Three letters to four

ANT-I	HAJ-I	PEN-I
ART-I	IMP-I	PER-I
BAN-I	KAK-I	PIP-I
BEN-I	LOB-I	PUR-I
BID-I	LOT-I	QUA-I
BUD-I	MAG-I	RAG-I
CAD-I	MAL-I	RAM-I
CAP-I	MAN-I	RAN-I
CHA-I	MAX-I	ROT-I
CON-I	MID-I	SAD-I
DAL-I	MIR-I	SAR-I
DEF-I	MOD-I	SAT-I
DEL-I	MOM-I	SIR-I
DEN-I	MOT-I	TAB-I
DIV-I	MUN-I	TAX-I
FEN-I	NID-I	TIP-I
FIN-I	NOD-I	TOP-I
GAD-I	NON-I	TOR-I
GAR-I	PAD-I	

Four letters to five

BASS-I	COMB-I	FUND-I
BAST-I	CORN-I	FUNG-I
BEST-I	CROC-I	GLOB-I
BIND-I	CULT-I	HADJ-I
BUFF-I	CURL-I	HAJJ-I
CAMP-I	DILL-I	HANG-I
CARD-I	DISC-I	HONG-I
CARP-I	FAST-I	HOUR-I
CELL-I	FERM-I	JINN-I
COAT-I	FILM-I	LASS-I

I

LENT-I PART-I SENT-I
LIMB-I POOR-I SWAM-I
LOGO-I PRIM-I TANG-I
LUNG-I PULL-I TARS-I
MACH-I PUTT-I TEMP-I
MYTH-I ROST-I VILL-I
PARK-I SENS-I VOLT-I

Five letters to six

ANNUL-I FRACT-I SCAMP-I
AVANT-I GARDA-I SENSE-I
CAROL-I GLUTE-I SHALL-I
CHICH-I HAIKA-I SILEN-I
CHILL-I JEHAD-I SMALT-I
COLON-I JIHAD-I SOLID-I
CUBIT-I KAIKA-I STELA-I
DENAR-I MANAT-I TAPET-I
DJINN-I POLYP-I YOGIN-I
EQUAL-I RHOMB-I

Six letters to seven

ACANTH-I DENARI-I REVERS-I
AFGHAN-I HALLAL-I RHYTHM-I
BANDAR-I JAMPAN-I SECOND-I
CHIASM-I MARTIN-I SHIKAR-I
DACTYL-I PAESAN-I SIGNOR-I
DEMENT-I QAWWAL-I TYMPAN-I

Seven letters to eight

BRAHMAN-I CONDUCT-I MARCHES-I
CALAMAR-I DRACHMA-I PARCHES-I
CAPITAN-I FASCISM-I PERFECT-I
CONCEPT-I FASCIST-I SIGNIOR-I
CONCERT-I HETAIRA-I TANDOOR-I

BLOCKERS

It is useful to know which words are blockers and can't therefore be extended before or after. You may want to play a blocker that your opponent can't extend, or you may want to avoid playing a blocker because you want to keep the board open.

Some four-letter blockers beginning with I

IBIS	IDLY	INLY

Some five-letter blockers beginning with I (except words ending in '-ED', '-J', '-S', '-X', '-Y' or '-Z')

ICTIC	IMSHI	INFRA
ILEAC	INAPT	INTIL
ILEAL	INBYE	INTRA
ILIAC	INCUT	INUST
IMIDO	INEPT	IODIC
IMINO	INERM	ISNAE

Some six-letter blockers beginning with I (except words ending in '-ED', '-J', '-S', '-X', '-Y' or '-Z')

ICEMEN	INFIMA	INWITH
ICONIC	INGRAM	INWORN
IDLEST	INKJET	IRATER
INANER	INLAID	IRIDAL
INBENT	INMESH	IRIDIC
INBORN	INMOST	IRITIC
INCUBI	INRUSH	IRREAL
INFELT	INTACT	ITSELF
INFERE	INTIRE	

BONUS WORDS

Bonus words on your rack can be hard to spot, especially for the less experienced player. One way to help find them is by using prefixes and suffixes.

Many larger words include a common prefix or suffix – remembering these and using them where you can is a good way to discover any longer words on your rack, including any potential bonus words. The key prefixes to remember beginning with I are IM-, IN- and ISO- and the key suffixes are -IBLE, -IFY, -INGS, -ISE, -ISH, -ISM, -IST, -ITY and -IUM.

Some words beginning with IM-
Seven-letter words

IM-AGERS	IM-BURSE	IM-MORAL
IM-AGING	IM-MENSE	IM-PACTS

IM-PAIRS
IM-PALAS
IM-PALED
IM-PALER
IM-PANEL
IM-PARTS
IM-PASSE

IM-PEACH
IM-PEDES
IM-PENDS
IM-PERIL
IM-PLANT
IM-PLIED
IM-PORTS

IM-POSED
IM-POUND
IM-PRESS
IM-PRINT
IM-PROVE
IM-PULSE
IM-PURER

Eight-letter words

IM-BARKED
IM-BODIED
IM-MATURE
IM-MOBILE
IM-MODEST
IM-MORTAL
IM-PAIRED
IM-PALING
IM-PARITY

IM-PARTED
IM-PENDED
IM-PLYING
IM-POLITE
IM-PORTED
IM-POSING
IM-POSTER
IM-POTENT
IM-PRISON

IM-PROPER
IM-PROVED
IM-PROVER
IM-PUDENT
IM-PURELY
IM-PUREST
IM-PURITY

Some words beginning with IN-

Seven-letter words

IN-BOUND
IN-BUILT
IN-CASED
IN-CENSE
IN-CITED
IN-COMER
IN-DENTS
IN-DEXES
IN-DICES
IN-DICTS
IN-DOORS
IN-DORSE
IN-DUCTS
IN-EXACT
IN-FAMED
IN-FESTS
IN-FIGHT
IN-FIRMS
IN-FLAME

IN-FORCE
IN-FORMS
IN-FRACT
IN-FUSED
IN-GESTS
IN-GRAIN
IN-GRATE
IN-GROWN
IN-HABIT
IN-HALED
IN-HUMAN
IN-LAYER
IN-MATES
IN-NARDS
IN-QUEST
IN-QUIRE
IN-ROADS
IN-SANER
IN-SECTS

IN-SIDER
IN-SIGHT
IN-SISTS
IN-SNARE
IN-SOFAR
IN-SOLES
IN-SPIRE
IN-STALL
IN-STATE
IN-STEAD
IN-STEPS
IN-STILL
IN-SURED
IN-TAKES
IN-TENDS
IN-TENSE
IN-TERNS
IN-TONER
IN-VADED

| IN-VALID | IN-VERSE | IN-VOLVE |
| IN-VENTS | IN-VESTS | IN-WARDS |

Eight-letter words

IN-ACTION	IN-EQUITY	IN-PUTTED
IN-ACTIVE	IN-EXPERT	IN-SANELY
IN-BREEDS	IN-FAMOUS	IN-SANITY
IN-CENSED	IN-FESTER	IN-SCRIBE
IN-CITING	IN-FILLED	IN-SECURE
IN-CLOSED	IN-FINITE	IN-SHRINE
IN-COMING	IN-FIRMER	IN-SISTER
IN-CREASE	IN-FLIGHT	IN-STANCE
IN-CURRED	IN-FORMAL	IN-STATED
IN-DEBTED	IN-FORMED	IN-TERNAL
IN-DECENT	IN-FRINGE	IN-THRALL
IN-DENTED	IN-FUSION	IN-TREPID
IN-DIGEST	IN-GROUND	IN-VENTED
IN-DIRECT	IN-GROWTH	IN-VIABLE
IN-DOLENT	IN-HUMANE	
IN-EDIBLE	IN-JURIES	

Some words beginning with ISO-

Seven-letter words

ISO-BARS	ISO-LATE	ISO-TOPE
ISO-DOSE	ISO-MERE	ISO-TRON
ISO-FORM	ISO-PODS	ISO-TYPE
ISO-GRAM	ISO-TONE	

Eight-letter words

ISO-BARIC	ISO-GRAPH	ISO-TONIC
ISO-BUTYL	ISO-LATED	ISO-TOPIC
ISO-GAMIC	ISO-MORPH	ISO-TYPIC
ISO-GENIC	ISO-NOMIC	
ISO-GRAFT	ISO-THERM	

Some words ending with -IBLE

Seven-letter words

ADD-IBLE	FUS-IBLE	RIS-IBLE
AUD-IBLE	LEG-IBLE	VIS-IBLE
DEL-IBLE	MIX-IBLE	
DOC-IBLE	PAT-IBLE	

Eight-letter words

CRED-IBLE
CRUC-IBLE
ELIG-IBLE
FALL-IBLE
FEAS-IBLE
FLEX-IBLE
FORC-IBLE

GULL-IBLE
HORR-IBLE
INED-IBLE
MAND-IBLE
POSS-IBLE
RINS-IBLE
RUNC-IBLE

SENS-IBLE
TANG-IBLE
TENS-IBLE
TERR-IBLE
VINC-IBLE

Some words ending with -IFY

Seven-letter words

ACID-IFY
AMPL-IFY
BEAT-IFY
CERT-IFY
CLAR-IFY
CRUC-IFY
DIGN-IFY
FALS-IFY
FORT-IFY
GLOR-IFY

GRAT-IFY
HORR-IFY
JUST-IFY
LIQU-IFY
MAGN-IFY
MORT-IFY
NULL-IFY
PETR-IFY
QUAL-IFY
RECT-IFY

REUN-IFY
SACR-IFY
SALS-IFY
SCAR-IFY
SIGN-IFY
SPEC-IFY
TERR-IFY
TEST-IFY
YUPP-IFY
ZOMB-IFY

Eight-letter words

BEAUT-IFY
CLASS-IFY
DETOX-IFY
EMULS-IFY
GENTR-IFY
HUMID-IFY
IDENT-IFY

PRETT-IFY
QUANT-IFY
REMOD-IFY
RENOT-IFY
REPUR-IFY
RESIN-IFY
RIGID-IFY

SANCT-IFY
SIMPL-IFY
SOLID-IFY
STRAT-IFY
STULT-IFY

Some words ending with -INGS

Seven-letter words

ACH-INGS
ARM-INGS
BID-INGS
BUS-INGS
CAN-INGS
COD-INGS
COM-INGS

DAT-INGS
DRY-INGS
EAR-INGS
END-INGS
FAD-INGS
FIX-INGS
GAP-INGS

GAT-INGS
HID-INGS
INN-INGS
LAD-INGS
MER-INGS
OUT-INGS
PAR-INGS

PAY-INGS
RAG-INGS
RAT-INGS
SAY-INGS

SPY-INGS
TIM-INGS
TOY-INGS
TRY-INGS

TUB-INGS
WAD-INGS
WAN-INGS

Eight-letter words

BAIT-INGS
BANG-INGS
BEAR-INGS
BEAT-INGS
BOMB-INGS
BOND-INGS
BOWL-INGS
BUCK-INGS
CAMP-INGS
CAST-INGS
COAT-INGS
COIN-INGS
COMB-INGS
DAWN-INGS
DEAL-INGS
DRAW-INGS
EARN-INGS
EDIT-INGS
ETCH-INGS
EVEN-INGS
FAIL-INGS
FAST-INGS
FEED-INGS
FIND-INGS
FISH-INGS
FOOT-INGS
GASP-INGS
GELD-INGS
GOLF-INGS

HEAD-INGS
HEAR-INGS
HINT-INGS
HUNT-INGS
JUMP-INGS
KILL-INGS
LAND-INGS
LASH-INGS
LEAN-INGS
LIMP-INGS
LIST-INGS
LOAN-INGS
LONG-INGS
MALT-INGS
MEAN-INGS
MEET-INGS
MOOR-INGS
MORN-INGS
NEST-INGS
ONGO-INGS
OUTS-INGS
PAIR-INGS
PARK-INGS
PAST-INGS
PELT-INGS
PRIM-INGS
RAIL-INGS
READ-INGS
REEL-INGS

RING-INGS
ROCK-INGS
ROLL-INGS
ROOF-INGS
ROUT-INGS
SACK-INGS
SEAL-INGS
SEAT-INGS
SHOW-INGS
SIGN-INGS
SING-INGS
SLID-INGS
SNIP-INGS
STAG-INGS
STAR-INGS
TRAD-INGS
TWIN-INGS
UNDO-INGS
UNIT-INGS
WARN-INGS
WASH-INGS
WEEP-INGS
WHIN-INGS
WHIT-INGS
WIND-INGS
WORK-INGS
WRIT-INGS

Some words ending with -ISE
Seven-letter words

AGON-ISE
ATOM-ISE

BAPT-ISE
CONC-ISE

DUAL-ISE
ICON-ISE

IDOL-ISE
IRON-ISE
ITEM-ISE
LION-ISE
MORT-ISE

ODOR-ISE
OXID-ISE
POET-ISE
PREC-ISE
PREM-ISE

PROM-ISE
REAL-ISE
REPR-ISE
UNIT-ISE

Eight-letter words

ACTIV-ISE
BANAL-ISE
CALOR-ISE
CANON-ISE
CIVIL-ISE
COLON-ISE
COLOR-ISE
DEMON-ISE
DEPUT-ISE
EQUAL-ISE
ETHER-ISE
EXERC-ISE

FINAL-ISE
HUMAN-ISE
IDEAL-ISE
IMMUN-ISE
LEGAL-ISE
LOCAL-ISE
MAXIM-ISE
MINIM-ISE
MORAL-ISE
MOTOR-ISE
ORGAN-ISE
PARAD-ISE

PENAL-ISE
POLAR-ISE
PRACT-ISE
SANIT-ISE
SATIR-ISE
TREAT-ISE
UNION-ISE
VAPOR-ISE
VITAL-ISE
VOCAL-ISE
VOWEL-ISE

Some words ending with -ISH
Seven-letter words

BOOK-ISH
BULL-ISH
COLD-ISH
DARK-ISH
FOOL-ISH
FOPP-ISH
GIRL-ISH
GOOD-ISH

HAWK-ISH
HOTT-ISH
LEFT-ISH
LONG-ISH
MORE-ISH
PECK-ISH
PEEV-ISH
REDD-ISH

RUBB-ISH
SELF-ISH
SLAV-ISH
SLOW-ISH
SOFT-ISH
TALL-ISH
VARN-ISH
WAIF-ISH

Eight-letter words

BLACK-ISH
BLOKE-ISH
BLOND-ISH
BLUNT-ISH
CHILD-ISH
CLOWN-ISH
DEVIL-ISH

FEVER-ISH
FIEND-ISH
GOLDF-ISH
LIGHT-ISH
NANNY-ISH
PLAIN-ISH
REFIN-ISH

ROUGH-ISH
SHARP-ISH
SHEEP-ISH
SMALL-ISH
SWEET-ISH
THICK-ISH
YOUNG-ISH

Some words ending with -ISM

Seven-letter words

BRUT-ISM	EGOT-ISM	SIZE-ISM
CULT-ISM	FASC-ISM	TOUR-ISM
DADA-ISM	IDOL-ISM	
DUAL-ISM	REAL-ISM	

Eight-letter words

ACTIV-ISM	FEMIN-ISM	NIHIL-ISM
ALARM-ISM	FUTUR-ISM	OPTIM-ISM
ALIEN-ISM	HEDON-ISM	ORGAN-ISM
ANEUR-ISM	HUMAN-ISM	PACIF-ISM
BOTUL-ISM	IDEAL-ISM	POPUL-ISM
CLASS-ISM	JINGO-ISM	ROYAL-ISM
CRONY-ISM	LOCAL-ISM	STOIC-ISM
CYNIC-ISM	LOYAL-ISM	TOKEN-ISM
DYNAM-ISM	LYRIC-ISM	UNION-ISM
EMBOL-ISM	MINIM-ISM	VEGAN-ISM
ESCAP-ISM	MORAL-ISM	
FATAL-ISM	NATIV-ISM	

Some words ending with -IST

Seven-letter words

ATOM-IST	DIET-IST	LEFT-IST
BASS-IST	DUAL-IST	PALM-IST
CELL-IST	DUEL-IST	PERS-IST
CHEM-IST	FLOR-IST	REAL-IST
DIAR-IST	HARP-IST	TOUR-IST

Eight-letter words

ALARM-IST	HUMAN-IST	MORAL-IST
ARSON-IST	HUMOR-IST	MOTOR-IST
BANJO-IST	IDEAL-IST	OPTIM-IST
CANOE-IST	JIHAD-IST	ORGAN-IST
CHART-IST	JINGO-IST	PACIF-IST
CLASS-IST	LOBBY-IST	PANEL-IST
COLOR-IST	LOYAL-IST	POPUL-IST
ESSAY-IST	LYRIC-IST	PUGIL-IST
FINAL-IST	MEDAL-IST	RALLY-IST
HOBBY-IST	MINIM-IST	REGAL-IST

RIGHT-IST   SHOOT-IST   TOTAL-IST
ROYAL-IST   STOCK-IST   TOTEM-IST

Some words ending with -ITY
Seven-letter words

ACID-ITY   DUAL-ITY   QUAL-ITY
AMEN-ITY   JOLL-ITY   REAL-ITY
ARID-ITY   NULL-ITY   TENS-ITY
CHAR-ITY   OBES-ITY   TRIN-ITY
DENS-ITY   PRIV-ITY   UTIL-ITY
DIGN-ITY   PROB-ITY   VACU-ITY

Eight-letter words

ACRID-ITY   HUMID-ITY   REGAL-ITY
ACTIV-ITY   HUMIL-ITY   RIGID-ITY
AFFIN-ITY   IDENT-ITY   RURAL-ITY
BANAL-ITY   IMMUN-ITY   SANCT-ITY
CALAM-ITY   INSAN-ITY   SECUR-ITY
CHAST-ITY   LEGAL-ITY   SENIL-ITY
CONIC-ITY   LIVID-ITY   SEREN-ITY
CUBIC-ITY   LOCAL-ITY   SEVER-ITY
ENORM-ITY   LUCID-ITY   SOLID-ITY
EQUAL-ITY   MAJOR-ITY   TIMID-ITY
FACIL-ITY   MINOR-ITY   TONAL-ITY
FATAL-ITY   MOBIL-ITY   TONIC-ITY
FIDEL-ITY   MORAL-ITY   TOTAL-ITY
FINAL-ITY   NATIV-ITY   TOXIC-ITY
FLUID-ITY   POLAR-ITY   VALID-ITY
FUTIL-ITY   PRIOR-ITY   VITAL-ITY
GRATU-ITY   RABID-ITY
HUMAN-ITY   RAPID-ITY

Some words ending with -IUM
Seven-letter words

CALC-IUM   IRID-IUM   RHOD-IUM
CRAN-IUM   LITH-IUM   STAD-IUM
FERM-IUM   PALL-IUM   TERT-IUM
GALL-IUM   PLAG-IUM   TRIT-IUM
HASS-IUM   PREM-IUM   URAN-IUM
HOLM-IUM   PROT-IUM   YTTR-IUM

Eight-letter words

ACTIN-IUM
AEROB-IUM
ALLUV-IUM
AMMON-IUM
AQUAR-IUM
BRACH-IUM
CHROM-IUM
CORON-IUM
DELIR-IUM
DILUV-IUM
EMPOR-IUM

EULOG-IUM
FRANC-IUM
GERAN-IUM
IMPER-IUM
INGEN-IUM
MOTOR-IUM
NOBEL-IUM
OSSAR-IUM
PHORM-IUM
POLON-IUM
REFUG-IUM

ROSAR-IUM
RUBID-IUM
SELEN-IUM
SOLAR-IUM
SOLAT-IUM
THALL-IUM
TITAN-IUM
TRILL-IUM
VIVAR-IUM

I

UNUSUAL LETTER COMBINATIONS

If you have an unusual combination of letters on your rack, or want to impress your opponent with an unusual word, a few words from World English can come in handy. Here are some beginning with I.

New Zealand word

IWI   a Maori tribe

Canadian word

ICEWINE   dessert wine made from frozen grapes

Urdu word

INQILAB   revolution

J
8

Essential info
Value: 8 points
Number in set: 1

POWER TILE

J alone is worth 8 points, making it an extremely valuable tile. However, it can be difficult to play: for example, there are only two two-letter words beginning with J (JA, a South African word for yes, and JO, a Scots word for sweetheart, both 9 points). When used in conjunction with the other power tiles X and Z, however, there is scope for huge scoring, especially if words are played judiciously on double- or triple-letter squares. Good short words to remember which use J alongside X and Z include JINX (18 points) and JAZY (23 points). Remember, as there is only one J tile in the Scrabble set, you will need a blank tile to take advantage of words with two Js (e.g. HAJJ, 13 points) or indeed a J and two of the same power tile letters (e.g. JAZZES, 21 points).

Two-letter words beginning with J

JA   JO

Some three-letter words beginning with J

JAG	JEU	JOL
JAI	JEW	JOR
JAK	JIB	JOW
JAP	JIN	JUD
JAY	JIZ	JUN
JEE	JOE	JUS

Some three-letter words using J

| GJU | RAJ |
| HAJ | TAJ |

Some four-letter words using J

Some four-letter words using J that you may not know are DOJO (room or hall for the practice of martial arts, 12 points), JEHU (a fast driver, 14 points), JIAO (Chinese currency unit, 11 points) and JIRD (another word for gerbil, 12 points)

AJAR	JEEP	JOLL
DJIN	JEER	JOLT
DOJO	JEEZ	JOMO
FUJI	JEFE	JONG
HADJ	JEFF	JOOK
HAJJ	JEHU	JOSH
JAAP	JELL	JOSS
JACK	JEON	JOTA
JADE	JERK	JOUK
JAFA	JESS	JOUR
JAGA	JEST	JOWL
JAGG	JETE	JUBA
JAIL	JEUX	JUBE
JAKE	JIAO	JUCO
JAMB	JIBB	JUDO
JANE	JIBE	JUDY
JANN	JIFF	JUGA
JAPE	JILL	JUJU
JARK	JILT	JUKE
JARL	JIMP	JUKU
JARP	JINK	JUMP
JASP	JINN	JUNK
JASS	JINS	JUPE
JASY	JINX	JURA
JATO	JIRD	JURE
JAUK	JIVE	JURY
JAUP	JIVY	JUST
JAVA	JOBE	JUTE
JAXY	JOCK	JUVE
JAZY	JOCO	JYNX
JAZZ	JOEY	KOJI
JEAN	JOHN	MOJO
JEAT	JOIN	RAJA
JEDI	JOKE	SOJA
JEED	JOKY	
JEEL	JOLE	

J

HOOKS

Hooking requires a subtle change in a player's thought process, in that they must look at words already on the board without becoming distracted by their pronunciation.

Some front-hooks
Two letters to three

J-AB	J-EE	J-OY
J-AG	J-ET	J-UG
J-AI	J-IN	J-UN
J-AM	J-OB	J-US
J-AR	J-OE	J-UT
J-AW	J-OR	
J-AY	J-OW	

Three letters to four

J-AGA	J-EAT	J-IVY
J-AIL	J-EEL	J-OBE
J-AKE	J-EFF	J-OKE
J-ANE	J-ELL	J-OLE
J-ANN	J-ERK	J-OUK
J-APE	J-ESS	J-OUR
J-ARK	J-EST	J-OWL
J-ASP	J-IFF	J-UDO
J-ASS	J-ILL	J-UKE
J-AUK	J-IMP	J-UMP
J-AVA	J-INK	J-URE
J-EAN	J-INN	J-UTE

Four letters to five

J-AGER	J-EMMY	J-OWED
J-ALAP	J-ESSE	J-OWLY
J-AMBO	J-IFFY	J-UMBO
J-APED	J-ILLS	J-UMPY
J-APER	J-IMMY	J-UNCO
J-AUNT	J-INGO	J-UNTO
J-AVEL	J-NANA	J-UPON
J-AWED	J-OINT	
J-EELY	J-OUST	

J

Five letters to six

J-ABBED	J-ASSES	J-OTTER
J-ACKER	J-AUNTY	J-OUNCE
J-AGGER	J-AWING	J-OWING
J-AILED	J-EANED	J-OWLED
J-AMBER	J-EFFED	J-OWLER
J-ANGLE	J-ESSES	J-UDDER
J-ANKER	J-ESTER	J-UGGED
J-APERY	J-IGGED	J-UMBLE
J-APING	J-IMPLY	J-UMPED
J-ARGON	J-INGLE	J-UNKED
J-ARRAH	J-INKED	J-UNKET
J-ASPER	J-INKER	

Six letters to seven

J-AGGIES	J-IMMIES	J-OUSTER
J-AILING	J-INGOES	J-OWLIER
J-ANGLED	J-INKING	J-OWLING
J-ANGLER	J-OCULAR	J-UGGING
J-AUNTIE	J-OINTED	J-UMPING
J-AWLESS	J-OLLIES	J-UNCATE
J-EFFING	J-OSTLER	J-UNCOES
J-IGGING	J-OUSTED	J-UNKING

Seven letters to eight

J-ANGLING	J-OUSTING	J-UNCTION
J-APERIES	J-OWLIEST	
J-OINTING	J-UDDERED	

Some end-hooks
Two letters to three

HA-J	TA-J

Three letters to four

BEN-J	HAD-J	HAJ-J

BLOCKERS

It is useful to know which words are blockers and can't therefore be extended before or after. You may want to play a blocker that your opponent can't extend, or you may want to avoid playing a blocker because you want to keep the board open.

Some four-letter blockers beginning with J

JASS	JEON	JOSH
JASY	JEUX	JOSS
JAZY	JINX	JURY
JEED	JIVY	JYNX
JEEZ	JOKY	

Some five-letter blockers beginning with J (except words ending in '-ED', '-J', '-S', '-X', '-Y' or '-Z')

JEUNE	JIRRE	JOMON
JINGO	JOKOL	JURAL

Some six-letter blockers beginning with J (except words ending in '-ED', '-J', '-S', '-X', '-Y' or '-Z')

JACENT	JINNEE	JOLING
JADING	JIVIER	JOVIAL
JADISH	JIVING	JOWING
JEEING	JOBING	JOYFUL
JEJUNE	JOCOSE	JOYING
JIBING	JOCUND	JUBATE
JIMPER	JOKIER	JUGATE
JIMSON	JOKING	JUKING

> **Handy Hint**
>
> When holding a power tile try looking beyond the easy two and three-letter words that might jump out at you. Also look for words that might score more embedding the power tile rather than starting with it – a few containing a J are RAJA (11 points), MAJOR (14), CAJOLE (15), OUIJA (12), BANJO (14).

Bonus words
Seven-letter words

JABBERS
JABBING
JACKALS
JACKASS
JACKDAW
JACKERS
JACKETS
JACKING
JACKPOT
JACKSIE
JADEDLY
JAGGERS
JAGGERY
JAGGIER
JAGGIES
JAGGING
JAGUARS
JAILERS
JAILING
JAILORS
JAMJARS
JAMLIKE
JAMMERS
JAMMIER
JAMMIES
JAMMING
JAMPOTS
JANDALS
JANGLED
JANGLER
JANGLES
JANITOR
JARFULS
JARGONS
JARGONY
JARHEAD
JARPING

JARRAHS
JARRING
JASMINE
JASPERS
JASPERY
JAUNTED
JAUNTEE
JAUNTIE
JAUPING
JAVELIN
JAWBONE
JAWINGS
JAWLESS
JAWLINE
JAYBIRD
JAYWALK
JAZZIER
JAZZILY
JAZZING
JAZZMAN
JAZZMEN
JEALOUS
JEEPERS
JEEPING
JEERERS
JEERING
JEHADIS
JELLIED
JELLIFY
JELLING
JEMIMAS
JEMMIED
JEMMIER
JEMMIES
JENNIES
JEOPARD
JERBILS

JERBOAS
JEREEDS
JERKERS
JERKIER
JERKIES
JERKILY
JERKING
JERKINS
JERRIES
JERSEYS
JESSIES
JESTEES
JESTERS
JESTFUL
JESTING
JESUITS
JETLAGS
JETLIKE
JETSAMS
JETSOMS
JETTIED
JETTIER
JETTIES
JETTING
JEWELED
JEWELER
JEWELRY
JEZEBEL
JIBBERS
JIBBING
JIFFIES
JIGGERS
JIGGIER
JIGGING
JIGGLED
JIGSAWS
JIHADIS

JILTERS	JOLLEYS	JUGGLER
JILTING	JOLLIED	JUGHEAD
JIMJAMS	JOLLIER	JUGSFUL
JIMMIED	JOLLIES	JUGULAR
JIMMIES	JOLLIFY	JUICERS
JIMMINY	JOLLILY	JUICIER
JINGLED	JOLLITY	JUICILY
JINGLER	JOLTILY	JUICING
JINGLET	JOLTING	JUJITSU
JINGOES	JONESED	JUJUIST
JINXING	JONESES	JUKEBOX
JITTERS	JOSHERS	JUMBLED
JITTERY	JOSHING	JUMBLER
JIVIEST	JOSTLED	JUMBUCK
JOANNAS	JOSTLER	JUMPERS
JOBBERS	JOTTERS	JUMPIER
JOBBING	JOTTING	JUMPILY
JOBLESS	JOURNAL	JUMPING
JOCKEYS	JOURNEY	JUNGLED
JOCULAR	JOURNOS	JUNGLES
JODHPUR	JOUSTED	JUNIORS
JOGGERS	JOUSTER	JUNIPER
JOGGING	JOWLIER	JUNKETS
JOHNNIE	JOWLING	JUNKIER
JOHNSON	JOYLESS	JUNKMAN
JOINERS	JOYRIDE	JUNKMEN
JOINERY	JUBILEE	JURISTS
JOINING	JUDASES	JURYING
JOINTED	JUDDERS	JURYMAN
JOINTER	JUDGERS	JURYMEN
JOINTLY	JUDGING	JUSTICE
JOISTED	JUDOIST	JUSTIFY
JOJOBAS	JUGFULS	JUTTING
JOKIEST	JUGGLED	

J

Eight-letter words

JABBERED	JACKEROO	JAGGEDLY
JABBERER	JACKETED	JAGGIEST
JACKAROO	JADELIKE	JAILABLE
JACKBOOT	JAGGEDER	JAILBAIT

JAILBIRD
JAILLESS
JALAPENO
JAMBOREE
JAMMABLE
JAMMIEST
JANGLIER
JANGLING
JANITRIX
JAPANISE
JAPANIZE
JAPINGLY
JARGONED
JAUNDICE
JAUNTIER
JAUNTILY
JAUNTING
JAVELINA
JAWBONED
JAWBONER
JAZZIEST
JAZZLIKE
JEALOUSY
JEANETTE
JEHADISM
JEHADIST
JELLYING
JEMMIEST
JEMMYING
JEOPARDY
JERKIEST
JEROBOAM
JERRICAN
JERRYCAN
JERSEYED
JESTBOOK
JESUITIC
JESUITRY
JIGGLIER
JIGGLING

JIGSAWED
JIHADISM
JIHADIST
JILLAROO
JIMCRACK
JIMMYING
JINGLIER
JINGLING
JINGOISM
JINGOIST
JITTERED
JOBSHARE
JOCKETTE
JOCKEYED
JOGGLING
JOINABLE
JOINTING
JOINTURE
JOISTING
JOKESOME
JOKESTER
JOKINESS
JOKINGLY
JOLLEYER
JOLLIEST
JOLLYING
JOLTHEAD
JOLTIEST
JONESING
JONGLEUR
JOSTLING
JOUNCIER
JOUNCING
JOUSTING
JOVIALLY
JOVIALTY
JOWLIEST
JOYFULLY
JOYOUSLY
JOYRIDER

JOYSTICK
JUBILANT
JUBILATE
JUDDERED
JUDGMENT
JUDICIAL
JUGGLERY
JUGGLING
JUGULATE
JUICIEST
JULIENNE
JUMBLIER
JUMBLING
JUMPABLE
JUMPIEST
JUMPSUIT
JUNCTION
JUNCTURE
JUNGLIER
JUNGLIST
JUNKETED
JUNKETER
JUNKIEST
JUNKYARD
JURASSIC
JURATORY
JURISTIC
JURYLESS
JURYMAST
JUSTICER
JUSTLING
JUSTNESS
JUTELIKE
JUTTYING
JUVENILE

J

UNUSUAL LETTER COMBINATIONS

If you have an unusual combination of letters on your rack,
or want to impress your opponent with an unusual word,
a few words from World English can come in handy.

Australian words

JARRAH	type of eucalyptus tree
JEFF	downsize or close down an organization
JUMBUCK	sheep

Canadian word

JOUAL	nonstandard Canadian French dialect

Hindi words

JAGGERY	coarse brown sugar
JAI	victory

J

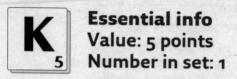

Essential info
Value: 5 points
Number in set: 1

K is a valuable tile at 5 points and is particularly useful if you also have a C on your rack because of the abundance of words ending in -CK. There is a selection of useful two-letter words beginning with K: KA, KI, KO (6 points each) and KY (9 points). Three-letter words beginning with K include common words such as KEG and KID (8 points) KIP (9 points), and KEY (10 points). Others tend to be more unusual words but nevertheless very useful: KEB (9 points). KEX (14 points), KIF (10 points).

Two-letter words beginning with K

KA	KO
KI	KY

Some three-letter words beginning with K

KAB	KED	KOA
KAE	KEF	KOB
KAF	KEN	KOI
KAI	KEP	KON
KAM	KET	KOP
KAT	KEX	KOR
KAW	KHI	KOW
KAY	KIF	KYE
KEA	KIN	KYU
KEB	KIR	

HOOKS

Hooking requires a subtle change in a player's thought process, in that they must look at words already on the board without becoming distracted by their pronunciation.

Some front-hooks
Two letters to three

K-AB	K-EF	K-OI
K-AE	K-ET	K-ON
K-AI	K-EX	K-OP
K-AM	K-HI	K-OR
K-AS	K-ID	K-OS
K-AT	K-IF	K-OW
K-AW	K-IN	K-YE
K-AY	K-IS	K-YU
K-EA	K-IT	
K-ED	K-OB	

Three letters to four

K-AGO	K-EEN	K-NAP
K-AID	K-ELL	K-NEE
K-AIL	K-ELT	K-NEW
K-AIM	K-ERF	K-NIT
K-AIN	K-ERN	K-NOT
K-AKA	K-EST	K-NOW
K-ALE	K-ETA	K-NUB
K-AMA	K-HAN	K-NUR
K-AMI	K-HAT	K-NUT
K-ANA	K-HET	K-OBO
K-ANE	K-ICK	K-OFF
K-ANT	K-IFF	K-ORA
K-ARK	K-ILL	K-ORE
K-ART	K-INK	K-SAR
K-AVA	K-IRK	K-UDO
K-AWA	K-ISH	K-UTA
K-BAR	K-IWI	K-UTU
K-EEK	K-LAP	K-YAK
K-EEL	K-NAG	

Four letters to five

K-ALIF	K-AWED	K-ERNE
K-ANGA	K-EDGE	K-ETCH
K-ARSY	K-EDGY	K-EVIL
K-ARTS	K-EECH	K-EYED
K-AVAS	K-EMPT	K-HETH

K-ICKY
K-INKY
K-LANG
K-LAPS
K-LICK
K-LONG
K-LOOF
K-LUGE
K-LUTZ
K-NAVE
K-NEED

K-NIFE
K-NISH
K-NOCK
K-NOLL
K-NOUT
K-NOWN
K-NURL
K-NURR
K-OKRA
K-OMBU
K-RAFT

K-RAIT
K-RANG
K-RILL
K-RONE
K-ROON
K-ULAN
K-VELL
K-YACK
K-YANG

Five letters to six

K-AINGA
K-ALONG
K-ANTAR
K-ANTED
K-ARKED
K-ARRIS
K-ARSEY
K-AWING
K-EBBED
K-EDGED
K-EDGER

K-EGGED
K-EGGER
K-EIGHT
K-EMBED
K-ENTIA
K-ERNED
K-ETTLE
K-EYING
K-ICKER
K-ILLER
K-INDIE

K-INGLE
K-INKED
K-INKLE
K-IRKED
K-ISHES
K-LATCH
K-LUGED
K-NAGGY
K-NIGHT
K-RATER
K-VETCH

Six letters to seven

K-ANTING
K-ARKING
K-EBBING
K-EDGERS
K-EDGIER
K-EDGING
K-EECHES
K-EGGING
K-ENOSIS
K-ERNING
K-ICKIER
K-IDLING

K-INKIER
K-INKING
K-INSHIP
K-IRKING
K-LAPPED
K-LINKER
K-LISTER
K-LUGING
K-LUTZES
K-NAPPED
K-NAPPER
K-NICKER

K-NISHES
K-NOBBLE
K-NOCKED
K-NUBBLE
K-NUBBLY
K-NURLED
K-ONNING
K-RATERS
K-RIMMER
K-RISING
K-VETCHY

K

Seven letters to eight

K-ALEWIFE	K-LAPPING	K-NOBBLED
K-EDGIEST	K-LATCHES	K-NOCKING
K-ETAMINE	K-NAGGIER	K-NUBBIER
K-ETCHING	K-NAPPING	K-NUBBLED
K-ICKIEST	K-NIGHTED	K-NURLING
K-INKIEST	K-NIGHTLY	K-OSMOSES
K-INSHIPS	K-NOBBIER	

Some end-hooks
Two letters to three

AR-K	IN-K	SI-K
AS-K	JA-K	TA-K
BO-K	KA-K	WO-K
DA-K	MA-K	YA-K
EE-K	NE-K	YO-K
EL-K	OI-K	YU-K
ER-K	OU-K	

Three letters to four

BAC-K	DOC-K	JUN-K
BAL-K	DOR-K	KIN-K
BAN-K	DUN-K	KIR-K
BAR-K	FAN-K	LAC-K
BAS-K	FIN-K	LAR-K
BON-K	FIR-K	LAW-K
BOO-K	FOR-K	LEA-K
BUN-K	FUN-K	LEE-K
BUR-K	GEE-K	LIN-K
BUS-K	GIN-K	LIS-K
CAR-K	GON-K	LOO-K
CAW-K	GUN-K	LUR-K
CHI-K	HAN-K	MAC-K
CON-K	HIC-K	MAR-K
COO-K	HOC-K	MAS-K
COR-K	HON-K	MAW-K
COW-K	HOO-K	MEE-K
DAN-K	HOW-K	MIL-K
DIN-K	HUN-K	MIR-K
DIS-K	JAR-K	MOC-K

MON-K
MOO-K
MUS-K
NOO-K
NOR-K
PAC-K
PAR-K
PEA-K
PEC-K
PEE-K
PER-K
PIC-K
PIN-K

PUN-K
RAN-K
REE-K
RIN-K
ROC-K
ROO-K
RUC-K
SAC-K
SAN-K
SEE-K
SIC-K
SIN-K
SOC-K

SUN-K
TAN-K
TAS-K
TEA-K
TEE-K
TIC-K
TOC-K
TON-K
TOO-K
WEE-K
WIN-K

Four letters to five

ABAC-K
ALEC-K
BLIN-K
BLOC-K
BRAN-K
BRIN-K
BRIS-K
BROO-K
BRUS-K
CHAL-K
CHIC-K
CHIN-K
CHOC-K
CLAN-K

CLON-K
CRAN-K
CREE-K
CROC-K
FLAN-K
FLIC-K
FLOC-K
FRIS-K
GREE-K
PLAN-K
SCUL-K
SHAN-K
SHIR-K
SHOO-K

SKIN-K
SLEE-K
SMIR-K
SPAN-K
SPAR-K
SPEC-K
SPIN-K
STAR-K
STIR-K
STUN-K
SWAN-K
THAN-K
THIN-K
TWIN-K

Five letters to six

ANTIC-K
ASPIC-K
BEGUN-K
DEBAR-K
EMBAR-K
IMBAR-K
JAMBO-K

KALPA-K
MEDIC-K
MELIC-K
MUSIC-K
PACHA-K
PANIC-K
REBEC-K

RESEE-K
SQUAW-K
UMIAC-K
UNBAR-K
ZEBEC-K

K

Six letters to seven

AMTRAC-K
BOOBOO-K
CALPAC-K
DISBAR-K

FINNAC-K
GWEDUC-K
LIMBEC-K
OOMIAC-K

OUTBAR-K
OUTRAN-K
TIETAC-K
TOMBAC-K

Seven letters to eight

ALMANAC-K
BALDRIC-K
BAUDRIC-K
FORERAN-K

OVERRAN-K
POLITIC-K
PRACTIC-K
SHELLAC-K

SHOEPAC-K
TAMARIS-K

BLOCKERS

It is useful to know which words are blockers and can't therefore be extended before or after. You may want to play a blocker that your opponent can't extend, or you may want to avoid playing a blocker because you want to keep the board open.

K

Three-letter blocker beginning with K

KEX

Some four-letter blockers beginning with K

KEPT
KEWL

KILD
KISH

KNEW
KRIS

Some five-letter blockers beginning with K (except words ending in '-ED', '-J', '-S', '-X', '-Y' or '-Z')

KEECH
KEMPT
KENCH
KIDGE

KINDA
KNELT
KNISH
KORAI

KOTCH
KRONA

Some six-letter blockers beginning with K (except words ending in '-ED', '-J', '-S', '-X', '-Y' or '-Z')

KAPUTT
KARMIC
KAWING
KEPPIT
KEWLER
KIBOSH

KIPPEN
KIRSCH
KLATCH
KNITCH
KONAKI
KOTARE

KOTUKU
KRONEN
KRONER
KULAKI
KUTCHA
KYBOSH

BONUS WORDS

Bonus words on your rack can be hard to spot, especially for the less experienced player. One way to help find them is by using prefixes and suffixes.

Many larger words include a common prefix or suffix – remembering these and using them where you can is a good way to discover any longer words on your rack, including any potential bonus words. The key suffix to remember beginning with K is -KIN.

Some words ending with -KIN

Seven-letter words

BUMP-KIN	LADY-KIN	MINI-KIN
CATS-KIN	LAMB-KIN	OILS-KIN
COWS-KIN	LORD-KIN	PIGS-KIN
DOES-KIN	LUMP-KIN	PUMP-KIN
FOXS-KIN	MANA-KIN	RAMA-KIN
GHER-KIN	MANI-KIN	WOLF-KIN

Eight-letter words

BEARS-KIN	FISHS-KIN	MUNCH-KIN
BOOTI-KIN	GOATS-KIN	SEALS-KIN
BUCKS-KIN	LAMBS-KIN	SWANS-KIN
CALFS-KIN	LARRI-KIN	TURNS-KIN
CIDER-KIN	MANNI-KIN	WINES-KIN
DEERS-KIN	MOLES-KIN	WOLFS-KIN
DEVIL-KIN	MOUSE-KIN	WOOLS-KIN

UNUSUAL LETTER COMBINATIONS

If you have an unusual combination of letters on your rack, or want to impress your opponent with an unusual word, a few words from World English can come in handy.

Australian words

KARRI	type of eucalyptus tree
KOALA	slow-moving arboreal marsupial
KYBO	temporary lavatory
KYLIE	boomerang that is flat on one side and convex on the other

Hindi words

KHADDAR   cotton cloth
KHEDA   enclosure for captured elephants
KOEL   parasitic cuckoo
KOS   Indian unit of distance
KRAIT   brightly coloured venomous snake
KULFI   Indian dessert
KURTA   long loose garment

New Zealand words

KAHAWAI   large fish
KAI   food
KARANGA   call or chant of welcome
KATIPO   small venomous spider
KAUPAPA   strategy, policy or cause
KAURI   coniferous tree
KAWA   protocol or etiquette
KIWI   flightless bird with long beak and no tail
KOHA   gift or donation
KORU   curved pattern
KOWHAI   small tree
KUIA   female elder
KURI   mongrel dog
KUTU   body louse

South African words

KEREL   chap or fellow
KRAAL   stockaded village
KWAITO   type of pop music

Urdu words

KAMEEZ   long tunic
KEBAB   dish of meat, onions, etc, grilled on skewers
KHARIF   crop harvested at beginning of winter
KHAYAL   kind of Indian classical vocal music
KINCOB   fine silk fabric embroidered with gold or silver threads
KOFTA   Indian dish of seasoned minced meat shaped into
            balls
KOFTGAR   person skilled in inlaying steel with gold
KOFTGARI   art of inlaying steel with gold
KORMA   Indian dish of meat or vegetables braised with
            yoghurt or cream

K

Handy Hint

The letter K features prominently in many variants of World English. Along with its frequency of use in the Maori-derived words of New Zealand English, the use of a double K is common in Australian English (QUOKKA, 18 points), Hindi (PUKKA, 10 points), Inuit words (MUKTUK, 11 points) and Urdu (KHAKI, 11 points). As there is only one K in the Scrabble set, you will need to have a handy blank tile to play these fascinating words.

Essential info
Value: 1 point
Number in set: 4

The **L** is a very flexible letter for playing words because it combines with many other consonants such as BL-, CL-, FL-, PL-. If you have two of them there are also many words enging in -LL to help you out. Be aware of the following two-letter words for making parallel plays involving an L: LA (in music, the sixth note of a major scale, 2 points), LI (a Chinese unit of length, 2 points) and LO (a command that means look, 2 points). There's a great selection of three-letter words for combining the L with another higher-scoring consonant such as: LAW, LAY, LOW and LYE, all worth 6 points. There are also quite a few words which use X: LAX, LEX, LOX and LUX, all worth 10 points.

Two-letter words beginning with L

LA	LI	LO

Some three-letter words beginning with L

LAB	LEX	LOX
LAC	LEZ	LOY
LAH	LIB	LUG
LAM	LIG	LUM
LAR	LIN	LUR
LAT	LOD	LUX
LAV	LOP	LUZ
LEA	LOR	LYE
LEE	LOS	LYM
LES	LOU	

HOOKS

Hooking requires a subtle change in a player's thought process, in that they must look at words already on the board without becoming distracted by their pronunciation.

Some front-hooks
Two letters to three

L-AB	L-ED	L-OP
L-AD	L-EE	L-OR
L-AG	L-ES	L-OS
L-AH	L-ET	L-OU
L-AM	L-EX	L-OW
L-AR	L-ID	L-OX
L-AS	L-IN	L-OY
L-AT	L-IS	L-UG
L-AW	L-IT	L-UM
L-AX	L-OB	L-UR
L-AY	L-OD	L-YE
L-EA	L-OO	

Three letters to four

L-ACE	L-EFT	L-OON
L-AID	L-END	L-OOP
L-AIN	L-ENS	L-OOT
L-AIR	L-ESS	L-OPE
L-AKE	L-EST	L-ORD
L-ALL	L-ICE	L-ORE
L-AMP	L-ICH	L-OSE
L-ANA	L-ICK	L-OUD
L-AND	L-IMP	L-OUP
L-ANE	L-INK	L-OUR
L-ARD	L-ION	L-OUT
L-ARK	L-OAF	L-OWE
L-ASH	L-OBE	L-OWN
L-ASS	L-OBO	L-OWT
L-ATE	L-OCH	L-UDO
L-AVA	L-ODE	L-UKE
L-AWN	L-OFT	L-UMP
L-EAN	L-ONE	L-URE
L-EAR	L-OOF	L-UTE
L-EEK	L-OOM	

L

Four letters to five

L-ACED	L-EAVE	L-LAMA
L-ACER	L-EDGE	L-OATH
L-AGER	L-EDGY	L-ONER
L-AIRY	L-EECH	L-OOSE
L-AKED	L-EERY	L-OPED
L-ANCE	L-EGAL	L-OTTO
L-APSE	L-EGGY	L-OVER
L-AWED	L-EISH	L-OWED
L-AWNY	L-ETCH	L-OWER
L-AYIN	L-EVER	L-OWLY
L-EACH	L-INCH	L-OWSE
L-EARN	L-INGO	L-UMPY
L-EASE	L-INKY	L-USER
L-EAST	L-ISLE	

Five letters to six

L-ACING	L-EASER	L-IZARD
L-ACKER	L-EAVED	L-OCKER
L-ADDER	L-EDGED	L-OCULI
L-AGGER	L-EDGER	L-OFTER
L-AIRED	L-EGGED	L-OLLER
L-AMBER	L-EGGER	L-ONELY
L-AMENT	L-ENDER	L-OOPED
L-AMPED	L-ETHAL	L-OPING
L-ANGER	L-ICKER	L-ORATE
L-ANKER	L-IGGED	L-OTHER
L-ARKED	L-IMBED	L-OTTER
L-ARVAL	L-IMPED	L-OUPED
L-ASHED	L-IMPLY	L-OUTED
L-ASTER	L-INKED	L-OWING
L-AWFUL	L-INKER	L-OWNED
L-AWING	L-INTEL	L-UGGED
L-EANED	L-INTER	L-UMBER
L-EARED	L-IRKED	L-UMPED
L-EASED	L-ITHER	L-USHER

L

Six letters to seven

L-AIDING	L-EDGIER	L-IONIZE
L-AIRIER	L-EECHED	L-IRKING
L-AIRING	L-EERIER	L-OCULAR
L-AMPING	L-EERILY	L-OOPING
L-ARKING	L-EFTEST	L-OUPING
L-ASHING	L-EGALLY	L-OUTING
L-AUDING	L-EGGIER	L-OVERED
L-AWLESS	L-EGGING	L-OVERLY
L-AWNIER	L-ENDING	L-OWLIER
L-EANING	L-ETCHED	L-OWNING
L-EARING	L-IGGING	L-OXYGEN
L-EARNED	L-IGNIFY	L-UGGING
L-EARNER	L-IMPING	L-ULLING
L-EASING	L-INKING	L-UMPING
L-EAVING	L-INNING	
L-ECHING	L-IONISE	

Seven letters to eight

L-ABILITY	L-EDGIEST	L-IONISER
L-ACERATE	L-EECHING	L-IONIZED
L-AIRIEST	L-EERIEST	L-IONIZER
L-AMBLING	L-EGALITY	L-ITERATE
L-ANGERED	L-EGGIEST	L-OCULATE
L-ANGUISH	L-ETCHING	L-OMENTUM
L-AUREATE	L-EVITATE	L-ONENESS
L-AWFULLY	L-IGNEOUS	L-OURIEST
L-AWNIEST	L-INCHPIN	L-OWLIEST
L-EARNING	L-IONISED	L-UMBERED

Some end-hooks
Two letters to three

AA-L	EE-L	OW-L
AI-L	EL-L	PA-L
AL-L	GU-L	PO-L
AW-L	JO-L	SO-L
BA-L	MA-L	TE-L
BE-L	ME-L	TI-L
DA-L	MI-L	ZO-L
DE-L	MO-L	
DO-L	OI-L	

L

Three letters to four

AXE-L	GAL-L	POL-L
BAL-L	GOA-L	PUL-L
BOW-L	HOW-L	PUR-L
CEL-L	JAI-L	SEA-L
COO-L	JOW-L	SOU-L
COW-L	MAL-L	TAI-L
CUR-L	MEL-L	TEA-L
DAH-L	MEW-L	TEL-L
DOL-L	MIL-L	TIL-L
DOW-L	MOL-L	TOO-L
DUE-L	NIL-L	VIA-L
EAR-L	ORA-L	WAI-L
FEE-L	OVA-L	WOO-L
FOU-L	PAL-L	YOW-L
FUR-L	PEA-L	ZEA-L

Four letters to five

ALKY-L	HAZE-L	QUAI-L
ALLY-L	HOTE-L	RAVE-L
ANNA-L	HOVE-L	RIVA-L
AURA-L	IDEA-L	ROTA-L
BABE-L	IDYL-L	RUBE-L
BRAW-L	KNEE-L	SCOW-L
CABA-L	LEVE-L	SHAW-L
CAME-L	LOCA-L	SNAR-L
CRAW-L	META-L	SPIE-L
CREE-L	MODE-L	UREA-L
CRUE-L	MORA-L	VASA-L
DRAW-L	MOTE-L	VENA-L
DURA-L	MURA-L	VINY-L
EASE-L	NAVE-L	VITA-L
FAVE-L	OCTA-L	WHEE-L
FETA-L	PANE-L	WHIR-L
GAVE-L	PEAR-L	YODE-L
GNAR-L	PERI-L	YOKE-L
GROW-L	PROW-L	ZONA-L
GRUE-L	PUPA-L	

Five letters to six

ANIMA-L	FLOTE-L	REDIA-L
AORTA-L	GRAVE-L	REGNA-L
APPAL-L	GROVE-L	SCRAW-L
ATRIA-L	LARVA-L	SEPTA-L
BARBE-L	MAMMA-L	SHOVE-L
BARRE-L	MANGE-L	SIGNA-L
CARTE-L	MEDIA-L	SPINA-L
CAUSA-L	MENTA-L	SWIVE-L
COSTA-L	MONGO-L	TASSE-L
DERMA-L	MORSE-L	TEASE-L
DORSA-L	MUSSE-L	TIBIA-L
DRIVE-L	NORMA-L	TRAVE-L
ENROL-L	PASTE-L	VANDA-L
EXTOL-L	PETRE-L	VESTA-L
FACIA-L	PORTA-L	VISTA-L
FAUNA-L	PRIMA-L	
FLORA-L	RECAL-L	

Six letters to seven

ANGINA-L	DISTIL-L	MIASMA-L
BARBEL-L	EPOCHA-L	MINIMA-L
CAMERA-L	FASCIA-L	NATURA-L
CAPITA-L	FEMORA-L	NOMINA-L
CENTRA-L	FULFIL-L	OPTIMA-L
CHANCE-L	GENERA-L	ORBITA-L
CHROMY-L	INSTAL-L	RETINA-L
COLONE-L	INSTIL-L	SALIVA-L
CORNEA-L	LATERA-L	STADIA-L
CORONA-L	LEXICA-L	STIGMA-L
CRESTA-L	LINGUA-L	TRIVIA-L
CUBICA-L	MAXIMA-L	

Seven letters to eight

ALLUVIA-L	CEREBRA-L	INERTIA-L
AMPHORA-L	CORPORA-L	MALARIA-L
ANTENNA-L	CRIMINA-L	MANDRIL-L
BRACHIA-L	ENTHRAL-L	MARSHAL-L
BRIMFUL-L	HYDROXY-L	MINUTIA-L
CAROUSE-L	IMPERIA-L	PERINEA-L

L

| PERSONA-L | SPECTRA-L | VISCERA-L |
| RESIDUA-L | STAMINA-L | |

BLOCKERS

It is useful to know which words are blockers and can't therefore be extended before or after. You may want to play a blocker that your opponent can't extend, or you may want to avoid playing a blocker because you want to keep the board open.

Some three-letter blockers beginning with L

| LOX | LUZ |

Some four-letter blockers beginning with L

| LACY | LEWD |
| LEVY | LYNX |

Some five-letter blockers beginning with L (except words ending in '-ED', '-J', '-S', '-X', '-Y' or '-Z')

LAXER	LEISH	LURCH
LEANT	LIVID	LURID
LEAPT	LOYAL	LYNCH
LEASH	LUCID	

Some six-letter blockers beginning with L (except words ending in '-ED', '-J', '-S', '-X', '-Y' or '-Z')

LACTIC	LAYMAN	LINEAR
LAKISH	LAYMEN	LIVEST
LAMEST	LEARNT	LOOSER
LARGER	LEFTER	LOUCHE
LARVAE	LEGMAN	LOUDER
LARVAL	LEWDER	LUBING
LAWFUL	LIMBIC	LURING
LAWMAN	LIMPID	
LAXEST	LINEAL	

BONUS WORDS

Bonus words on your rack can be hard to spot, especially for the less experienced player. One way to help find them is by using prefixes and suffixes.

Many larger words include a common prefix or suffix –
remembering these and using them where you can is a good
way to discover any longer words on your rack, including any
potential bonus words. The key suffixes to remember beginning
with L are -LAND, -LESS, -LET, -LIKE, -LOGY and -LY.

Some words ending with -LAND
Seven-letter words

BAD-LAND	HIE-LAND	NOR-LAND
BOG-LAND	HOL-LAND	OUT-LAND
DRY-LAND	LAW-LAND	SUN-LAND
FEN-LAND	LOW-LAND	WET-LAND
GAR-LAND	MID-LAND	

Eight-letter words

BACK-LAND	GANG-LAND	PEAT-LAND
BOOK-LAND	HEAD-LAND	PINE-LAND
BUSH-LAND	HIGH-LAND	PORT-LAND
CLUB-LAND	HOME-LAND	SHET-LAND
CROP-LAND	LAKE-LAND	SNOW-LAND
DOCK-LAND	MAIN-LAND	TIDE-LAND
DUNE-LAND	MOOR-LAND	WILD-LAND
FARM-LAND	OVER-LAND	WOOD-LAND
FLAT-LAND	PARK-LAND	YARD-LAND

Some words ending with -LESS
Seven-letter words

AGE-LESS	GOD-LESS	LEG-LESS
AIM-LESS	GUN-LESS	MAP-LESS
AIR-LESS	GUT-LESS	RIB-LESS
ARM-LESS	HAP-LESS	SEX-LESS
ART-LESS	HAT-LESS	SUN-LESS
BAG-LESS	IRE-LESS	USE-LESS
EAR-LESS	JOB-LESS	WIT-LESS
END-LESS	JOY-LESS	ZIP-LESS
EYE-LESS	LAW-LESS	

L

Eight-letter words

BACK-LESS
BONE-LESS
CARE-LESS
CASH-LESS
CHIN-LESS
CLUE-LESS
CORD-LESS
DEBT-LESS
FACE-LESS
FEAR-LESS
FLAW-LESS
FORM-LESS

GAIN-LESS
GOAL-LESS
HAIR-LESS
HARM-LESS
HEAD-LESS
HELP-LESS
LIFE-LESS
LIST-LESS
LOVE-LESS
MIND-LESS
NAME-LESS
PAIN-LESS

PEER-LESS
REST-LESS
RUTH-LESS
SEAM-LESS
SEED-LESS
SELF-LESS
TACT-LESS
TAIL-LESS
TIME-LESS
WIRE-LESS

Some words ending with -LET

Seven-letter words

BOOK-LET
COUP-LET
DOUB-LET
EPAU-LET
LAKE-LET
LEAF-LET
NECK-LET

NOTE-LET
OVER-LET
RING-LET
RIVU-LET
ROOT-LET
SCAR-LET
SERV-LET

SING-LET
SKIL-LET
STAR-LET
TART-LET
TRIO-LET

Eight-letter words

BRACE-LET
COVER-LET
FRUIT-LET
GAUNT-LET

GLOBU-LET
PAMPH-LET
PISTO-LET
PLATE-LET

UNDER-LET
VALVE-LET

Some words ending with -LIKE

Seven-letter words

APE-LIKE
BAT-LIKE
CAT-LIKE
DIS-LIKE
DOG-LIKE
FAN-LIKE

GOD-LIKE
HOG-LIKE
MAN-LIKE
MIS-LIKE
POD-LIKE
SKY-LIKE

TOY-LIKE
WAR-LIKE
WAX-LIKE
WIG-LIKE

L

Eight-letter words

AUNT-LIKE	HAWK-LIKE	REED-LIKE
BEAR-LIKE	HERD-LIKE	ROCK-LIKE
BIRD-LIKE	KING-LIKE	SILK-LIKE
CLAW-LIKE	LADY-LIKE	SWAN-LIKE
DOME-LIKE	LIFE-LIKE	TWIG-LIKE
FISH-LIKE	LORD-LIKE	VICE-LIKE
GAME-LIKE	MAZE-LIKE	WHIP-LIKE
GERM-LIKE	OVEN-LIKE	WOLF-LIKE

Some words ending with -LOGY

Seven-letter words

ANA-LOGY	GEO-LOGY	URO-LOGY
APO-LOGY	NEO-LOGY	ZOO-LOGY
BIO-LOGY	TRI-LOGY	
ECO-LOGY	UFO-LOGY	

Eight-letter words

AERO-LOGY	ONTO-LOGY	TYPO-LOGY
AUTO-LOGY	PYRO-LOGY	VENO-LOGY
HOMO-LOGY	SINO-LOGY	VIRO-LOGY
IDEO-LOGY	THEO-LOGY	
ONCO-LOGY	TOPO-LOGY	

Some words ending with -LY

Seven-letter words

ACUTE-LY	DEATH-LY	LARGE-LY
AGILE-LY	EAGER-LY	LEGAL-LY
AWFUL-LY	ELDER-LY	LITHE-LY
BEAST-LY	FAINT-LY	LOCAL-LY
BLACK-LY	FALSE-LY	MISER-LY
BLANK-LY	FLUID-LY	MONTH-LY
BLUNT-LY	FRESH-LY	MUTED-LY
BRAVE-LY	GHOST-LY	NASAL-LY
BROAD-LY	GREAT-LY	NIGHT-LY
CHEAP-LY	GROSS-LY	ORDER-LY
CHIEF-LY	HARSH-LY	PLAIN-LY
CLEAR-LY	IDEAL-LY	PRICK-LY
CRACK-LY	INEPT-LY	QUICK-LY
DAZED-LY	JOINT-LY	QUIET-LY

RAPID-LY   STATE-LY   TWINK-LY
RIGHT-LY   STERN-LY   USUAL-LY
ROUGH-LY   TACIT-LY   UTTER-LY
SHAPE-LY   TENSE-LY   VAGUE-LY
SIGHT-LY   TOTAL-LY   VIRAL-LY
SMART-LY   TOUGH-LY   WEIRD-LY
SOUND-LY   TRICK-LY   WORLD-LY

Eight-letter words

ABRUPT-LY   GINGER-LY   PROPER-LY
ABSURD-LY   HEATED-LY   QUAINT-LY
ACTIVE-LY   HEAVEN-LY   RECENT-LY
AUGUST-LY   INSANE-LY   REMOTE-LY
BENIGN-LY   JOYFUL-LY   SCARCE-LY
BOYISH-LY   KNIGHT-LY   SECOND-LY
BRUTAL-LY   LAWFUL-LY   SECURE-LY
CANDID-LY   MANFUL-LY   SOLEMN-LY
CASUAL-LY   MANNER-LY   TRIBAL-LY
DEMURE-LY   MANUAL-LY   TURGID-LY
DIRECT-LY   MENTAL-LY   UNEVEN-LY
ENTIRE-LY   MINUTE-LY   UNFAIR-LY
EXPERT-LY   NATIVE-LY   VERBAL-LY
FACIAL-LY   ONWARD-LY   WESTER-LY
FORMAL-LY   PATENT-LY   WINTER-LY
FRIEND-LY   PRIMAL-LY   WOODEN-LY

L

UNUSUAL LETTER COMBINATIONS

If you have an unusual combination of letters on your rack, or want to impress your opponent with an unusual word, a few words from World English can come in handy.

Australian words

LOPPY   man employed to do maintenance work on a ranch

LOWAN   ground-dwelling bird

Canadian words

LOGAN   backwater

LOONIE   Canadian dollar coin with loon bird on one face

Hindi words

LAKH   100,000
LANGUR   arboreal monkey
LASSI   yoghurt drink
LATHI   long heavy stick used as a weapon
LUNGI   long piece of cloth worn as loincloth or turban

South African word

LEGUAAN   large monitor lizard

Urdu word

LASCAR   sailor from the East Indies

Handy Hint: Do Your Homework

A game of Scrabble can go either way and a less prepared player will always be at a disadvantage. A few simple steps can improve your chances before even starting the game, for example:

- Learn two and three-letter words, especially those with a tile worth 4 or more points (FHJKQVWXYZ), for scoring well in tight situations and milking the premium squares

- Don't forget using all your letters at once gets you a 50-point bonus

L

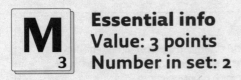

Essential info
Value: 3 points
Number in set: 2

M is a good letter for forming short words as it begins a two-letter word with every vowel, as well as with Y and with another M. M combines well with power tiles X and Z: MAX, MIX and MUX (an old American word meaning to make a mess of something) are all worth 12 points and MIZ (informal short form of misery) is worth 14. It is also worth remembering the three-letter words ending in W: MAW, MEW and MOW (8 points each).

Two-letter words beginning with M

MA	MM	MY
ME	MO	
MI	MU	

Some three-letter words beginning with M

MAA	MEW	MOG
MAC	MHO	MOI
MAE	MIB	MOL
MAG	MIC	MOM
MAK	MID	MON
MAL	MIG	MOR
MAM	MIL	MOT
MAW	MIM	MOU
MAX	MIR	MOY
MED	MIZ	MOZ
MEE	MNA	MUN
MEG	MOA	MUT
MEL	MOC	MUX
MEM	MOD	MYC
MEU	MOE	

HOOKS

Hooking requires a subtle change in a player's thought process, in that they must look at words already on the board without becoming distracted by their pronunciation.

Some front-hooks
Two letters to three

M-AA	M-EE	M-OM
M-AD	M-EL	M-ON
M-AE	M-EM	M-OO
M-AG	M-EN	M-OP
M-AL	M-ES	M-OR
M-AM	M-ET	M-OS
M-AN	M-HO	M-OU
M-AR	M-ID	M-OW
M-AS	M-IS	M-OY
M-AT	M-NA	M-UG
M-AW	M-OB	M-UM
M-AX	M-OD	M-UN
M-AY	M-OE	M-US
M-ED	M-OI	M-UT

Three letters to four

M-ACE	M-ARK	M-ERE
M-ACH	M-ART	M-ESS
M-AGE	M-ARY	M-ETA
M-AID	M-ASH	M-ETH
M-AIL	M-ASK	M-ICE
M-AIM	M-ASS	M-IFF
M-AIN	M-ATE	M-ILK
M-AIR	M-EAN	M-ILL
M-AKE	M-EAT	M-INK
M-ALE	M-EEK	M-IRE
M-ALL	M-ELD	M-IRK
M-ALT	M-ELL	M-ISO
M-AMA	M-ELT	M-OAT
M-ANE	M-EME	M-ODE
M-ANY	M-EMO	M-OKE
M-ARE	M-END	M-OLD

M-OLE	M-OPE	M-UMP
M-ONO	M-ORE	M-UMU
M-OON	M-ORT	M-USE
M-OOR	M-OWN	M-UTE
M-OOT	M-ULE	

Four letters to five

M-ACED	M-AXIS	M-ORAL
M-ACER	M-ETIC	M-OSES
M-ACHE	M-IFFY	M-OTTO
M-AGMA	M-IRED	M-OUCH
M-AMBO	M-ITCH	M-OULD
M-ANGA	M-ODAL	M-OURN
M-ANNA	M-OLDY	M-OUST
M-ANTA	M-OLLA	M-OVER
M-ARCH	M-ONER	M-OWED
M-ASHY	M-ONIE	M-OWER
M-AWED	M-OOSE	M-USED
M-AXED	M-OPED	M-USER
M-AXES	M-OPUS	

M

Five letters to six

M-ACERS	M-ANTIS	M-ENDED
M-ACING	M-ANTRA	M-ENDER
M-ADDED	M-ARKED	M-ERING
M-ADDER	M-ARROW	M-ESSES
M-ADMAN	M-ASCOT	M-ESTER
M-ADMEN	M-ASHED	M-ETHOS
M-AGISM	M-ASHES	M-ETHYL
M-AIDED	M-ASKED	M-ETTLE
M-AILED	M-ASKER	M-ICKLE
M-AIMED	M-ASTER	M-ILLER
M-AIMER	M-AWING	M-INGLE
M-AKING	M-AXING	M-INION
M-ALIGN	M-EAGER	M-INTER
M-ALLOW	M-EAGRE	M-IRING
M-AMMON	M-EANED	M-ISLED
M-ANGEL	M-EASED	M-ITHER
M-ANGER	M-EASLE	M-OCKER
M-ANGLE	M-ELDER	M-OILED
M-ANTIC	M-EMBER	M-OILER

M-OLDER   M-OUGHT   M-UMBLE
M-OLLIE   M-OUPED   M-UMPED
M-OPING   M-OUTER   M-UNIFY
M-ORGAN   M-OWING   M-UNITE
M-ORGUE   M-OZZIE   M-USHER
M-ORRIS   M-UDDER   M-USING
M-OTHER   M-UGGED   M-UTTER

Six letters to seven

M-ADDING   M-ASKING   M-OPUSES
M-AGNATE   M-EANING   M-ORALLY
M-AIDING   M-EARING   M-ORPHIC
M-AILING   M-EASING   M-OUCHED
M-AIMING   M-ELDING   M-OUCHES
M-ANGLED   M-ENDING   M-OULDER
M-ANGLER   M-ETHANE   M-OUPING
M-ARCHED   M-ETHOXY   M-OUSTED
M-ARCHER   M-ETTLED   M-OUTHER
M-ARCHES   M-ICKLER   M-OZZIES
M-ARGENT   M-IFFIER   M-UGGING
M-ARKING   M-ITCHED   M-ULLING
M-ARROWY   M-OILING   M-UMPING
M-ASHIER   M-OMENTA   M-UNITED
M-ASHING   M-ONEYER   M-USEFUL

Seven letters to eight

M-ACERATE   M-EAGERLY   M-OORIEST
M-ADWOMAN   M-ENOLOGY   M-ORALISM
M-ADWOMEN   M-ERISTIC   M-ORALIST
M-AGISTER   M-ETHANOL   M-ORALITY
M-AIDLESS   M-ETHOXYL   M-ORATORY
M-ALIGNED   M-ETHYLIC   M-UNIFIED
M-ALIGNER   M-ICKLEST   M-UNITING
M-ANGLING   M-IFFIEST   M-UNITION
M-ARCHING   M-ISOGAMY   M-UTTERED
M-ARRIAGE   M-ITCHING   M-UTTERER
M-ARROWED   M-OATLIKE
M-ASHIEST   M-OMENTUM

M

Some end-hooks
Two letters to three

AI-M	HO-M	OO-M
AR-M	IS-M	PA-M
BA-M	JA-M	PO-M
DA-M	KA-M	RE-M
DI-M	LA-M	SI-M
DO-M	MA-M	SO-M
EL-M	ME-M	TA-M
FE-M	MI-M	TO-M
GU-M	MO-M	UM-M
HA-M	MU-M	WE-M
HE-M	NA-M	YA-M
HI-M	NO-M	YO-M
HM-M	OH-M	YU-M

Three letters to four

BAL-M	GOR-M	ROO-M
BAR-M	HAE-M	SEA-M
BOO-M	HAW-M	SEE-M
BOR-M	HER-M	SHA-M
CHA-M	IDE-M	SKI-M
COO-M	LEA-M	SOW-M
COR-M	LOO-M	SPA-M
DEE-M	MAL-M	TEA-M
DOO-M	MAR-M	TEE-M
DOR-M	MUM-M	THE-M
FAR-M	NEE-M	TOO-M
FER-M	NOR-M	WAR-M
FIL-M	PAL-M	WAS-M
FIR-M	PER-M	WEE-M
FOR-M	PLU-M	WHA-M
FRO-M	PRE-M	WHO-M
GAU-M	PRO-M	ZOO-M

Four letters to five

ABRI-M	BROO-M	FLAM-M
ABYS-M	CHAR-M	FLEA-M
ALAR-M	CHAS-M	FORA-M
BREE-M	DENI-M	GOLE-M

M

HAKA-M	PASH-M	SHAW-M
HARE-M	PURI-M	SPAS-M
HAUL-M	REAL-M	STUM-M
MALA-M	REAR-M	THAR-M
MAXI-M	RETE-M	THRU-M
MINI-M	SATE-M	TOTE-M
MODE-M	SEIS-M	

Five letters to six

BALSA-M	MALIS-M	SADIS-M
BESEE-M	MERIS-M	SCRAW-M
CENTU-M	MESTO-M	SHTUM-M
CHIAS-M	MONTE-M	SPIRE-M
CONDO-M	MURRA-M	TELES-M
COPAL-M	MUTIS-M	YOGIS-M
DODGE-M	PARTI-M	
LINGA-M	PURIS-M	

Six letters to seven

ANIMIS-M	GOPURA-M	MISTER-M
BUCKRA-M	MANTRA-M	PREWAR-M
FASCIS-M	MISSEE-M	SENSIS-M

Seven letters to eight

CLASSIS-M	FINALIS-M	JIHADIS-M
CYMBALO-M	JEHADIS-M	TITANIS-M

M

BLOCKERS

It is useful to know which words are blockers and can't therefore be extended before or after. You may want to play a blocker that your opponent can't extend, or you may want to avoid playing a blocker because you want to keep the board open.

Three-letter blocker beginning with M

MUX

Some four-letter blockers beginning with M

MADE	MATY	MIXY
MANY	MAZY	MOBY
MARY	MINX	MONY

MOPY	MOWN
MOSH	MOZZ

Some five-letter blockers beginning with M (except words ending in '-ED', '-J', '-S', '-X', '-Y' or '-Z')

MACHI	MENSH	MUCHO
MARCH	MERCH	MULCH
MARIA	MICRA	MULSH
MAYAN	MITCH	MUNCH
MEANT	MOOSE	MUTER

Some six-letter blockers beginning with M (except words ending in '-ED', '-J', '-S', '-X', '-Y' or '-Z')

MACING	MEEKER	MIXING
MADMAN	MEIKLE	MODISH
MADMEN	MEREST	MODULI
MAGYAR	MERMAN	MONACT
MAINER	MERMEN	MOOING
MALIBU	METING	MOPIER
MANATU	MEWING	MOPING
MANFUL	MILDER	MORBID
MANTIC	MILKEN	MORISH
MAOMAO	MIMING	MURKER
MATIER	MINIER	MUTEST
MAXING	MIRING	MUTING
MAYEST	MISDID	MYSELF
MAYHAP	MISLIT	MYTHIC
MAZIER	MITRAL	
MEAGER	MIXIER	

M

M is for Mnemonic

You may find it useful to use memory aids when trying to remember long lists of Scrabble words. Some more experienced players prefer to remember words in their entirety, but for beginners a mnemonic or two can be a great help. Eg, the initial letters of the words in the mnemonic: Please Don't Holler So, Be Nice For Once gives the front hooks for the two-letter word OH.

BONUS WORDS

Bonus words on your rack can be hard to spot, especially for the less experienced player. One way to help find them is by using prefixes and suffixes.

Many larger words include a common prefix or suffix – remembering these and using them where you can is a good way to discover any longer words on your rack, including any potential bonus words. The key prefixes to remember beginning with M are MAN- and MIS- and the key suffixes are -MAN and -MEN.

Some words beginning with MAN-

Seven-letter words

MAN-AGED	MAN-HOLE	MAN-LIKE
MAN-AGER	MAN-HOOD	MAN-MADE
MAN-DATE	MAN-HUNT	MAN-TIDS
MAN-GING	MAN-JACK	MAN-TRAP
MAN-GLED	MAN-KIER	MAN-URES
MAN-GOES	MAN-KIND	MAN-WARD
MAN-GOLD	MAN-LIER	

Eight-letter words

MAN-AGING	MAN-FULLY	MAN-SWORN
MAN-DATED	MAN-GROVE	MAN-URIAL
MAN-DRAKE	MAN-POWER	
MAN-DRILL	MAN-SHIFT	

Some words beginning with MIS-

Seven-letter words

MIS-ALLY	MIS-FITS	MIS-SILE
MIS-CALL	MIS-GIVE	MIS-SING
MIS-CAST	MIS-HAPS	MIS-STEP
MIS-CODE	MIS-HEAR	MIS-TAKE
MIS-CUED	MIS-LAID	MIS-TIME
MIS-DEED	MIS-LEAD	MIS-TING
MIS-DIAL	MIS-MARK	MIS-TOOK
MIS-DOER	MIS-NAME	MIS-USED
MIS-FILE	MIS-READ	
MIS-FIRE	MIS-RULE	

Eight-letter words

MIS-ALIGN
MIS-APPLY
MIS-BEGOT
MIS-CARRY
MIS-CHIEF
MIS-CHOSE
MIS-COLOR
MIS-COUNT
MIS-FILED
MIS-FIRED
MIS-GIVEN
MIS-GUIDE

MIS-HEARD
MIS-JUDGE
MIS-MATCH
MIS-PLACE
MIS-PRICE
MIS-PRINT
MIS-QUOTE
MIS-RULED
MIS-SABLE
MIS-SHAPE
MIS-SPEAK
MIS-SPELL

MIS-SPEND
MIS-SPOKE
MIS-TAKEN
MIS-TIMED
MIS-TREAT
MIS-TRESS
MIS-TRIAL
MIS-TRUST
MIS-TRUTH
MIS-USAGE
MIS-USING

Some words ending with -MAN

Seven-letter words

AUTO-MAN
BATS-MAN
BIRD-MAN
BOAT-MAN
BOND-MAN
BUSH-MAN
CAVE-MAN
COAL-MAN
CREW-MAN
DEAD-MAN
DOOR-MAN
DUST-MAN
FIRE-MAN

FOOT-MAN
FORE-MAN
FREE-MAN
FROG-MAN
HANG-MAN
HARD-MAN
HEAD-MAN
JAZZ-MAN
JURY-MAN
KINS-MAN
LENS-MAN
LINE-MAN
MAIL-MAN

MILK-MAN
NEWS-MAN
OARS-MAN
OTTO-MAN
PLOW-MAN
POST-MAN
REPO-MAN
SAND-MAN
SHOW-MAN
SNOW-MAN
SWAG-MAN
WING-MAN
WORK-MAN

M

Eight-letter words

BAILS-MAN
BLUES-MAN
BOATS-MAN
BOGEY-MAN
BONDS-MAN
BRINK-MAN
CHAIR-MAN
CLANS-MAN
CLASS-MAN

COACH-MAN
EARTH-MAN
EVERY-MAN
FERRY-MAN
FRESH-MAN
FRONT-MAN
GAMES-MAN
HANDY-MAN
HELMS-MAN

HENCH-MAN
HERDS-MAN
HUNTS-MAN
KNIFE-MAN
LANDS-MAN
LINES-MAN
MARKS-MAN
NOBLE-MAN
POINT-MAN

RIFLE-MAN	SPACE-MAN	TRASH-MAN
SALES-MAN	STUNT-MAN	WATCH-MAN
SHORE-MAN	SWORD-MAN	WHEEL-MAN
SOUND-MAN	TALIS-MAN	WOODS-MAN

Some words ending with -MEN
Seven-letter words

ABDO-MEN	DOOR-MEN	LENS-MEN
ALBU-MEN	DUST-MEN	LINE-MEN
BATS-MEN	FOOT-MEN	RAIL-MEN
BIRD-MEN	FORE-MEN	REGI-MEN
BITU-MEN	FREE-MEN	REPO-MEN
BOAT-MEN	FROG-MEN	SHIP-MEN
BOOK-MEN	HANG-MEN	SHOW-MEN
BUSH-MEN	HARD-MEN	SNOW-MEN
CAVE-MEN	HEAD-MEN	SWAG-MEN
COAL-MEN	HILL-MEN	WING-MEN
CREW-MEN	JAZZ-MEN	WORK-MEN
DEAD-MEN	KINS-MEN	

Eight-letter words

BAILS-MEN	FREED-MEN	POINT-MEN
BARGE-MEN	GAMES-MEN	RANCH-MEN
BLUES-MEN	HANDY-MEN	RIFLE-MEN
BOATS-MEN	HELMS-MEN	ROADS-MEN
BONDS-MEN	HENCH-MEN	SALES-MEN
BOOGY-MEN	HERDS-MEN	SHORE-MEN
BRINK-MEN	HORSE-MEN	SOUND-MEN
CHAIR-MEN	HUNTS-MEN	SPACE-MEN
CLANS-MEN	KNIFE-MEN	STUNT-MEN
COACH-MEN	LINES-MEN	SUPER-MEN
DOORS-MEN	MARKS-MEN	WATCH-MEN
EVERY-MEN	MERRY-MEN	WHEEL-MEN
FERRY-MEN	NOBLE-MEN	WOODS-MEN

UNUSUAL LETTER COMBINATIONS

If you have an unusual combination of letters on your rack, or want to impress your opponent with an unusual word, a few words from World English can come in handy.

Australian words

MALLEE	low shrubby eucalyptus tree
MARRI	type of eucalyptus
MIDDY	middle-sized glass of beer
MILKO	milkman
MOLOCH	spiny lizard
MOPOKE	small spotted owl
MOZ	hoodoo or hex
MUGGA	eucalyptus tree with pink flowers
MULGA	acacia shrub
MULLOCK	waste material from a mine
MUSO	musician
MYALL	acacia with hard scented wood
MYXO	myxomatosis

Canadian words

| MUCKAMUCK | food |
| MUKTUK | beluga skin used as food |

Hindi words

MACHAN	platform used in tiger hunting
MAHOUT	elephant driver
MAHSEER	large freshwater fish
MANDI	big market
MANDIR	Hindu or Jain temple
MAUND	unit of weight
MELA	cultural or religious festival
MOHUR	old gold coin
MONAL	Asian pheasant
MORCHA	hostile demonstration
MRIDANG	drum used in Indian music
MYNAH	tropical starling

New Zealand words

MANUKA	myrtaceous tree
MATAI	evergreen tree
MIHI	ceremonial greeting
MOA	extinct large flightless bird
MOKI	edible sea fish
MOKO	Maori tattoo or tattoo pattern
MOOLOO	person from Waikato
MOPOKE	small spotted owl
MUNGA	army canteen

M

South African words

MEERKAT	sociable mongoose
MENEER	Mr or Sir
MEVROU	Mrs or Madam
MOOI	pleasing
MUTI	herbal medicine

Urdu words

MAIDAN	open space used for meetings and sports
MASALA	mixed spices ground into a paste
MOOLVI	Muslim doctor of the law

M

Essential info
Value: 1 point
Number in set: 6

There are six **N** tiles in the Scrabble set, making it one of the most common consonants. N is very useful for short words to facilitate parallel plays as it begins a two-letter word with every vowel except I. While three-letter words beginning with N are common, there are fewer high-scoring ones than you might think. These include NAB (5 points) and NAY, NEW and NOW (all 6 points). N is one of the letters of the RETAIN set and is therefore a good letter to keep if trying to get a bonus word.

Two-letter words beginning with N

NA	NO	NY
NE	NU	

Some three-letter words beginning with N

NAE	NEK	NOO
NAH	NEP	NOR
NAM	NID	NOT
NAT	NIS	NOX
NAW	NIT	NOY
NAY	NIX	NUB
NEB	NOB	NUR
NED	NOG	NYE
NEE	NOH	NYS
NEF	NOM	
NEG	NON	

HOOKS

Hooking requires a subtle change in a player's thought process, in that they must look at words already on the board without becoming distracted by their pronunciation.

Some front-hooks
Two letters to three

N-AB	N-EE	N-OO
N-AE	N-EF	N-OR
N-AG	N-ET	N-OS
N-AH	N-ID	N-OW
N-AM	N-IS	N-OX
N-AN	N-IT	N-OY
N-AS	N-OB	N-UN
N-AT	N-OD	N-UR
N-AW	N-OH	N-US
N-AY	N-OM	N-UT
N-ED	N-ON	N-YE

Three letters to four

N-AFF	N-EAT	N-ODE
N-AGA	N-EON	N-ONE
N-AIL	N-ERK	N-OON
N-ANA	N-ESS	N-OPE
N-ANE	N-EST	N-OSE
N-APE	N-EUK	N-OUS
N-ARC	N-EWT	N-OUT
N-ARE	N-ICE	N-OVA
N-ARK	N-ICK	N-OWL
N-ARY	N-ILL	N-OWN
N-AVE	N-ISH	N-OWT
N-EAR	N-ITS	N-UKE

Four letters to five

N-ACHE	N-EMPT	N-ONCE
N-AILS	N-EVER	N-ONES
N-AKED	N-EWER	N-OOSE
N-APED	N-ICER	N-OPAL
N-ARCO	N-ICKY	N-OULD
N-AUNT	N-IFFY	N-OUPS
N-AVAL	N-ODAL	N-OVEL
N-AVEL	N-OILY	N-OVUM
N-EATH	N-OINT	N-OWED
N-EDDY	N-OMEN	

Five letters to six

N-ABBED	N-EATER	N-ODDER
N-AGGER	N-EBBED	N-OGGIN
N-AILED	N-ESSES	N-OSIER
N-APERY	N-ESTER	N-OTARY
N-APING	N-ETHER	N-OTHER
N-APRON	N-ETTLE	N-OUGHT
N-ARKED	N-EWEST	N-UMBER
N-ARROW	N-ICHED	N-UMPTY
N-AUGHT	N-ICKER	N-UNCLE
N-EARED	N-ICKLE	N-UTTER
N-EARLY	N-IMBED	
N-EATEN	N-ITHER	

Six letters to seven

N-AILING	N-EMESES	N-OVATED
N-APHTHA	N-EMESIS	N-OYESES
N-ARKING	N-EOLITH	N-ULLING
N-ASCENT	N-ETTLED	N-UNDINE
N-ATRIUM	N-ICHING	N-UNHOOD
N-EARING	N-IFFIER	N-UNLIKE
N-EBBING	N-OINTED	N-UNSHIP
N-EDDISH	N-ONUSES	
N-EITHER	N-OOLOGY	

Seven letters to eight

N-AINSELL	N-EARLIER	N-OVATION
N-APERIES	N-ETTLING	N-ULLINGS
N-ARRASES	N-IFFIEST	N-UMBERED
N-ARROWED	N-OINTING	N-YAFFING
N-ATRIUMS	N-OTARIES	

Some end-hooks
Two letters to three

AI-N	BO-N	EE-N
AN-N	DA-N	ER-N
AW-N	DE-N	FA-N
BA-N	DI-N	FE-N
BE-N	DO-N	GI-N
BI-N	EA-N	GO-N

N

GU-N	MO-N	SO-N
HA-N	MU-N	TA-N
HE-N	NA-N	TE-N
HI-N	NO-N	TI-N
HO-N	NU-N	TO-N
IN-N	OO-N	UR-N
IO-N	OW-N	WE-N
KI-N	PA-N	WO-N
KO-N	PE-N	YE-N
LI-N	PI-N	YO-N
MA-N	RE-N	
ME-N	SI-N	

Three letters to four

BAR-N	GOO-N	RAI-N
BEE-N	GUR-N	SAW-N
BOO-N	HEW-N	SEE-N
BOR-N	HOO-N	SEW-N
BRA-N	JIN-N	SKI-N
BUR-N	LAW-N	SOW-N
CHI-N	LEA-N	SPA-N
COR-N	LIE-N	TEE-N
DAW-N	LOO-N	THE-N
DEE-N	MOA-N	TOO-N
DOO-N	MOO-N	TOR-N
DOW-N	MOR-N	TOW-N
EAR-N	MOW-N	UPO-N
EVE-N	NOO-N	YAR-N
FAW-N	OPE-N	YAW-N
FER-N	PAW-N	

N

Handy Hint

Use a dictionary when playing Scrabble to check the validity of
words when a play is challenged (and to avoid any arguments!).
We recommend Collins Official Scrabble Dictionary, where you
will find the meanings for all the words listed in this book.

Four letters to five

BLOW-N	GROW-N	SARI-N
BRAW-N	HALO-N	SATI-N
BROW-N	HERO-N	SHAW-N
CHAI-N	HOSE-N	SHOW-N
CLOW-N	HUMA-N	SIRE-N
COVE-N	KNOW-N	SPAW-N
CROW-N	LADE-N	SPUR-N
DEMO-N	LEAR-N	STOW-N
DJIN-N	LIKE-N	TAKE-N
DOVE-N	LINE-N	TOKE-N
DOZE-N	LOGO-N	TWEE-N
DRAW-N	MAYA-N	VEGA-N
FLOW-N	RAVE-N	WAKE-N
FROW-N	RIPE-N	WIDE-N
GIVE-N	RISE-N	WOKE-N
GNAW-N	RIVE-N	WOVE-N
GREE-N	ROMA-N	YEAR-N

Five letters to six

ALTER-N	GLUTE-N	RESOW-N
ARISE-N	GRAVE-N	ROTTE-N
ASTER-N	HASTE-N	SCREE-N
AWAKE-N	HEAVE-N	SHAKE-N
AWOKE-N	HOOVE-N	SHAMA-N
BABOO-N	INTER-N	SHAPE-N
BARRE-N	LARGE-N	SHAVE-N
BITTE-N	LEAVE-N	SPOKE-N
BRAZE-N	LOOSE-N	STOLE-N
BROKE-N	MACRO-N	STONE-N
CARBO-N	MEDIA-N	STRAW-N
CARVE-N	MICRO-N	STREW-N
CAVER-N	MODER-N	STROW-N
CHOSE-N	NORMA-N	SYLVA-N
CLOVE-N	PHOTO-N	THRAW-N
COMMO-N	PROVE-N	THROW-N
CRAVE-N	RATIO-N	WHITE-N
DRIVE-N	RESEE-N	WICCA-N
FROZE-N	RESEW-N	

N

Six letters to seven

ACKNOW-N	PATTER-N	SMIDGE-N
ALKALI-N	POSTER-N	STONER-N
BRONZE-N	PREWAR-N	STRIVE-N
CAPITA-N	PROTEA-N	STROKE-N
CHASTE-N	PROTEI-N	TERTIA-N
COARSE-N	REDRAW-N	THRIVE-N
EASTER-N	REFLOW-N	TRUDGE-N
EMBRYO-N	REGIME-N	UNDRAW-N
ENVIRO-N	REGIVE-N	UNWOVE-N
GELATI-N	REGROW-N	UPGROW-N
HOARSE-N	RERISE-N	UPRISE-N
JIGSAW-N	RESHOW-N	UPTAKE-N
MEDUSA-N	RETAKE-N	URANIA-N
NUCLEI-N	REWAKE-N	UTOPIA-N
OUTSEE-N	REWOVE-N	WESTER-N
PAPAYA-N	RIPSAW-N	WRITHE-N
PASTER-N	SIERRA-N	ZITHER-N

Seven letters to eight

AQUARIA-N	FORGIVE-N	OVERSEE-N
ARCADIA-N	FORSAKE-N	PANACEA-N
AURELIA-N	HACKSAW-N	PARAZOA-N
BEREAVE-N	LEATHER-N	PARTAKE-N
BESPOKE-N	MAGNETO-N	PRESHOW-N
BESTREW-N	MALARIA-N	QUARTER-N
BOHEMIA-N	MISDRAW-N	REAWAKE-N
CODRIVE-N	MISGIVE-N	REFROZE-N
COLLAGE-N	MISGROW-N	REGALIA-N
DEFROZE-N	MISKNOW-N	RESHAVE-N
DILUVIA-N	MISTAKE-N	ROSARIA-N
DISLIKE-N	NORTHER-N	RUBELLA-N
ELECTRO-N	OUTDRAW-N	SLATTER-N
ENGRAVE-N	OUTFLOW-N	SOUTHER-N
ENLARGE-N	OUTGIVE-N	UNBROKE-N
FLYBLOW-N	OUTGROW-N	UNFROZE-N
FORESEE-N	OUTTAKE-N	UNSPOKE-N

N

BLOCKERS

It is useful to know which words are blockers and can't therefore be extended before or after. You may want to play a blocker that your opponent can't extend, or you may want to avoid playing a blocker because you want to keep the board open.

Some three-letter blockers beginning with N

NAE	NOH	NTH
NAH	NOX	

Some four-letter blockers beginning with N

NAVY	NOPE	NOUS
NESS	NOSH	
NIXY	NOSY	

Some five-letter blockers beginning with N (except words ending in '-ED', '-J', '-S', '-X', '-Y' or '-Z')

NATAL	NEWER	NOMEN
NAVAL	NICER	NUTSO
NEVER	NOHOW	

Some six-letter blockers beginning with N (except words ending in '-ED', '-J', '-S', '-X', '-Y' or '-Z')

NAFFER	NEWEST	NONMEN
NAIFER	NEWISH	NONPAR
NAIVER	NICEST	NORDIC
NAPING	NICISH	NOSIER
NEARER	NIGHER	NOSTRO
NEATER	NITRIC	NOTING
NEBISH	NIXING	NOTOUR
NERVAL	NOBLER	NOUNAL
NETHER	NONFAT	NOWISE
NEURAL	NONMAN	NUKING

N

BONUS WORDS

Bonus words on your rack can be hard to spot, especially for the less experienced player. One way to help find them is by using prefixes and suffixes.

Many larger words include a common prefix or suffix – remembering these and using them where you can is a good way to discover any longer words on your rack, including any potential bonus words. The key suffix to remember beginning with N is -NESS.

Some words ending with -NESS
Seven-letter words

APT-NESS
BAD-NESS
BIG-NESS
COY-NESS
DIM-NESS
DRY-NESS
FAT-NESS
FIT-NESS
FUL-NESS
HAR-NESS

HIP-NESS
HOT-NESS
ICI-NESS
ILL-NESS
LIO-NESS
LOW-NESS
MAD-NESS
NEW-NESS
ODD-NESS
OLD-NESS

ONE-NESS
RAW-NESS
RED-NESS
SAD-NESS
SHY-NESS
WET-NESS
WIT-NESS
WRY-NESS

Eight-letter words

AGED-NESS
ARCH-NESS
BALD-NESS
BARE-NESS
BOLD-NESS
BUSI-NESS
CALM-NESS
COLD-NESS
COSI-NESS
CURT-NESS
DAMP-NESS
DARK-NESS
DEAF-NESS
DEFT-NESS
DEMO-NESS
EVIL-NESS
FAIR-NESS
FIRM-NESS

FOND-NESS
GLAD-NESS
GOOD-NESS
GREY-NESS
HARD-NESS
HIGH-NESS
HUGE-NESS
IDLE-NESS
KIND-NESS
LATE-NESS
LIKE-NESS
MEAN-NESS
MILD-NESS
MUCH-NESS
NEAT-NESS
NUMB-NESS
OPEN-NESS
PALE-NESS

POSH-NESS
PURE-NESS
RARE-NESS
RIPE-NESS
SAME-NESS
SICK-NESS
SLOW-NESS
SURE-NESS
TALL-NESS
TAME-NESS
TAUT-NESS
VAST-NESS
WARM-NESS
WEAK-NESS
WELL-NESS
WILD-NESS

UNUSUAL LETTER COMBINATIONS

If you have an unusual combination of letters on your rack, or want to impress your opponent with an unusual word, a few words from World English can come in handy.

Australian words

NARDOO	cloverlike fern
NEDDY	horse
NOAH	shark
NONG	stupid or incompetent person
NUMBAT	small marsupial with long snout

Canadian word

NANOOK	polar bear

Hindi words

NAUCH	intricate Indian dance
NAWAB	Muslim prince in India
NEEM	large tree
NILGAI	large Indian antelope
NULLAH	stream or drain
NUMDAH	coarse felt

New Zealand words

NGAIO	small tree
NGATI	tribe or clan
NIKAU	palm tree

South African words

NAARTJIE	tangerine
NEK	mountain pass
NKOSI	master or chief

N

Essential info
Value: 1 point
Number in set: 8

O is a common letter in Scrabble, with eight tiles in the set. It forms a two-letter word with every other vowel except for A, and is useful when it comes to forming short words in order to score in two directions at once using premium squares, or in tight corners, or for parallel plays, for example OB, OM and OP (4 points each) and OF, OH, OW (5 points each). O also combines well with X to form short words such as OXO (10 points) and OXY (13 points).

Two-letter words beginning with O

OB	OM	OU
OD	ON	OW
OE	OO	OX
OF	OP	OY
OH	OR	
OI	OS	

Some three-letter words beginning with O

OBA	ONY	ORF
OBE	OOF	ORT
OBI	OOH	OSE
OBO	OOM	OUD
OCH	OON	OUK
ODA	OOP	OUP
OFF	OOR	OUS
OFT	OOT	OWT
OHM	OPE	OXO
OHO	ORA	OXY
OIK	ORB	OYE
OKA	ORC	
ONO	ORD	

HOOKS

Hooking requires a subtle change in a player's thought process, in that they must look at words already on the board without becoming distracted by their pronunciation.

Some front-hooks
Two letters to three

O-AR	O-HO	O-OS
O-AT	O-KA	O-PE
O-BA	O-NE	O-RE
O-BE	O-NO	O-UP
O-BI	O-NY	O-UR
O-BO	O-OF	O-US
O-CH	O-OH	O-UT
O-DA	O-OM	O-WE
O-DE	O-ON	O-YE
O-ES	O-OP	
O-HM	O-OR	

Three letters to four

O-ARY	O-GEE	O-PEN
O-BEY	O-INK	O-PUS
O-BIT	O-KAY	O-RAD
O-CHE	O-LEA	O-RES
O-DAH	O-LES	O-SAR
O-DAL	O-LID	O-TIC
O-DOR	O-MEN	O-URN
O-DSO	O-OSE	O-VUM
O-FAY	O-PAL	O-WED
O-GAM	O-PED	O-YES

Four letters to five

O-AKED	O-GIVE	O-OPED
O-ARED	O-GLED	O-OSES
O-AVES	O-HING	O-PINE
O-BANG	O-LIVE	O-PING
O-BOLE	O-LOGY	O-PIUM
O-CHER	O-MEGA	O-RACH
O-DOUR	O-OBIT	O-RACY
O-FLAG	O-OHED	O-RANG

O

O-RANT
O-RATE
O-READ
O-RIEL
O-SCAR

O-UNCE
O-UNDY
O-VARY
O-VERT
O-VINE

O-VOID
O-WING
O-ZONE

Five letters to six

O-BITER
O-BLAST
O-BLATE
O-BOLUS
O-CELLI
O-EDEMA
O-GAMIC
O-GIVES
O-INKED
O-LINGO
O-LIVER

O-MENED
O-MENTA
O-OHING
O-OLOGY
O-OPING
O-OSIER
O-PALED
O-PENED
O-PINED
O-PUSES
O-RACHE

O-RALLY
O-RANGE
O-RANGY
O-RATED
O-STEAL
O-STENT
O-TITIS
O-UNCES
O-WRIER
O-YESES

Six letters to seven

O-CARINA
O-CELLAR
O-CREATE
O-DONATE
O-DORISE
O-DORIZE
O-ESTRAL
O-ESTRUM
O-INKING
O-KIMONO
O-LOGIES
O-MENING

O-MENTAL
O-MENTUM
O-MICRON
O-MIKRON
O-PACIFY
O-PENING
O-PINING
O-PINION
O-POSSUM
O-RANGER
O-RATING
O-RATION

O-ROTUND
O-STRICH
O-UGLIED
O-UGLIES
O-UTMOST
O-VARIES
O-VERBID
O-VERSET
O-WRIEST
O-YESSES
O-ZONATE

Seven letters to eight

O-DORISED
O-DORIZED
O-ECOLOGY
O-EDEMATA
O-ENOLOGY
O-ESTRIOL
O-ESTRONE

O-ESTROUS
O-MISSION
O-MISSIVE
O-OLOGIES
O-OLOGIST
O-RANGIER
O-STOMATE

O-UROLOGY
O-VARIOLE
O-VARIOUS
O-ZONATED

Some end-hooks
Two letters to three

AB-O	GO-O	ON-O
AD-O	HA-O	OX-O
AG-O	HO-O	PO-O
BI-O	IS-O	RE-O
BO-O	LO-O	TA-O
DO-O	MO-O	TO-O
EM-O	NO-O	UP-O
EX-O	OB-O	WO-O
GI-O	OH-O	ZO-O

Three letters to four

ALS-O	FIN-O	MON-O
ALT-O	HER-O	MUS-O
ANN-O	HOB-O	PES-O
BIT-O	HYP-O	PIS-O
BOH-O	JUD-O	POL-O
BOY-O	KAY-O	RED-O
BUB-O	KIN-O	REG-O
BUD-O	LID-O	REP-O
CAM-O	LIN-O	ROT-O
CAP-O	LIP-O	SAD-O
CIT-O	LOB-O	SAG-O
DAD-O	LOG-O	SOH-O
DIN-O	LOT-O	SOL-O
DOC-O	LUD-O	SUM-O
DOD-O	MAK-O	TAR-O
ECH-O	MAN-O	TOP-O
ERG-O	MAY-O	TOR-O
FAR-O	MEM-O	VEG-O
FID-O	MIC-O	VET-O
FIG-O	MIL-O	VIN-O
FIL-O	MIS-O	WIN-O

Four letters to five

AMIN-O	BENT-O	BOMB-O
BANC-O	BERK-O	BONG-O
BARD-O	BIFF-O	BUCK-O
BASH-O	BING-O	BUFF-O
BEAN-O	BOFF-O	BUNK-O

O

167

BURR-O   GISM-O   PEST-O
CACA-O   GUAN-O   PHON-O
CAME-O   GUST-O   PHOT-O
CARB-O   HALL-O   PIAN-O
CELL-O   HELL-O   PINK-O
CHIA-O   HILL-O   PINT-O
CHIC-O   HOWS-O   PONG-O
CHIN-O   HULL-O   POSH-O
CHOC-O   JELL-O   POTT-O
COMB-O   JOCK-O   PRIM-O
COMM-O   KEEN-O   PROM-O
COMP-O   LASS-O   PROS-O
COND-O   LENT-O   PULA-O
CORN-O   LIMB-O   PUNT-O
CRED-O   LING-O   RODE-O
CUFF-O   MACH-O   RUMP-O
DECK-O   MANG-O   SANT-O
DING-O   MENT-O   SICK-O
DIPS-O   METH-O   SOCK-O
DISC-O   MEZZ-O   STEN-O
DITT-O   MILK-O   TANG-O
DRAC-O   MIME-O   TEMP-O
DUMB-O   MOTT-O   TORS-O
FANG-O   MUCH-O   VERS-O
FATS-O   NACH-O   VIDE-O
FUNG-O   NARC-O   WACK-O
GAMB-O   NUTS-O   WALD-O
GECK-O   PANT-O   WHAM-O

Five letters to six

AMMON-O   CONCH-O   HULLO-O
BILLY-O   CRYPT-O   LIBER-O
BRILL-O   DINER-O   LIVED-O
BRONC-O   DORAD-O   MEDIC-O
CARDI-O   DUETT-O   MORPH-O
CHARR-O   ERING-O   NYMPH-O
CHEAP-O   FASCI-O   PEDAL-O
CHEER-O   FRANC-O   PLONK-O
CHOCK-O   HALLO-O   PREST-O
CHURR-O   HOLLO-O   PSEUD-O

O

PSYCH-O	SHACK-O	TOLED-O
QUART-O	SHEEP-O	TRILL-O
RABAT-O	SOLAN-O	VIGOR-O
RANCH-O	SPEED-O	WEIRD-O
REECH-O	STERE-O	WHACK-O
RIGHT-O	STINK-O	WHATS-O
ROMAN-O	THICK-O	

Six letters to seven

BANDIT-O	MOMENT-O	RABBIT-O
BATTER-O	NITROS-O	REVERS-O
BRACER-O	PAESAN-O	SECOND-O
BUDGER-O	PAISAN-O	SERRAN-O
CANTIC-O	PAMPER-O	TAMARA-O
CYMBAL-O	PIMENT-O	TYMPAN-O
GRADIN-O	PRIMER-O	VERISM-O
MAGNET-O	PUMMEL-O	WHERES-O

Seven letters to eight

ARMIGER-O	FASCISM-O	PRELUDI-O
CAPITAN-O	FLAMING-O	RANCHER-O
CLASSIC-O	INTAGLI-O	SESTETT-O
COMMAND-O	LEGGIER-O	SOMBRER-O
CONCERT-O	MONTANT-O	STAMPED-O
CORNETT-O	PEEKABO-O	VIGOROS-O
COURANT-O	PERFECT-O	ZECCHIN-O
EXPRESS-O	POLITIC-O	

O

BLOCKERS

It is useful to know which words are blockers and can't therefore be extended before or after. You may want to play a blocker that your opponent can't extend, or you may want to avoid playing a blocker because you want to keep the board open.

Three-letter blocker beginning with O

OXO

Some four-letter blockers beginning with O

| OAKY | ONYX | OYEZ |
| OCCY | ORYX | |

Some five-letter blockers beginning with O (except words ending in '-ED', '-J', '-S', '-X', '-Y' or '-Z')

OATEN	ORGIC	OUTDO
OLEIC	OSSIA	OUTGO

Some six-letter blockers beginning with O (except words ending in '-ED', '-J', '-S', '-X', '-Y' or '-Z')

OAFISH	OILMEN	OUTBYE
OAKIER	OMIGOD	OUTDID
OBESER	ONRUSH	OUTSAT
OBITER	OPTING	OUTSAW
OBTECT	ORBIER	OUTWON
OCTOPI	ORGANA	OWLISH
ODDEST	ORGIAC	OXIDIC
ODDISH	OSTEAL	OZONIC
OGRISH	OSTIAL	
OILMAN	OSTIUM	

O

BONUS WORDS

Bonus words on your rack can be hard to spot, especially for the less experienced player. One way to help find them is by using prefixes and suffixes.

Many larger words include a common prefix or suffix – remembering these and using them where you can is a good way to discover any longer words on your rack, including any potential bonus words. The key prefixes to remember beginning with O are OUT- and OVER- and the key suffixes are -OID, -OR, -OUS and -OUT.

Some words beginning with OUT-
Seven-letter words

OUT-ACTS	OUT-DOER	OUT-FITS
OUT-AGES	OUT-DONE	OUT-FLOW
OUT-BACK	OUT-DOOR	OUT-FOOT
OUT-BIDS	OUT-DRAW	OUT-GAVE
OUT-CAST	OUT-EARN	OUT-GOER
OUT-COME	OUT-FALL	OUT-GROW
OUT-CROP	OUT-FISH	OUT-GUNS

OUT-GUSH
OUT-KEEP
OUT-LAID
OUT-LAND
OUT-LAST
OUT-LAWS
OUT-LAYS
OUT-LETS
OUT-LIES
OUT-LIVE
OUT-LOOK
OUT-MODE

OUT-PACE
OUT-PLAY
OUT-POST
OUT-PUTS
OUT-RAGE
OUT-RANK
OUT-RIDE
OUT-RUNS
OUT-SELL
OUT-SIDE
OUT-SING
OUT-SIZE

OUT-SOLD
OUT-SPAN
OUT-STAY
OUT-TAKE
OUT-TALK
OUT-VOTE
OUT-WAIT
OUT-WARD
OUT-WITH
OUT-WITS

Eight-letter words

OUT-ACTED
OUT-ARGUE
OUT-BOARD
OUT-BOUND
OUT-BREAK
OUT-CHARM
OUT-CLASS
OUT-CRIES
OUT-DANCE
OUT-DATED
OUT-DOING
OUT-DRINK
OUT-FACED

OUT-FENCE
OUT-FIELD
OUT-FLANK
OUT-FOXED
OUT-GOING
OUT-GROWN
OUT-LAWED
OUT-LINED
OUT-MATCH
OUT-PACED
OUT-PRICE
OUT-RAGED
OUT-REACH

OUT-RIDER
OUT-SCORE
OUT-SIDER
OUT-SIZED
OUT-SPEAK
OUT-SPOKE
OUT-STAND
OUT-STARE
OUT-SWEPT
OUT-THINK
OUT-VOICE
OUT-WEIGH

O

Some words beginning with OVER-
Seven-letter words

OVER-ACT
OVER-AGE
OVER-ALL
OVER-ATE
OVER-AWE
OVER-CUT
OVER-DID

OVER-DUB
OVER-DUE
OVER-EAT
OVER-EGG
OVER-FED
OVER-JOY
OVER-LAP

OVER-LAY
OVER-PAY
OVER-RAN
OVER-SAW
OVER-SEE
OVER-TAX
OVER-USE

Eight-letter words

OVER-ARCH
OVER-AWED

OVER-BEAR
OVER-BITE

OVER-BRED
OVER-BUSY

OVER-CAME	OVER-HEAR	OVER-PLAY
OVER-CAST	OVER-HEAT	OVER-RATE
OVER-COAT	OVER-HYPE	OVER-RODE
OVER-COME	OVER-IDLE	OVER-RULE
OVER-COOK	OVER-KEEN	OVER-SEEN
OVER-DOES	OVER-KILL	OVER-SELL
OVER-DONE	OVER-LAID	OVER-SHOT
OVER-DOSE	OVER-LAND	OVER-SIZE
OVER-EASY	OVER-LEAF	OVER-STAY
OVER-FEED	OVER-LOAD	OVER-STEP
OVER-FILL	OVER-LONG	OVER-TAKE
OVER-GOES	OVER-LOOK	OVER-TIME
OVER-GROW	OVER-LORD	OVER-TONE
OVER-HAND	OVER-PACK	OVER-TOOK
OVER-HANG	OVER-PAGE	OVER-TURN
OVER-HAUL	OVER-PAID	OVER-WORK

Some words ending with -OID

Seven-letter words

ADEN-OID	FACT-OID	SPOR-OID
ANDR-OID	FUNG-OID	STER-OID
COSM-OID	GLOB-OID	TABL-OID
CYST-OID	HYDR-OID	THYR-OID
DELT-OID	NEUR-OID	TYPH-OID
DISC-OID	SAUR-OID	

Eight-letter words

ALKAL-OID	LYMPH-OID	RESIN-OID
AMOEB-OID	MANAT-OID	RETIN-OID
BLAST-OID	MEDUS-OID	RHOMB-OID
CAMEL-OID	MELAN-OID	SCHIZ-OID
CENTR-OID	NEMAT-OID	SLEAZ-OID
DENDR-OID	NUCLE-OID	SPHER-OID
GROUP-OID	PARAN-OID	TETAN-OID
HEMAT-OID	PLASM-OID	VARIC-OID
HUMAN-OID	POLYP-OID	VIRUS-OID
LEMUR-OID	PSYCH-OID	

O

Some words ending with -OR
Seven-letter words

ADAPT-OR
ADVIS-OR
AUDIT-OR
AVIAT-OR
BICOL-OR
CREAT-OR
CURAT-OR
DEBIT-OR
DILUT-OR
EJECT-OR
ELECT-OR

EMPER-OR
ENACT-OR
EQUAT-OR
EXCIT-OR
GRANT-OR
IGNIT-OR
JANIT-OR
NEGAT-OR
OFFER-OR
QUEST-OR
REACT-OR

ROTAT-OR
SCISS-OR
SENAT-OR
SETTL-OR
SPONS-OR
SQUAL-OR
TRACT-OR
TRAIT-OR
TRUST-OR
VISIT-OR

Eight-letter words

ABDUCT-OR
ACCENT-OR
ACCEPT-OR
ADJUST-OR
AGITAT-OR
ANIMAT-OR
ASSESS-OR
ASSIGN-OR
BEHAVI-OR
BISECT-OR
CAVEAT-OR
CODEBT-OR
CONVEN-OR
CONVEY-OR
CORRID-OR
CREDIT-OR
DEFECT-OR
DEPICT-OR

DETECT-OR
DICTAT-OR
DIRECT-OR
EFFECT-OR
ELEVAT-OR
ENDEAV-OR
EXECUT-OR
GOVERN-OR
IMITAT-OR
IMPOST-OR
INFECT-OR
INJECT-OR
INVENT-OR
INVEST-OR
ISOLAT-OR
METAPH-OR
NARRAT-OR
NEIGHB-OR

OBJECT-OR
OBSESS-OR
PREDAT-OR
PROVID-OR
PURVEY-OR
RADIAT-OR
REDUCT-OR
REJECT-OR
RESIST-OR
SCULPT-OR
SECRET-OR
SELECT-OR
STRESS-OR
SURVEY-OR
TESTAT-OR
VIOLAT-OR

Some words ending with -OUS
Seven-letter words

AMOR-OUS
ARDU-OUS
BILI-OUS
BULB-OUS

CALL-OUS
CURI-OUS
DEVI-OUS
DUBI-OUS

ENVI-OUS
FATU-OUS
FERR-OUS
FIBR-OUS

FURI-OUS	OBVI-OUS	TEDI-OUS
GIBB-OUS	ODOR-OUS	TENU-OUS
GLOB-OUS	OMIN-OUS	TIME-OUS
HEIN-OUS	ONER-OUS	VACU-OUS
HIDE-OUS	PITE-OUS	VARI-OUS
IGNE-OUS	POMP-OUS	VICI-OUS
JEAL-OUS	RAUC-OUS	ZEAL-OUS
NITR-OUS	RIOT-OUS	
NOXI-OUS	RUIN-OUS	

Tile Tracking

This means being aware of what tiles have already been played and therefore what might remain in the bag or on your opponent's rack. Tile tracking can be useful to manage your expectations of what common vowels or consonants you are likely to pick from the bag, and whether there are any goodies (blanks Ss JQXZ) left. At the end of a game it could even enable you to know what your opponent is holding. This practice is more common at club and tournament level.

Eight-letter words

O

ARSON-OUS	GRACI-OUS	RIGOR-OUS
BIBUL-OUS	GRIEV-OUS	SENSU-OUS
CHROM-OUS	LIBEL-OUS	SQUAM-OUS
COUSC-OUS	LUMIN-OUS	STUDI-OUS
COVET-OUS	LUSCI-OUS	TIMOR-OUS
DECOR-OUS	LUSTR-OUS	TORTU-OUS
DESIR-OUS	MUTIN-OUS	ULCER-OUS
DEXTR-OUS	NITRE-OUS	UNCTU-OUS
ENORM-OUS	NUMER-OUS	VAPOR-OUS
FABUL-OUS	ORDUR-OUS	VENOM-OUS
FACTI-OUS	PERIL-OUS	VIGOR-OUS
FEVER-OUS	POPUL-OUS	VIRTU-OUS
GENER-OUS	PRECI-OUS	WONDR-OUS
GORGE-OUS	PREVI-OUS	

Some words ending with -OUT
Seven-letter words

BACK-OUT	HAND-OUT	SHUT-OUT
BAIL-OUT	HANG-OUT	SPIN-OUT
BESP-OUT	HIDE-OUT	TAKE-OUT
BLOW-OUT	LOCK-OUT	TIME-OUT
BURN-OUT	LOOK-OUT	TURN-OUT
CAMP-OUT	MISS-OUT	WALK-OUT
COOK-OUT	PASS-OUT	WASH-OUT
DROP-OUT	PULL-OUT	WITH-OUT
FADE-OUT	READ-OUT	WORK-OUT
FALL-OUT	ROLL-OUT	
FOLD-OUT	SELL-OUT	

Eight-letter words

BLACK-OUT	OUTSH-OUT	SPEAK-OUT
BREAK-OUT	PHASE-OUT	STAKE-OUT
CARRY-OUT	PRINT-OUT	STAND-OUT
CHECK-OUT	RUNAB-OUT	STICK-OUT
FLAME-OUT	SEASC-OUT	THERE-OUT
FREAK-OUT	SEATR-OUT	UNDEV-OUT
INDEV-OUT	SHAKE-OUT	WATCH-OUT
KNOCK-OUT	SHOOT-OUT	WHITE-OUT
LAYAB-OUT	SLEEP-OUT	

O

UNUSUAL LETTER COMBINATIONS

If you have an unusual combination of letters on your rack, or want to impress your opponent with an unusual word, a few words from World English can come in handy.

Australian word

OCKER   uncultivated or boorish Australian

Hindi word

OONT   camel

South African words

OKE   man
OOM   title of respect

P
3

Essential info
Value: 3 points
Number in set: 2

There are two-letter words beginning with **P** for each vowel except U which, combined with OP and UP, make it very flexible for short words such as PE (the 17th letter in the Hebrew alphabet, 4 points) and PO (an informal word for chamber pot, also 4 points). P also combines well with X, forming three-letter words PAX, PIX and POX (12 points each) and also Z, for example the three-letter POZ (an old-fashioned short form of positive, 14 points).

Two-letter words beginning with P

PA	PI
PE	PO

Some three-letter words beginning with P

PAC	PHO	POZ
PAH	PHT	PRE
PAM	PIA	PSI
PAP	PIC	PST
PAR	PIR	PUG
PAV	PIU	PUH
PAX	PIX	PUR
PEC	POA	PUS
PED	POH	PUY
PEH	POI	PYA
PEP	POL	PYE
PER	POM	PYX
PEW	POW	
PHI	POX	

HOOKS

Hooking requires a subtle change in a player's thought process, in that they must look at words already on the board without becoming distracted by their pronunciation.

Some front-hooks
Two letters to three

P-AD	P-EN	P-OS
P-AH	P-ER	P-OW
P-AL	P-ES	P-OX
P-AM	P-ET	P-RE
P-AN	P-HI	P-SI
P-AR	P-HO	P-ST
P-AS	P-IN	P-UG
P-AT	P-IS	P-UH
P-AW	P-IT	P-UN
P-AX	P-OD	P-UP
P-AY	P-OH	P-UR
P-EA	P-OI	P-US
P-ED	P-OM	P-UT
P-EE	P-OO	P-YA
P-EH	P-OP	P-YE

Three letters to four

P-ACE	P-AWN	P-LAT
P-ACT	P-EAR	P-LAY
P-AGE	P-EAT	P-LEA
P-AID	P-EEK	P-LED
P-AIL	P-EEL	P-LEX
P-AIN	P-EEN	P-LIE
P-AIR	P-ELT	P-LOD
P-AIS	P-END	P-LOP
P-ALE	P-EON	P-LOT
P-ALL	P-ERE	P-LOW
P-ALP	P-ERK	P-LOY
P-AND	P-EST	P-LUG
P-ANE	P-HAT	P-LUM
P-ANT	P-HEW	P-OKE
P-ARE	P-HUT	P-OLE
P-ARK	P-ICK	P-ONE
P-ART	P-ILL	P-ONY
P-ASH	P-IMP	P-OOR
P-ASS	P-INK	P-OPE
P-ATE	P-ION	P-ORE
P-AVE	P-ITA	P-ORT

P

P-OSE	P-RAY	P-ROD
P-OUR	P-REP	P-ROM
P-OUT	P-REZ	P-ROW
P-OXY	P-RIG	P-UKE
P-RAM	P-RIM	P-UMP
P-RAT	P-ROB	P-URE

Four letters to five

P-ACED	P-INTO	P-RANG
P-ACER	P-ITCH	P-RANK
P-AEON	P-LACE	P-RAWN
P-AGED	P-LACK	P-REEN
P-AGER	P-LAID	P-RICE
P-ALAS	P-LAIN	P-RICY
P-ALLY	P-LANE	P-RIDE
P-APER	P-LANK	P-RIMA
P-ARCH	P-LANT	P-RIME
P-ARED	P-LAST	P-RISE
P-ARIS	P-LATE	P-ROBE
P-ARTY	P-LEAD	P-ROLE
P-AVER	P-LEAT	P-ROLL
P-AWED	P-LIED	P-RONG
P-EACH	P-LIER	P-ROOF
P-EARL	P-LINK	P-ROSE
P-EASE	P-LUCK	P-ROVE
P-EGGY	P-LUMP	P-RUDE
P-ESKY	P-LUSH	P-RUNE
P-HONE	P-OINT	P-SHAW
P-ICKY	P-OLIO	P-UNTO
P-INCH	P-OUCH	P-URGE
P-INKY	P-OWER	

Five letters to six

P-ACING	P-ALATE	P-AWING
P-ACKER	P-ANTED	P-AWNED
P-ADDED	P-ARISH	P-AWNER
P-ADDER	P-ARKED	P-EASED
P-ADDLE	P-ARLED	P-EGGED
P-AGING	P-ARSON	P-ELVES
P-AIRED	P-ASHED	P-ENDED
P-AIRER	P-ASTER	P-ESTER

P-HONED	P-LOWED	P-RESET
P-HONER	P-LOWER	P-RETAX
P-HONEY	P-LUCKY	P-REVUE
P-HOOEY	P-LUMMY	P-RICED
P-ICKER	P-LUMPY	P-RICER
P-ICKLE	P-LUNGE	P-RIEVE
P-IGGED	P-LYING	P-RIMED
P-IMPLY	P-ODIUM	P-RIMER
P-INION	P-OLDER	P-RISER
P-INKED	P-OSIER	P-RIVET
P-INKER	P-OTTER	P-ROBED
P-INNED	P-OUNCE	P-ROPER
P-INNER	P-OUPED	P-ROSED
P-IRATE	P-OUTED	P-ROTON
P-ITCHY	P-OUTER	P-ROVED
P-LACED	P-RAISE	P-ROVEN
P-LACER	P-RANCE	P-ROVER
P-LATED	P-RAYED	P-ROWER
P-LATER	P-REACH	P-RUNED
P-LAYED	P-REACT	P-UMPED
P-LAYER	P-REBUY	P-UPPED
P-LEASE	P-RECUT	P-URGED
P-LEDGE	P-REFER	P-URGER
P-LODGE	P-REFIX	P-USHER
P-LOUGH	P-REMIX	P-UTTER
P-LOVER	P-REPAY	

P

Six letters to seven

P-ADDING	P-AWNING	P-ICKLER
P-ADDLED	P-EANING	P-INCASE
P-AIRING	P-EASING	P-INCHED
P-ANTHER	P-EERIER	P-INCHER
P-ANTING	P-EGGING	P-INKING
P-ANTLER	P-ENDING	P-INNING
P-ARABLE	P-ENFOLD	P-ITCHED
P-ARCHED	P-HATTER	P-LACING
P-ARKING	P-HONIED	P-LAIDED
P-ARLING	P-HONING	P-LANKED
P-ARTIER	P-ICKIER	P-LANNER
P-ASHING	P-ICKILY	P-LASTER

179

P-LATINA	P-ORCINE	P-REPAID
P-LATTER	P-OUCHED	P-REPONE
P-LAYING	P-OUTING	P-RESALE
P-LAYOFF	P-RAISED	P-RESELL
P-LEADED	P-RAISER	P-RESENT
P-LEADER	P-RANCED	P-RESHIP
P-LEASED	P-RANGED	P-RESIDE
P-LEASER	P-RANKED	P-RESOLD
P-LEDGED	P-RANKLE	P-RESUME
P-LEDGER	P-RATTED	P-RETELL
P-LIABLE	P-RATTLE	P-RETOLD
P-LODGED	P-RAYING	P-REVERB
P-LOTTED	P-REAVER	P-REVIEW
P-LOTTER	P-REBILL	P-REWASH
P-LOWING	P-REBOOK	P-REWORN
P-LUCKED	P-RECAST	P-RICIER
P-LUGGED	P-RECEDE	P-RICKLE
P-LUGGER	P-RECEPT	P-RICKLY
P-LUMBER	P-RECOOK	P-RIDING
P-LUMPED	P-REDATE	P-RISING
P-LUMPEN	P-REDIAL	P-ROBING
P-LUMPER	P-REFACE	P-RODDED
P-LUNGED	P-REFECT	P-ROOFED
P-LUNGER	P-REHEAT	P-ROOFER
P-LUNKER	P-REMADE	P-ROSILY
P-LUSHER	P-REMISE	P-ROVING
P-LUSHLY	P-REMOVE	P-RUDISH
P-OINTED	P-RENAME	P-UPPING
P-OODLES	P-REPACK	P-URGING

Seven letters to eight

P-ADDLING	P-ENLIGHT	P-ITCHIER
P-ALIMONY	P-ENOLOGY	P-ITCHILY
P-ALTERED	P-ENTICED	P-ITCHING
P-ARCHING	P-HARMING	P-LAIDING
P-ARTICLE	P-HISHING	P-LANKING
P-ARTISAN	P-HONEYED	P-LAYBACK
P-ARTWORK	P-ICKIEST	P-LAYTIME
P-EARLIER	P-INCHING	P-LEADING
P-ENCHANT	P-INKIEST	P-LEASING

P

P-LEASURE	P-REAPPLY	P-RESERVE
P-LIGHTED	P-REARMED	P-RESHOWN
P-LIGHTER	P-REBIRTH	P-RESIDED
P-LOTTING	P-REBOUND	P-RESIDER
P-LUCKILY	P-REBUILD	P-RESUMED
P-LUCKING	P-REBUILT	P-RESUMER
P-LUGGING	P-RECEDED	P-RETRAIN
P-LUGHOLE	P-RECITED	P-RETRIAL
P-LUMPING	P-RECLEAN	P-RETYPED
P-LUMPISH	P-RECURED	P-REUNION
P-LUNGING	P-REDATED	P-REUNITE
P-LUSHEST	P-REDRAFT	P-REVALUE
P-LUSHIER	P-REELECT	P-REVISED
P-OTTERED	P-REFACED	P-REVISIT
P-OUCHING	P-REFIXED	P-REWEIGH
P-RAISING	P-REGNANT	P-REWIRED
P-RANCING	P-REJUDGE	P-RICIEST
P-RANGING	P-REMIXED	P-RIGGISH
P-RANKING	P-REMORSE	P-RILLING
P-RANKISH	P-REMOVED	P-RODDING
P-RATTLED	P-REORDER	P-ROOFING
P-RATTLER	P-REPAVED	P-ROSIEST
P-REACHED	P-REPLACE	P-UNITIVE
P-REACHER	P-REPOSED	P-UTTERED
P-READAPT	P-REPRICE	P-UTTERER
P-READMIT	P-REPRINT	

Some end-hooks
Two letters to three

AL-P	HA-P	MO-P
AM-P	HE-P	NA-P
AS-P	HI-P	NE-P
BA-P	HO-P	OO-P
BO-P	JA-P	OU-P
DA-P	KI-P	PA-P
DI-P	KO-P	PE-P
DO-P	LA-P	PI-P
FA-P	LI-P	PO-P
GI-P	LO-P	RE-P
GU-P	MA-P	SI-P

P

SO-P   UM-P   YE-P
TA-P   UR-P   YU-P
TI-P   WO-P   ZA-P
TO-P   YA-P

```
........................................................
:  **Celebrity Scrabble Players**
:  include Mel Gibson, Nicole Kidman, Chris Martin, Madonna
:  and Sting.
........................................................
```

Three letters to four

BEE-P	HAS-P	PER-P
BUM-P	HEM-P	POM-P
BUR-P	HOO-P	PRE-P
CAM-P	HUM-P	PRO-P
CAR-P	JEE-P	PUL-P
CHA-P	LAM-P	RAM-P
CHI-P	LEA-P	RAS-P
COO-P	LEE-P	ROM-P
COW-P	LIS-P	RUM-P
DAM-P	LOO-P	SEE-P
DEE-P	LOU-P	SKI-P
FRA-P	LOW-P	SUM-P
GAS-P	LUM-P	TAR-P
GOO-P	MUM-P	WAR-P
GUL-P	PAR-P	WAS-P
GUM-P	PEE-P	WIS-P

Four letters to five

BICE-P	GRAM-P	SLEE-P
BLEE-P	GRUM-P	SLUM-P
CHAM-P	PLUM-P	SLUR-P
CHUM-P	POLY-P	STUM-P
CLAM-P	PRIM-P	SWAM-P
CRAM-P	SCAM-P	SWEE-P
CREE-P	SCAR-P	TRAM-P
CRIM-P	SCUL-P	WHOM-P
CRIS-P	SKIM-P	

P

Five letters to six

ESCAR-P	SCRUM-P	TRICE-P
SCRAW-P	SHLEP-P	
SCRIM-P	THREE-P	

Six letters to seven

BEDLAM-P	MANTRA-P	SCHLEP-P

Seven letters to eight

AUTOCAR-P	MINICAM-P

BLOCKERS

It is useful to know which words are blockers and can't therefore be extended before or after. You may want to play a blocker that your opponent can't extend, or you may want to avoid playing a blocker because you want to keep the board open.

Some three-letter blockers beginning with P

PAX	PLY	PST
PHT	POH	PYX

Some four-letter blockers beginning with P

PFFT	PLEX	PREZ
PHAT	POCO	PSST
PHEW	POKY	PUKA
PHIZ	PONY	PUNY
PITY	POSY	

Some five-letter blockers beginning with P (except words ending in '-ED', '-J', '-S', '-X', '-Y' or '-Z')

PACTA	PILAR	PUKKA
PADRI	PILCH	PULMO
PAISE	PINCH	PUPAE
PALER	POOCH	PUPAL
PAOLO	PORCH	PURER
PAPAL	PROST	PUTID
PENAL	PROUD	PYRAL
PERCH	PUBIC	PYRIC

P

Some six-letter blockers begining with P (except words ending in '-ED', '-J', '-S', '-X', '-Y' or '-Z')

PACTUM	PHONAL	POTMAN
PAIRER	PHYLUM	POTMEN
PALEAL	PIEING	POXIER
PALEST	PIEMAN	POXING
PALISH	PIEMEN	PRELAW
PALLID	PIPIER	PRIMAL
PANINI	PITMEN	PROGUN
PARISH	PLACID	PRONER
PARTIM	PLANAR	PRONTO
PASSEE	PLIANT	PROWAR
PASSIM	POKIER	PROWER
PAUSAL	POLISH	PULPAL
PAWING	POLYPI	PUNIER
PENMAN	POSHER	PUNISH
PENMEN	POSIER	PUREST
PEPFUL	POTASH	PURING
PERISH	POTATO	PUTRID
PERTER	POTING	

BONUS WORDS

Bonus words on your rack can be hard to spot, especially for the less experienced player. One way to help find them is by using prefixes and suffixes.

Many larger words include a common prefix or suffix – remembering these and using them where you can is a good way to discover any longer words on your rack, including any potential bonus words. The key prefixes to remember beginning with P are PER-, PRE- and PRO-.

Some words beginning with PER-
Seven-letter words

PER-CENT	PER-FUME	PER-KING
PER-CHER	PER-HAPS	PER-MING
PER-CUSS	PER-JURE	PER-PLEX
PER-FORM	PER-JURY	PER-SIST

PER-SONS
PER-TAIN
PER-TAKE

PER-USED
PER-USER
PER-VADE

PER-VERT

Eight-letter words

PER-FUMED
PER-ISHES
PER-MUTED
PER-OXIDE

PER-SPIRE
PER-SUING
PER-TAKEN
PER-USING

PER-VADED
PER-VERSE

Some words beginning with PRE-

Seven-letter words

PRE-ACHY
PRE-BOIL
PRE-BOOK
PRE-CAST
PRE-CEDE
PRE-CODE
PRE-COOK
PRE-DATE
PRE-DAWN
PRE-DIAL
PRE-DICT
PRE-EMPT

PRE-FACE
PRE-LATE
PRE-LOAD
PRE-LUDE
PRE-MADE
PRE-MISE
PRE-PACK
PRE-PAID
PRE-PARE
PRE-PLAN
PRE-SAGE
PRE-SALE

PRE-SENT
PRE-SHOW
PRE-SIDE
PRE-TEEN
PRE-TEND
PRE-TERM
PRE-TEXT
PRE-VAIL
PRE-VIEW
PRE-WARN
PRE-WASH
PRE-WORN

P

Eight-letter words

PRE-ADAPT
PRE-AMBLE
PRE-BIRTH
PRE-BUILT
PRE-CEDED
PRE-CITED
PRE-CURED
PRE-DATED
PRE-ELECT
PRE-EXIST
PRE-FACED
PRE-FIXED

PRE-JUDGE
PRE-MOLAR
PRE-ORDER
PRE-OWNED
PRE-PARED
PRE-PLANT
PRE-POSED
PRE-PRESS
PRE-PRINT
PRE-SAGER
PRE-SERVE
PRE-SHAPE

PRE-SIDED
PRE-SLEEP
PRE-SOLVE
PRE-STORE
PRE-TASTE
PRE-TENSE
PRE-TRIAL
PRE-TYPED
PRE-VALUE
PRE-VISED

Some words beginning with PRO-

Seven-letter words

PRO-BALL	PRO-FESS	PRO-PONE
PRO-BATE	PRO-FILE	PRO-POSE
PRO-BING	PRO-FUSE	PRO-SING
PRO-CESS	PRO-GRAM	PRO-TEST
PRO-CURE	PRO-LONG	PRO-VERB
PRO-DRUG	PRO-MISE	PRO-VIDE
PRO-DUCE	PRO-MOTE	PRO-WEST
PRO-DUCT	PRO-NOUN	
PRO-FANE	PRO-PANE	

Eight-letter words

PRO-BATED	PRO-MISER	PRO-STATE
PRO-CLAIM	PRO-MOTED	PRO-STYLE
PRO-CURED	PRO-MOTOR	PRO-TEASE
PRO-FILED	PRO-PHASE	PRO-TRACT
PRO-FILER	PRO-POSED	PRO-TRADE
PRO-FOUND	PRO-POUND	PRO-UNION
PRO-LAPSE	PRO-RATED	PRO-VISOR

UNUSUAL LETTER COMBINATIONS

If you have an unusual combination of letters on your rack, or want to impress your opponent with an unusual word, a few words from World English can come in handy.

Australian words

PINDAN	desert region of Western Australia
PLONKO	alcoholic, especially one who drinks wine
PODDY	handfed calf or lamb
POKIE	poker machine
POSSIE	position
PRELOVED	second-hand

Canadian words

PARFLECHE	dried rawhide
PARKADE	building used as a car park
PARKETTE	small public park
PLEW	beaver skin used as a standard unit
POGEY	financial relief for the unemployed

POKELOGAN	backwater
POUTINE	chipped potatoes topped with curd cheese and tomato sauce
PUNG	horse-drawn sleigh

Hindi words

PACHISI	game resembling backgammon
PAISA	one hundredth of a rupee
PAKORA	dish of deep-fried chicken or vegetables
PANEER	soft white cheese
PARATHA	flat unleavened bread
PEEPUL	tree similar to the banyan
PUNKAH	fan made of palm leaves
PURDAH	custom of keeping women secluded
PURI	unleavened flaky bread
PUTTEE	strip of cloth wound around the leg

New Zealand words

PAKAHI	acid soil or land
PAKOKO	small freshwater fish
PAUA	edible abalone
PIKAU	rucksack
PIPI	shellfish
PIUPIU	leaf skirt
POI	ball of woven flax
PONGA	tall tree fern
PORAE	edible sea fish
PORANGI	crazy
PORINA	moth larva
POTAE	hat
POWHIRI	welcoming ceremony
PUGGY	sticky
PUHA	sow thistle
PUKEKO	wading bird
PURIRI	forest tree

South African words

| PADKOS | snacks for a long journey |
| PLAAS | farm |

P

Q
10

Essential info
Value: 10 points
Number in set: 1

POWER TILE

Along with Z, **Q** is the highest-scoring letter in the Scrabble set. However, unlike Z, Q can prove difficult to use if it is not accompanied by the letter U. The best method of getting around this is to commit to memory all the short words beginning with Q which do not require a U. This is easier than it sounds, as there is only one two-letter word beginning with Q: QI (vital energy believed to circulate around the body, 11 points). There are three three-letter words (12 points each, and only one of these uses a U): QUA (in the capacity of), QAT (evergreen shrub of Africa and Asia whose leaves have narcotic properties) and QIS (plural of QI). The fourth three-letter word containing a Q is SUQ.

Two-letter word beginning with Q

QI

Three-letter words beginning with Q

QAT   QUA

Three-letter word using Q

SUQ

Four-letter words

Some four-letter words using Q with which you may not be familiar include QUAG (short form of quagmire, 14 points), QUEY (a young cow, 16 points) and WAQF (endowment in Muslim law, 19 points).

AQUA	QUAT	QUIT
QADI	QUAY	QUIZ
QAID	QUEP	QUOD
QOPH	QUEY	QUOP
QUAD	QUID	SUQS
QUAG	QUIN	WAQF
QUAI	QUIP	

HOOKS

Hooking requires a subtle change in a player's thought process, in that they must look at words already on the board without becoming distracted by their pronunciation.

Some front-hooks
Two letters to three

Q-AT   Q-IS

Three letters to four

Q-AID   Q-UEY

Four letters to five

Q-AIDS   Q-UEYS

Some end-hooks
Four letters to five

TALA-Q

Q

BLOCKERS

It is useful to know which words are blockers and can't therefore be extended before or after. You may want to play a blocker that your opponent can't extend, or you may want to avoid playing a blocker because you want to keep the board open.

Three-letter blocker beginning with Q

QIS

Four-letter blocker beginning with Q

QUEP

Some five-letter blockers beginning with Q (except words ending in '-ED', '-J', '-S', '-X', '-Y' or '-Z')

QUALE	QUAYD	QURSH
QUASI	QUOAD	

Some six-letter blockers beginning with Q (except words ending in '-ED', '-J', '-S', '-X', '-Y' or '-Z')

QUAINT	QUENCH	QUOTHA
QUALIA	QUETCH	QURUSH
QUATCH	QUINIC	
QUEINT	QUOOKE	

Bonus words

Seven-letter words

QABALAH	QUAMASH	QUAVERY
QAWWALI	QUANGOS	QUAYAGE
QAWWALS	QUANNET	QUEENED
QIGONGS	QUANTAL	QUEENIE
QINDARS	QUANTED	QUEENLY
QINTARS	QUANTIC	QUEESTS
QUACKED	QUANTUM	QUELLED
QUACKER	QUAREST	QUELLER
QUACKLE	QUARREL	QUEMING
QUADDED	QUARTAN	QUERIDA
QUADRAT	QUARTER	QUERIED
QUADRIC	QUARTES	QUERIER
QUAERED	QUARTET	QUERIES
QUAERES	QUARTIC	QUERIST
QUAFFED	QUARTOS	QUESTED
QUAFFER	QUARTZY	QUESTER
QUAGGAS	QUASARS	QUESTOR
QUAICHS	QUASHED	QUETZAL
QUAIGHS	QUASHEE	QUEUERS
QUAILED	QUASHER	QUEUING
QUAKERS	QUASHES	QUIBBLE
QUAKIER	QUASHIE	QUICHED
QUAKILY	QUASSIA	QUICHES
QUAKING	QUASSIN	QUICKEN
QUALIFY	QUATRES	QUICKER
QUALITY	QUAVERS	QUICKIE

QUICKLY	QUINNAT	QUIVERS
QUIDAMS	QUINOAS	QUIVERY
QUIDDIT	QUINOID	QUIXOTE
QUIESCE	QUINOLS	QUIZZED
QUIETED	QUINONE	QUIZZER
QUIETEN	QUINTAL	QUIZZES
QUIETER	QUINTAN	QUODDED
QUIETLY	QUINTAR	QUODLIN
QUIETUS	QUINTAS	QUOHOGS
QUIGHTS	QUINTES	QUOIFED
QUILLAI	QUINTET	QUOINED
QUILLED	QUINTIC	QUOISTS
QUILLET	QUINTIN	QUOITED
QUILLON	QUINZES	QUOITER
QUILTED	QUIPPED	QUOKKAS
QUILTER	QUIPPER	QUOMODO
QUINARY	QUIPPUS	QUONDAM
QUINATE	QUIRING	QUONKED
QUINCES	QUIRKED	QUOPPED
QUINCHE	QUIRTED	QUORATE
QUINELA	QUITING	QUORUMS
QUINIES	QUITTAL	QUOTERS
QUININA	QUITTED	QUOTING
QUININE	QUITTER	QUOTUMS
QUININS	QUITTOR	QWERTYS

Eight-letter words

QABALISM	QUADRANT	QUAKIEST
QABALIST	QUADRATE	QUALMIER
QALAMDAN	QUADRIGA	QUALMING
QINDARKA	QUADROON	QUALMISH
QUAALUDE	QUAESTOR	QUANDANG
QUACKERY	QUAFFING	QUANDARY
QUACKIER	QUAGGIER	QUANDONG
QUACKING	QUAGMIRE	QUANTIFY
QUACKISH	QUAGMIRY	QUANTILE
QUACKISM	QUAICHES	QUANTING
QUACKLED	QUAILING	QUANTISE
QUADDING	QUAINTER	QUANTITY
QUADPLEX	QUAINTLY	QUANTIZE

QUANTONG	QUESTION	QUINONES
QUARRIAN	QUETCHED	QUINSIED
QUARRIED	QUETCHES	QUINSIES
QUARRIER	QUETHING	QUINTAIN
QUARRIES	QUEUEING	QUINTETS
QUARRION	QUIBBLED	QUINTETT
QUARTERN	QUIBBLER	QUINTICS
QUARTETT	QUIBBLES	QUINTILE
QUARTIER	QUICHING	QUIPPIER
QUARTILE	QUICKEST	QUIPPING
QUARTZES	QUICKIES	QUIPPISH
QUASHIES	QUICKSET	QUIPSTER
QUASHING	QUIDDANY	QUIRKIER
QUASSIAS	QUIDDITY	QUIRKILY
QUATCHED	QUIDDLED	QUIRKING
QUATORZE	QUIDDLER	QUIRKISH
QUATRAIN	QUIDNUNC	QUIRTING
QUAVERED	QUIESCED	QUISLING
QUAVERER	QUIESCES	QUITCHED
QUAYLIKE	QUIETEST	QUITCHES
QUAYSIDE	QUIETING	QUITRENT
QUAZZIER	QUIETISM	QUITTALS
QUEACHES	QUIETIST	QUITTERS
QUEASIER	QUIETIVE	QUITTING
QUEASILY	QUIETUDE	QUIVERED
QUEAZIER	QUIGHTED	QUIVERER
QUEENITE	QUILLAIA	QUIXOTES
QUEENLET	QUILLAJA	QUIXOTIC
QUELCHED	QUILLING	QUIXOTRY
QUELCHES	QUILLMAN	QUIZZERY
QUELLING	QUILLMEN	QUIZZIFY
QUENCHED	QUILTING	QUIZZING
QUENCHER	QUINCHED	QUODDING
QUENCHES	QUINCHES	QUODLINS
QUENELLE	QUINCUNX	QUOIFING
QUERCINE	QUINELLA	QUOINING
QUERYING	QUINIELA	QUOITERS
QUESTANT	QUININES	QUOITING
QUESTERS	QUINOIDS	QUONKING
QUESTING	QUINOLIN	QUOPPING

Q

QUOTABLE   QUOTIENT
QUOTABLY   QWERTIES

UNUSUAL LETTER COMBINATIONS

If you have an unusual combination of letters on your rack, or want to impress your opponent with an unusual word, a few words from World English can come in handy.

Australian words

QUOKKA   small wallaby
QUOLL   native cat

Urdu word

QORMA   Indian dish of meat or vegetables braised with yoghurt or cream

QUIZ show

If you are lucky enough to have the letters Q, U, I and Z on your rack, or with one of them in a usable place on the board, the obvious choice would be to play QUIZ, an extremely useful and high-scoring word (22 points). Should your opponent be the lucky one to play QUIZ then perhaps you can then reap the benefits of front-hooking it with an S to make SQUIZ (23 points).

Q

Essential info
Value: 1 point
Number in set: 6

R is one of the most common consonants in Scrabble but, surprisingly, only begins one two-letter word: RE (2 points). Some useful three-letter words to remember include ROW and RAY (6 points each) and there are also more unusual words such as RAX (a Scots word for stretch or extend, 10 points) and REZ (a short informal word for reservation, 12 points) which use power tiles. R is one of the letters of the RETAIN set and is therefore a good letter to keep if trying to get a bonus word.

Two-letter word beginning with R

RE

Some three-letter words beginning with R

RAD	REH	RHO
RAH	REI	RHY
RAI	REM	RIF
RAJ	REN	RIN
RAS	REO	RIT
RAX	REP	RIZ
REB	RET	ROM
REC	REW	ROO
REE	REX	RYA
REG	REZ	

HOOKS

Hooking requires a subtle change in a player's thought process, in that they must look at words already on the board without becoming distracted by their pronunciation.

Some front-hooks

Two letters to three

R-AD	R-EF	R-OD
R-AG	R-EH	R-OE
R-AH	R-EM	R-OM
R-AI	R-EN	R-OO
R-AM	R-ES	R-OW
R-AN	R-ET	R-UG
R-AS	R-EX	R-UM
R-AT	R-HO	R-UN
R-AW	R-ID	R-UT
R-AX	R-IF	R-YA
R-AY	R-IN	R-YE
R-ED	R-IT	
R-EE	R-OB	

Three letters to four

R-ACE	R-ATE	R-INK
R-AFF	R-AVE	R-OAR
R-AFT	R-AWN	R-OBE
R-AGE	R-EAR	R-ODE
R-AID	R-EEK	R-OIL
R-AIL	R-EEL	R-OLE
R-AIN	R-EFT	R-OOF
R-AKE	R-END	R-OOM
R-ALE	R-EST	R-OOT
R-AMP	R-ICE	R-OPE
R-AND	R-ICH	R-OSE
R-ANT	R-ICK	R-OUT
R-APT	R-ICY	R-ULE
R-ARE	R-IDE	R-UMP
R-ASH	R-IFF	R-USE
R-ASP	R-IGG	R-YES

Four letters to five

R-ABID	R-AKED	R-AVER
R-ACED	R-ALLY	R-EACH
R-ACER	R-AMEN	R-EAVE
R-AGED	R-ARED	R-EDDY
R-AGER	R-AVEL	R-EGAL

R

R-EMIT
R-ENEW
R-ETCH
R-ICED
R-OARY

R-OAST
R-OILY
R-OPED
R-OUST
R-OVEN

R-OVER
R-OWED
R-OWER

Five letters to six

R-ABIES
R-ACING
R-ADDER
R-ADIOS
R-AFTER
R-AGING
R-AIDED
R-AIDER
R-AILED
R-AKING
R-AMBLE
R-AMPED
R-ANGER
R-ANKER
R-ANKLE
R-ANTED
R-APPEL
R-APTLY
R-AREFY
R-ASHED
R-ASPER
R-AUGHT

R-AVINE
R-AZURE
R-EARED
R-EAVED
R-EBOOK
R-EDUCE
R-EFFED
R-EGRET
R-EJECT
R-ELATE
R-EMAIL
R-EMOTE
R-EMOVE
R-ENDED
R-ENTER
R-ESTER
R-ETAPE
R-EVERT
R-EVERY
R-EVOKE
R-ICIER
R-ICING

R-ICKLE
R-ICTAL
R-ICTUS
R-IGGED
R-INKED
R-OARED
R-OCKER
R-OILED
R-OLLER
R-OPING
R-OSIER
R-OTARY
R-OTTER
R-OUGHT
R-OUNCE
R-OUPED
R-OUTED
R-OUTER
R-OWING
R-UDDER
R-USHER
R-UTTER

Six letters to seven

R-ABIDER
R-ADDLED
R-AIDING
R-AILING
R-ALLIED
R-AMBLED
R-AMBLER
R-AMPING
R-ANKLED
R-ANTING

R-APPORT
R-ASHING
R-ASPISH
R-EARING
R-EAVING
R-EDDISH
R-EDUCED
R-EFFING
R-EGALLY
R-EGENCE

R-EGENCY
R-EGRESS
R-ELAPSE
R-ELATED
R-ELATER
R-EMERGE
R-EMOTER
R-EMOVED
R-ENDING
R-ENEWED

R-EPRISE	R-ICHING	R-OUSTED
R-ESTATE	R-ICIEST	R-OUSTER
R-ETCHED	R-IGGING	R-OUTING
R-EVILER	R-INKING	R-OYSTER
R-EVOKED	R-OARING	R-UGGING
R-EVOKER	R-OILING	R-UNLESS
R-EVOLVE	R-OUGHLY	

Seven letters to eight

R-ADDLING	R-ELATING	R-ENOUNCE
R-ALLYING	R-ELATION	R-ESTATED
R-AMBLING	R-ELATIVE	R-ETCHING
R-ANKLING	R-EMAILED	R-EVERTED
R-APTNESS	R-EMERGED	R-EVOKING
R-AREFIED	R-EMITTED	R-EVOLVED
R-ECLOSED	R-EMITTER	R-EVOLVER
R-EDUCING	R-EMOTION	R-EVULSED
R-EGALITY	R-EMOVING	R-UNROUND
R-EJECTED	R-ENEWING	R-URALITE
R-ELAPSED	R-ENFORCE	

Handy Hint

JAR (10 points) is an obvious word to spot on the rack. If it won't play then remember that JAR backwards makes the word RAJ which might fit in. RAJ is an Indian word for government and it also takes a useful A hook for RAJA, which then can take an H for RAJAH. Other short reversible words beginning with R are RAW/WAR (6 points) RAP/PAR (5 points) RIM/MIR (5 points).

R

Some end-hooks
Two letters to three

AI-R	GO-R	LO-R
BA-R	GU-R	MA-R
BO-R	HE-R	MI-R
DO-R	JA-R	MO-R
EA-R	JO-R	NO-R
ER-R	KI-R	NU-R
FA-R	KO-R	OO-R
FE-R	LA-R	OU-R

PA-R	SI-R	YA-R
PE-R	TA-R	
PI-R	TO-R	

Three letters to four

ACE-R	EWE-R	OWE-R
AGA-R	EYE-R	PEA-R
AGE-R	FEE-R	PIE-R
APE-R	FIE-R	PUR-R
AVE-R	FOU-R	SEA-R
BEE-R	GOE-R	SEE-R
BOA-R	HOA-R	SOU-R
BOO-R	HOE-R	SPA-R
BRR-R	HUE-R	SUE-R
BUR-R	ICE-R	TEA-R
CHA-R	JEE-R	TEE-R
CHE-R	LEA-R	TIE-R
DEE-R	LEE-R	USE-R
DOE-R	LIE-R	VEE-R
DOO-R	MEE-R	VIE-R
DYE-R	MOO-R	YEA-R
EVE-R	ONE-R	YOU-R

Four letters to five

ABLE-R	CHAI-R	DIVE-R
BAKE-R	CIDE-R	DONE-R
BARE-R	CITE-R	DOPE-R
BASE-R	CODE-R	DOSE-R
BIDE-R	COME-R	DOVE-R
BIKE-R	COPE-R	DOZE-R
BITE-R	COVE-R	EASE-R
BLUE-R	CUBE-R	EDGE-R
BORE-R	CURE-R	FACE-R
CAGE-R	CUTE-R	FADE-R
CANE-R	DARE-R	FAKE-R
CAPE-R	DATE-R	FILE-R
CARE-R	DECO-R	FINE-R
CATE-R	DICE-R	FIRE-R
CAVE-R	DINE-R	FIVE-R

R

FREE-R	LUTE-R	ROTO-R
FUME-R	MACE-R	ROVE-R
GAME-R	MAKE-R	RUDE-R
GATE-R	MANO-R	RULE-R
GAZE-R	MATE-R	SABE-R
GIVE-R	MAYO-R	SAFE-R
GONE-R	METE-R	SAGE-R
HATE-R	MINE-R	SANE-R
HAVE-R	MITE-R	SAVE-R
HAZE-R	MOVE-R	SHOE-R
HIDE-R	MUSE-R	SIDE-R
HIKE-R	NAME-R	SIZE-R
HIRE-R	NICE-R	SOLA-R
HOME-R	NOSE-R	SORE-R
HOPE-R	NOTE-R	SUPE-R
HOVE-R	OCHE-R	SURE-R
HUGE-R	ONCE-R	TAKE-R
HYPE-R	PACE-R	TAME-R
IDLE-R	PAGE-R	TAPE-R
JIVE-R	PALE-R	TIGE-R
JOKE-R	PATE-R	TIME-R
LACE-R	PIKE-R	TONE-R
LAKE-R	PIPE-R	TRUE-R
LAME-R	POKE-R	TUBE-R
LASE-R	POSE-R	TUNE-R
LATE-R	PUKE-R	UNDE-R
LEVE-R	PURE-R	VILE-R
LIFE-R	RACE-R	VINE-R
LIKE-R	RARE-R	VOTE-R
LINE-R	RATE-R	WADE-R
LIVE-R	RAVE-R	WAGE-R
LONE-R	RAZE-R	WAKE-R
LOSE-R	RICE-R	WAVE-R
LOVE-R	RIDE-R	WIDE-R
LUGE-R	RIPE-R	WIPE-R
LUNA-R	RISE-R	WISE-R
LURE-R	ROPE-R	ZONE-R

R

Five letters to six

ABIDE-R	DROVE-R	PARSE-R
ACUTE-R	EERIE-R	PASSE-R
ADORE-R	ELATE-R	PIECE-R
AGILE-R	ERASE-R	PLACE-R
AMPLE-R	EVADE-R	PLANE-R
AMUSE-R	EXILE-R	PRIME-R
ANGLE-R	FALSE-R	PROVE-R
ARGUE-R	FENCE-R	QUAKE-R
BADGE-R	FLAKE-R	REAVE-R
BARBE-R	FLAME-R	RECTO-R
BATHE-R	FORCE-R	RIFLE-R
BINGE-R	GLAZE-R	RINSE-R
BLAME-R	GLIDE-R	ROUTE-R
BLAZE-R	GLOVE-R	SAUCE-R
BOMBE-R	GORGE-R	SCALE-R
BOOZE-R	GOUGE-R	SCORE-R
BRAVE-R	GRADE-R	SERVE-R
BRIBE-R	GRAVE-R	SHAKE-R
BULGE-R	GUIDE-R	SHAPE-R
CARVE-R	GUISE-R	SHARE-R
CAUSE-R	HEAVE-R	SHAVE-R
CHAFE-R	HOUSE-R	SHINE-R
CHASE-R	IRATE-R	SINGE-R
CLEVE-R	ISSUE-R	SLATE-R
CLONE-R	JUDGE-R	SLIDE-R
CLOSE-R	JUICE-R	SPARE-R
CLOVE-R	KNIFE-R	SPICE-R
CONDO-R	LANCE-R	STATE-R
CRATE-R	LARGE-R	STONE-R
CRUDE-R	LATHE-R	SWIPE-R
CURSE-R	LATTE-R	TASTE-R
CYCLE-R	LEASE-R	TEASE-R
DANCE-R	LEAVE-R	TITLE-R
DENSE-R	LODGE-R	TRACE-R
DODGE-R	LUNGE-R	TRADE-R
DOUSE-R	MERGE-R	TWICE-R
DRIVE-R	MINCE-R	UNITE-R
DRONE-R	NOOSE-R	VAGUE-R

R

| VALUE-R | WAIVE-R | WHITE-R |
| VERGE-R | WASTE-R | |

Six letters to seven

ACCUSE-R	FREEZE-R	OBLIGE-R
ADMIRE-R	GAMBLE-R	OBTUSE-R
ADVISE-R	GENTLE-R	OFFICE-R
AVENGE-R	GROOVE-R	OPPOSE-R
BABBLE-R	GROUSE-R	PEOPLE-R
BAFFLE-R	HANDLE-R	PERUSE-R
BOTTLE-R	HUDDLE-R	PICKLE-R
BOUNCE-R	HUMBLE-R	PIERCE-R
BROWSE-R	HURDLE-R	PLEASE-R
BUNDLE-R	HUSTLE-R	PLEDGE-R
CACKLE-R	IGNITE-R	POLITE-R
CHANGE-R	IMPALE-R	PRAISE-R
CHARGE-R	IMPOSE-R	QUARTE-R
CHEQUE-R	IMPURE-R	RAMBLE-R
CLEAVE-R	INCITE-R	RATTLE-R
COARSE-R	INCOME-R	REDUCE-R
CREASE-R	INHALE-R	REFINE-R
CRINGE-R	INSANE-R	REMOTE-R
CRUISE-R	INSIDE-R	RESCUE-R
DAMAGE-R	INSURE-R	REVISE-R
DANGLE-R	INVADE-R	RUSTLE-R
DEBASE-R	IONISE-R	SAMPLE-R
DEBATE-R	IONIZE-R	SAVAGE-R
DECIDE-R	JUGGLE-R	SECURE-R
DEFINE-R	KINDLE-R	SEDUCE-R
DIVIDE-R	LOATHE-R	SNOOZE-R
DOUBLE-R	LOCATE-R	SPARSE-R
ENABLE-R	LOUNGE-R	SQUARE-R
ENCODE-R	MANAGE-R	STRIKE-R
ENDURE-R	MARINE-R	STRIPE-R
ESCAPE-R	MENACE-R	TODDLE-R
EVOLVE-R	MINUTE-R	TROUSE-R
EXPOSE-R	MUZZLE-R	TRUDGE-R
FIERCE-R	NEEDLE-R	TUMBLE-R
FLEECE-R	NOTICE-R	UNIQUE-R
FORAGE-R	NUZZLE-R	UNSAFE-R

R

UNSURE-R WAFFLE-R WOBBLE-R
UPDATE-R WHEEZE-R
VOYAGE-R WIGGLE-R

Seven letters to eight

ACHIEVE-R GRUMBLE-R RECLINE-R
ADVANCE-R IMAGINE-R RECYCLE-R
AIRLINE-R IMMENSE-R REPLACE-R
ARRANGE-R IMPROVE-R RESERVE-R
BALANCE-R INQUIRE-R RESTORE-R
BANDAGE-R INTRUDE-R REVERSE-R
BELIEVE-R JOYRIDE-R REVOLVE-R
BICYCLE-R JUSTICE-R REWRITE-R
BREATHE-R LECTURE-R SERVICE-R
CAPTURE-R LICENCE-R SHUTTLE-R
CAROUSE-R LICENSE-R SILENCE-R
CHUCKLE-R MEASURE-R SINCERE-R
COMBINE-R MISTAKE-R STICKLE-R
COMMUTE-R NARRATE-R STRANGE-R
COMPUTE-R NEWCOME-R SURVIVE-R
CONJURE-R NURTURE-R TEENAGE-R
CONSUME-R OBSCURE-R TOASTIE-R
DECEIVE-R OBSERVE-R TOPLINE-R
DECLINE-R OUTLINE-R TORTURE-R
DIFFUSE-R OUTSIDE-R TROUBLE-R
DISABLE-R PERJURE-R TWINKLE-R
DISPOSE-R PILLAGE-R UPGRADE-R
ENDORSE-R POLLUTE-R UPSTATE-R
ENFORCE-R PRECISE-R VENTURE-R
ENHANCE-R PREFACE-R VILLAGE-R
EXAMINE-R PREPARE-R WELCOME-R
EXECUTE-R PRODUCE-R WHISTLE-R
EXPLORE-R PROFILE-R WHITTLE-R
FORGIVE-R PROMOTE-R
FRAGILE-R PROPOSE-R
GESTURE-R PROVIDE-R
GRAPPLE-R RECEIVE-R

R

BLOCKERS

It is useful to know which words are blockers and can't therefore be extended before or after. You may want to play a blocker that your opponent can't extend, or you may want to avoid playing a blocker because you want to keep the board open.

Some three-letter blockers beginning with R

RAX   RHY

Some four-letter blockers beginning with R

RAZZ	RELY	ROUX
REFT	ROPY	RUBY

Some five-letter blockers beginning with R (except words ending in '-ED', '-J', '-S', '-X', '-Y' or '-Z')

RABID	REDID	RESAT
RADII	RELIT	RIFER
RARER	RENAL	RUNIC
RASTA	RERAN	

Some six-letter blockers beginning with R (except words ending in '-ED', '-J', '-S', '-X', '-Y' or '-Z')

RACIAL	REDONE	RESHOD
RACIER	REDREW	RESHOT
RADDER	REFLEW	RETOOK
RADGER	REGAVE	RETORN
RADISH	REGNAL	RETROD
RAKISH	REGREW	RICHER
RANCID	REHASH	RIDDEN
RAREST	REHUNG	RIFEST
RARING	RELAID	RIPEST
RATHER	RELISH	ROPIER
RAVISH	RESAID	RUEFUL
RAWISH	RESEEN	

R

BONUS WORDS

Bonus words on your rack can be hard to spot, especially for the less experienced player. One way to help find them is by using prefixes and suffixes.

Many larger words include a common prefix or suffix – remembering these and using them where you can is a good way to discover any longer words on your rack, including any potential bonus words. The key prefixes to remember beginning with R are RE- and RED-.

Some words beginning with RE-
Seven-letter words

RE-ACTED
RE-ADAPT
RE-AGENT
RE-ALIGN
RE-APING
RE-APPLY
RE-BATED
RE-BIRTH
RE-BOOTS
RE-BOUND
RE-BRAND
RE-BUILD
RE-CALLS
RE-CEDED
RE-CITAL
RE-CITED
RE-CLAIM
RE-COILS
RE-CORDS
RE-COUNT
RE-COVER
RE-CYCLE
RE-DEEMS
RE-DOUBT
RE-DRAFT
RE-DRESS
RE-DUCES
RE-ELECT
RE-ENACT
RE-ENTRY

RE-FILLS
RE-FINED
RE-FORMS
RE-FRESH
RE-FUSED
RE-GALES
RE-GENTS
RE-GROUP
RE-GROWN
RE-HOUSE
RE-INTER
RE-ISSUE
RE-JOINS
RE-KEYED
RE-LAPSE
RE-LAXER
RE-LEASE
RE-LIVED
RE-LOADS
RE-LYING
RE-MAINS
RE-MARKS
RE-MATCH
RE-MINDS
RE-MIXED
RE-MORSE
RE-MOVED
RE-NEWER
RE-ORDER
RE-PAINT

RE-PASTS
RE-PEALS
RE-PEATS
RE-PLACE
RE-PLAYS
RE-PLIES
RE-PORTS
RE-PRESS
RE-PRINT
RE-QUEST
RE-READS
RE-ROUTE
RE-SEALS
RE-SERVE
RE-SIDED
RE-SIGNS
RE-SISTS
RE-SOLVE
RE-SOUND
RE-SPIRE
RE-SPITE
RE-START
RE-STATE
RE-STING
RE-STORE
RE-TAILS
RE-TAPED
RE-TEACH
RE-THINK
RE-TIRED

R

RE-TRACT
RE-TREAD
RE-TREAT
RE-TURNS
RE-UNIFY

RE-UNION
RE-UNITE
RE-VENGE
RE-VERSE
RE-VISED

RE-VOLVE
RE-WORKS
RE-WOUND
RE-WRITE

Eight-letter words

RE-ABSORB
RE-ACTION
RE-ADJUST
RE-APPEAR
RE-ASSESS
RE-BOOTED
RE-BUFFED
RE-BUTTED
RE-CALLED
RE-CAPPED
RE-CEDING
RE-CHARGE
RE-CITING
RE-COILED
RE-COMMIT
RE-CONNED
RE-CORDED
RE-COUPED
RE-COURSE
RE-CYCLED
RE-DEEMED
RE-DEFINE
RE-DEPLOY
RE-DESIGN
RE-DOUBLE
RE-DUBBED
RE-EMERGE
RE-ENGAGE
RE-ENLIST
RE-FILLED
RE-FINERY
RE-FITTED

RE-FLEXED
RE-FORMAT
RE-FORMED
RE-FUELED
RE-FUNDED
RE-GAINED
RE-GROWTH
RE-HEARSE
RE-HEATED
RE-IGNITE
RE-INVENT
RE-ISSUED
RE-JOINED
RE-KINDLE
RE-LAPSED
RE-LAUNCH
RE-LAYING
RE-LEASED
RE-LIABLE
RE-LOADED
RE-LOCATE
RE-MAKING
RE-MARKED
RE-MASTER
RE-MEMBER
RE-MINDED
RE-MOVING
RE-OCCUPY
RE-OFFEND
RE-PAIRED
RE-PEALED
RE-PHRASE

RE-PLACED
RE-PORTER
RE-PRISED
RE-PUBLIC
RE-QUITED
RE-RECORD
RE-ROUTED
RE-SEALED
RE-SEARCH
RE-SECURE
RE-SIDING
RE-SISTER
RE-SOLVED
RE-SORTED
RE-STORED
RE-STRICT
RE-TAILED
RE-TIRING
RE-TRACED
RE-TURNED
RE-UNITED
RE-USABLE
RE-VALUED
RE-VERSED
RE-VIEWER
RE-VISING
RE-VISION
RE-WARDED
RE-WINDER
RE-WRITER

R

Some words beginning with RED-
Seven-letter words

RED-BACK	RED-EYES	RED-RAWN
RED-BIRD	RED-FISH	RED-ROOT
RED-CAPS	RED-FOOT	RED-TAIL
RED-COAT	RED-HEAD	RED-TOPS
RED-DENS	RED-LINE	RED-WING
RED-DING	RED-NECK	RED-WOOD
RED-DISH	RED-NESS	

Eight-letter words

RED-BELLY	RED-OLENT	RED-SHIRT
RED-BRICK	RED-SHANK	RED-START
RED-HORSE	RED-SHIFT	RED-WATER
RED-LINED	RED-SHIRE	

UNUSUAL LETTER COMBINATIONS

If you have an unusual combination of letters on your rack, or want to impress your opponent with an unusual word, a few words from World English can come in handy.

Australian words

RAZOO	imaginary coin
REGO	registration of a motor vehicle
RESTO	restored antique, vintage car, etc
ROO	kangaroo
ROUGHIE	something unfair, especially a trick

Canadian words

REDEYE	drink incorporating beer and tomato juice
RUBABOO	soup made by boiling pemmican
RUBBY	rubbing alcohol mixed with cheap wine for drinking

Hindi words

RAGGEE	cereal grass
RAITA	yoghurt-and-vegetable dish served with curry
RAJ	government
RAJAH	ruler or landlord
RAMTIL	African plant grown in India

R

RANI	queen or princess
RATHA	four-wheeled carriage drawn by horses or bullocks
ROTI	type of unleavened bread
RUPEE	standard monetary unit of India
RUPIAH	standard monetary unit of Indonesia
RYOT	peasant or tenant farmer

New Zealand words

RAHUI	Maori prohibition
RATA	myrtaceous forest tree
RAUPATU	seizure of land
RAURIKI	sow thistle

South African word

| ROOIKAT | lynx |

Urdu word

| RABI | crop harvested at the end of winter |

R

Essential info
Value: 1 point
Number in set: 4

The **S** is such a valuable letter for making longer plays, especially a seven-letter bonus word, that it ought not to be squandered in a short two-letter word play. The four twos that begin with S could assist in hooking your play onto an existing word: SH (a sound people make to request silence or quiet, 5 points) and SI, SO and ST (2 each). Quite a few three-letter words which use no vowels begin with S (although you will need a Y), including: SHY (9 points), SKY (10) and SPY (8). S also forms various three-letter words using X, one for each vowel except for U: SAX, SEX, SIX and SOX (10 points each).

Two-letter words beginning with S

SH	SO
SI	ST

Some three-letter words beginning with S

SAB	SEZ	SOL
SAE	SHA	SOM
SAI	SHH	SOT
SAL	SIB	SOU
SAM	SIC	SOV
SAN	SIF	SOX
SAR	SIK	SOY
SAX	SIM	SUQ
SAY	SKA	SUR
SAZ	SMA	SUS
SED	SNY	SWY
SEL	SOC	SYE
SEN	SOG	
SER	SOH	

HOOKS

Examples of S as end hooks are not included in this book due to their ease of use as the simple plural form of the word originally played. We recommend checking the Collins Scrabble Dictionary (or the dictionary you are using) if you are in any doubt.

Some front-hooks
Two letters to three

S-AB	S-EN	S-OH
S-AD	S-ER	S-OM
S-AE	S-ET	S-ON
S-AG	S-EX	S-OP
S-AI	S-HA	S-OS
S-AL	S-HE	S-OU
S-AM	S-IF	S-OW
S-AN	S-IN	S-OX
S-AR	S-IS	S-OY
S-AT	S-IT	S-PA
S-AW	S-KA	S-UM
S-AX	S-KI	S-UN
S-AY	S-KY	S-UP
S-EA	S-MA	S-UR
S-ED	S-NY	S-US
S-EE	S-OB	S-YE
S-EL	S-OD	

Three letters to four

S-ADO	S-ARK	S-CAT
S-AGA	S-ARS	S-CRY
S-AGE	S-ASH	S-CUD
S-AGO	S-ASS	S-CUM
S-AID	S-ATE	S-EAR
S-AIL	S-AVE	S-EAT
S-AIR	S-AWN	S-EEK
S-AKE	S-CAB	S-EEN
S-ALE	S-CAG	S-ELF
S-ALT	S-CAM	S-ELL
S-AND	S-CAN	S-END
S-ANE	S-CAR	S-HAH

S

S-HAM	S-LOP	S-PAY
S-HAW	S-LOT	S-PEC
S-HEW	S-LOW	S-PEW
S-HIN	S-LUG	S-PIN
S-HIP	S-LUM	S-PIT
S-HOD	S-LUR	S-POT
S-HOE	S-MOG	S-PRY
S-HOP	S-MUG	S-PUD
S-HOT	S-MUT	S-PUN
S-HOW	S-NAG	S-PUR
S-HUN	S-NAP	S-TAB
S-HUT	S-NIB	S-TAG
S-ICK	S-NIP	S-TAR
S-IDE	S-NOB	S-TAT
S-ILK	S-NOT	S-TAY
S-ILL	S-NOW	S-TEN
S-INK	S-OAK	S-TET
S-IRE	S-OAR	S-TEW
S-KID	S-ODA	S-TOP
S-KIN	S-OFT	S-TOT
S-KIP	S-OIL	S-TOW
S-KIT	S-OLD	S-TUB
S-LAB	S-OLE	S-TUN
S-LAM	S-OON	S-UMP
S-LAP	S-OOT	S-URE
S-LAT	S-ORE	S-WAB
S-LAY	S-ORT	S-WAG
S-LED	S-OUP	S-WAN
S-LEW	S-OUR	S-WAP
S-LID	S-OWN	S-WAT
S-LIP	S-PAM	S-WAY
S-LIT	S-PAN	S-WIG
S-LOB	S-PAR	S-WOP
S-LOG	S-PAT	

Four letters to five

S-ABLE	S-AVER	S-CAPE
S-AGER	S-AWED	S-CARE
S-ALLY	S-CAMP	S-CART
S-AUNT	S-CANT	S-COFF

S

S-COLD	S-HOOK	S-NAIL
S-CONE	S-HOOT	S-NIFF
S-COOP	S-HORN	S-OILY
S-COOT	S-HOVE	S-OWED
S-COPE	S-HUCK	S-PACE
S-CORE	S-HUNT	S-PAIN
S-CORN	S-HUSH	S-PARE
S-COWL	S-IDLE	S-PARK
S-CRAM	S-IRED	S-PATE
S-CRAN	S-KELP	S-PAWN
S-CREW	S-KILL	S-PEAK
S-CROW	S-KINK	S-PEAR
S-CUFF	S-LACK	S-PECK
S-CULL	S-LAIN	S-PELT
S-EDGE	S-LAKE	S-PEND
S-EVEN	S-LANG	S-PIKE
S-EVER	S-LASH	S-PILL
S-EWER	S-LATE	S-PINE
S-EXED	S-LEEK	S-PLAY
S-HACK	S-LEET	S-POKE
S-HAFT	S-LICE	S-POOL
S-HAKE	S-LICK	S-PORE
S-HALE	S-LIME	S-PORT
S-HALL	S-LOAN	S-POUT
S-HALT	S-LOPE	S-PRAY
S-HAME	S-LOTH	S-PROG
S-HANK	S-LUMP	S-QUAD
S-HARD	S-LUNG	S-QUID
S-HARE	S-LUNK	S-TACK
S-HARK	S-LUSH	S-TAKE
S-HARP	S-MACK	S-TALE
S-HAVE	S-MALL	S-TALK
S-HEAR	S-MART	S-TALL
S-HELL	S-MASH	S-TANK
S-HERE	S-MELL	S-TART
S-HILL	S-MELT	S-TATE
S-HIRE	S-MILE	S-TEAK
S-HOCK	S-MITE	S-TEAL
S-HOED	S-MOCK	S-TEAM
S-HONE	S-MOKE	S-TEED

S

S-TEEL	S-TOUT	S-WELL
S-TERN	S-TOWN	S-WELT
S-TICK	S-TRAP	S-WEPT
S-TIFF	S-TRAY	S-WILL
S-TILE	S-TRIP	S-WINE
S-TILL	S-TUCK	S-WING
S-TINT	S-URGE	S-WIPE
S-TOCK	S-WARM	S-WISH
S-TONE	S-WEAR	S-WORD
S-TOOK	S-WEEP	S-WORE
S-TOOL	S-WEER	

Five letters to six

S-ADDER	S-HANDY	S-MITER
S-ADDLE	S-HARPY	S-MOGGY
S-AILED	S-HAVEN	S-NAKED
S-ALLOW	S-HAVER	S-NAPPY
S-ALTER	S-HEATH	S-NATCH
S-AMPLE	S-HIRED	S-NIFFY
S-AVANT	S-HOVED	S-OAKED
S-AWING	S-HOVEL	S-OARED
S-CABBY	S-HOVER	S-OFTEN
S-CARED	S-ICKER	S-OILED
S-CATTY	S-ICKLE	S-OLDER
S-COPED	S-IDLED	S-OMBRE
S-CORED	S-INKER	S-OUGHT
S-CRAWL	S-INNER	S-OUPED
S-CREAM	S-KIDDY	S-OWING
S-CREED	S-KITED	S-PACED
S-CRIED	S-LAKED	S-PARED
S-CRIMP	S-LATER	S-PARKY
S-CURRY	S-LAYER	S-PARSE
S-CURVY	S-LEDGE	S-PAYED
S-EARED	S-LIGHT	S-PIKER
S-EATER	S-LIMED	S-PINED
S-EDUCE	S-LOPED	S-POKED
S-ELECT	S-LOWER	S-PORED
S-ENDER	S-LOWLY	S-POTTY
S-ENTRY	S-MIDGE	S-PRINT
S-EXIST	S-MILER	S-QUASH

S

S-TABLE	S-TRIKE	S-URGED
S-TARRY	S-TRIPE	S-WAGER
S-TENCH	S-TROLL	S-WAYED
S-TICKY	S-TROVE	S-WEEPY
S-TILED	S-TRUCK	S-WIPED
S-TITCH	S-TUBBY	S-WITCH
S-TONED	S-UNDER	S-WOOSH
S-TOWED	S-UNLIT	
S-TRAIN	S-UPPER	

Six letters to seven

S-ADDLED	S-HARING	S-LIMIER
S-AILING	S-HARKED	S-LINGER
S-ALLIED	S-HARPER	S-LINKED
S-AMPLER	S-HATTER	S-LITHER
S-CABBED	S-HAVING	S-LOGGED
S-CAMPER	S-HIPPED	S-LOPING
S-CANNED	S-HOOTER	S-LOWEST
S-CANTER	S-HOPPED	S-LUGGED
S-CARING	S-HOVING	S-LUMBER
S-CARPER	S-HUNTED	S-LUMPED
S-COFFER	S-HUSHED	S-LUSHED
S-COLDER	S-INKING	S-MASHED
S-COOPER	S-KIDDED	S-MATTER
S-COOTER	S-KILLED	S-MELLED
S-COPING	S-KIPPED	S-MELTED
S-CORING	S-KIPPER	S-MITTEN
S-CORNED	S-KITING	S-MOCKED
S-CORNER	S-LACKED	S-MOLDER
S-CRUMMY	S-LAKING	S-MOTHER
S-CUDDLE	S-LAMMED	S-MUGGER
S-CUFFED	S-LANDER	S-NAGGED
S-CUPPER	S-LAPPED	S-NAILED
S-CUTTLE	S-LASHED	S-NAPPED
S-EATING	S-LASHER	S-NIPPED
S-EDUCED	S-LAYING	S-OILING
S-ELFISH	S-LEDGED	S-PACING
S-ENDING	S-LEDGER	S-PANNER
S-HACKED	S-LENDER	S-PARING
S-HALLOW	S-LICKED	S-PARKED

S

S-PARSER	S-TACKED	S-TOPPED
S-PATTER	S-TAGGER	S-TUMBLE
S-PAWNED	S-TAKING	S-UNLESS
S-PAYING	S-TALKED	S-UNLIKE
S-PLAYED	S-TALKER	S-URGING
S-PONGED	S-TAMPER	S-WAGGER
S-POOLED	S-TEAMED	S-WALLOW
S-PORTED	S-TICKER	S-WARMED
S-POTTED	S-TICKLE	S-WAYING
S-PRAYED	S-TILTED	S-WEEPER
S-PURRED	S-TINGED	S-WIPING
S-TABBED	S-TINKER	S-WITHER
S-TABLED	S-TONING	S-WORDED

Seven letters to eight

S-ADDLING	S-HUSHING	S-PILLING
S-ALLOWED	S-HUTTING	S-PINNING
S-ALLYING	S-KIDDING	S-PITTING
S-CANNING	S-KILLING	S-PLATTER
S-CARLESS	S-KINLESS	S-PLAYING
S-CRAMMED	S-KIPPING	S-POOLING
S-CRAWLED	S-LACKING	S-PORTING
S-CREAMED	S-LAPPING	S-POTTING
S-CRUMPLE	S-LASHING	S-PRAYING
S-CRUNCHY	S-LIGHTLY	S-PRINTED
S-CUFFING	S-LOWDOWN	S-QUASHED
S-CURRIED	S-LOWNESS	S-TABBING
S-EDITION	S-LUGGING	S-TABLING
S-ELECTED	S-MASHING	S-TACKING
S-HACKING	S-MELTING	S-TAKEOUT
S-HACKLED	S-MOOCHED	S-TALKING
S-HARKING	S-MOULDER	S-TEAMING
S-HEARING	S-NAPPING	S-TICKING
S-HEATHER	S-NIPPING	S-TICKLED
S-HILLING	S-OFTENER	S-TILTING
S-HIPPING	S-PANNING	S-TOPPING
S-HOCKING	S-PARKING	S-TOWAWAY
S-HOOTING	S-PAWNING	S-TRAINED
S-HOPPING	S-PEAKING	S-TRAPPED
S-HUNTING	S-PILLAGE	S-TRESSED

S-TRIDENT	S-UNBAKED	S-WEEPING
S-TRIPPED	S-UNBLOCK	S-WILLING
S-TRUMPET	S-WADDLED	S-WINGING
S-TUMBLED	S-WARMING	S-WORDING

Some end-hooks
Two letters to three

AA-S	GO-S	OH-S
AB-S	GU-S	OM-S
AD-S	HA-S	ON-S
AG-S	HE-S	OO-S
AH-S	HI-S	OP-S
AI-S	HO-S	OR-S
AL-S	ID-S	OU-S
AR-S	IF-S	OY-S
AS-S	IN-S	PA-S
AY-S	IO-S	PE-S
BA-S	IT-S	PI-S
BE-S	KA-S	PO-S
BI-S	KI-S	QI-S
BO-S	KO-S	RE-S
BY-S	LA-S	SI-S
DA-S	LI-S	SO-S
DI-S	LO-S	TA-S
DPO-S	MA-S	TE-S
EA-S	ME-S	TI-S
ED-S	MI-S	UG-S
EF-S	MI-S	UN-S
EH-S	MO-S	UP-S
EL-S	MU-S	UT-S
EM-S	NA-S	WO-S
EN-S	NO-S	XI-S
ER-S	NU-S	YE-S
ES-S	NY-S	YO-S
FA-S	OB-S	YU-S
FE-S	OD-S	ZA-S
GI-S	OE-S	ZO-S

S

BLOCKERS

It is useful to know which words are blockers and can't therefore be extended before or after. You may want to play a blocker that your opponent can't extend, or you may want to avoid playing a blocker because you want to keep the board open.

Some three-letter blockers beginning with S

SAE	SHH	SMA
SAZ	SIX	SOX
SEZ	SLY	SWY

Some four-letter blockers beginning with S

SAGY	SEWN	SOON
SASH	SEXY	SPED
SAWN	SHMO	SPRY
SCRY	SHOD	SUCH
SECO	SIZY	SUNG
SEEN	SOHO	SUSS
SESH	SOME	SWUM

Some five-letter blockers beginning with S (except words ending in '-ED', '-J', '-S', '-X', '-Y' or '-Z')

SAFER	SLIPT	STOOD
SANER	SLUNG	STUNG
SHALT	SLUNK	STUNK
SHAWN	SLYER	SUPRA
SHERE	SMASH	SWANG
SHEWN	SMOTE	SWAPT
SHONE	SMUSH	SWEPT
SHORN	SNUCK	SWOPT
SHOWN	SOCKO	SWORE
SHUSH	SORBO	SWORN
SINCE	SORER	SWUNG
SITKA	SPAKE	
SKINT	SPENT	
SLAIN	STAID	
SLASH	STASH	
SLEPT	STEPT	

S

Some six-letter blockers ending with S (except words ending in '-ED', '-J', '-S', '-X', '-Y' or '-Z')

SADDER	SHAZAM	SORDID
SAFEST	SHEESH	SOREST
SAFING	SHOULD	SOUGHT
SAGEST	SHRANK	SOURER
SAGIER	SHREWD	SPEECH
SAIRER	SHRUNK	SPLOSH
SAMIER	SHYEST	SPOILT
SANCTA	SHYING	SPOKEN
SANEST	SHYISH	SPRUNG
SANING	SICKER	SPRYER
SAPFUL	SINFUL	STALER
SATING	SIRING	STINKO
SAYEST	SITING	STITCH
SCOOCH	SKOOSH	STOLEN
SCOOSH	SKYING	STREWN
SCORCH	SKYLIT	STRODE
SCOTCH	SLEAZO	STRONG
SEAMAN	SLIEST	STRUCK
SEAMEN	SLOWER	STRUNG
SEARCH	SLYEST	SUABLE
SEARER	SLYISH	SUAVER
SEDENT	SMOOSH	SUBSEA
SELDOM	SNIDER	SUNKEN
SEMPER	SOAKEN	SUNLIT
SEXIER	SOBFUL	SUPERB
SHAKEN	SOFTER	SUREST
SHAPEN	SOLEMN	SWOOSH
SHAVEN	SOLING	

S

•••

Handy Hint: saving the S for last

If you can earn 10 points more by playing the S then do so, otherwise consider holding it back as an investment for better scores later in the game. More experienced players tend to save S tiles instead of playing them immediately. This is because S is easy to play at the end of a six-letter word, thus making it much easier to score a 50-point bonus word by using all your tiles in one go.

BONUS WORDS

Bonus words on your rack can be hard to spot, especially for the less experienced player. One way to help find them is by using prefixes and suffixes.

Many larger words include a common prefix or suffix – remembering these and using them where you can is a good way to discover any longer words on your rack, including any potential bonus words. The key prefixes to remember beginning with S are SEA-, SUB- and SUN- and the key suffixes are -SET, -SHIP, -SKIN, -SMAN and -SOME.

Some words beginning with SEA-

Seven-letter words

SEA-BANK	SEA-LANT	SEA-SICK
SEA-BEDS	SEA-LIFT	SEA-SIDE
SEA-BIRD	SEA-LINE	SEA-SING
SEA-DOGS	SEA-LING	SEA-SONS
SEA-FOLK	SEA-MAID	SEA-TING
SEA-FOOD	SEA-MING	SEA-WALL
SEA-FOWL	SEA-PORT	SEA-WARD
SEA-GULL	SEA-REST	SEA-WEED
SEA-HAWK	SEA-RING	SEA-ZING

Eight-letter words

SEA-BEACH	SEA-FRONT	SEA-SCAPE
SEA-BOARD	SEA-GOING	SEA-SCOUT
SEA-BORNE	SEA-HORSE	SEA-SHELL
SEA-COAST	SEA-HOUND	SEA-SHORE
SEA-CRAFT	SEA-MANLY	SEA-SPEAK
SEA-DROME	SEA-MOUNT	SEA-TRAIN
SEA-FARER	SEA-PLANE	SEA-TROUT
SEA-FLOOR	SEA-QUAKE	SEA-WATER

Some words beginning with SUB-

Seven-letter words

SUB-AQUA	SUB-CELL	SUB-DUES
SUB-ARID	SUB-CODE	SUB-EDIT
SUB-ATOM	SUB-CULT	SUB-FILE
SUB-BASS	SUB-DUCE	SUB-ITEM
SUB-BING	SUB-DUED	SUB-JOIN

SUB-LETS
SUB-LIME
SUB-MISS
SUB-PLOT
SUB-RENT
SUB-RULE
SUB-SECT

SUB-SETS
SUB-SIDE
SUB-SIST
SUB-SOIL
SUB-TASK
SUB-TEND
SUB-TEXT

SUB-TONE
SUB-TYPE
SUB-UNIT
SUB-URBS
SUB-VERT
SUB-WAYS
SUB-ZERO

Eight-letter words

SUB-ADULT
SUB-AGENT
SUB-BASIN
SUB-CHORD
SUB-CLAIM
SUB-CLASS
SUB-DUING
SUB-DURAL
SUB-ENTRY
SUB-EQUAL
SUB-FLOOR
SUB-GENRE
SUB-GRADE
SUB-GROUP

SUB-HUMAN
SUB-INDEX
SUB-LEASE
SUB-LEVEL
SUB-LIMED
SUB-MERGE
SUB-POLAR
SUB-SCALE
SUB-SENSE
SUB-SERVE
SUB-SIDED
SUB-SIDER
SUB-SKILL
SUB-SONIC

SUB-SPACE
SUB-STAGE
SUB-STATE
SUB-TITLE
SUB-TOPIC
SUB-TOTAL
SUB-TRACT
SUB-URBAN
SUB-URBIA
SUB-VERSE
SUB-WAYED
SUB-WORLD

Some words beginning with SUN-
Seven-letter words

SUN-BACK
SUN-BAKE
SUN-BEAM
SUN-BEDS
SUN-BELT
SUN-BURN
SUN-DIAL
SUN-DOWN

SUN-FISH
SUN-HATS
SUN-LAMP
SUN-LESS
SUN-NIES
SUN-RAYS
SUN-RISE
SUN-ROOF

SUN-SETS
SUN-SPOT
SUN-TANS
SUN-TRAP
SUN-WARD
SUN-WISE

S

Eight-letter words

SUN-BAKED
SUN-BATHE
SUN-BERRY
SUN-BLOCK
SUN-BURNT

SUN-BURST
SUN-DERED
SUN-DRESS
SUN-DRILY
SUN-GLASS

SUN-LIGHT
SUN-PROOF
SUN-SHADE
SUN-SHINE
SUN-SHINY

Some words ending with -SET

Seven-letter words

BACK-SET	HAND-SET	MOON-SET
BONE-SET	HARD-SET	OVER-SET
BRAS-SET	HEAD-SET	TOOL-SET
CHIP-SET	LOCK-SET	TWIN-SET
FILM-SET	MIND-SET	TYPE-SET

Eight-letter words

EARTH-SET	PHOTO-SET	THICK-SET
HEAVY-SET	QUICK-SET	THORN-SET
MARMO-SET	SOMER-SET	UNDER-SET

Some words ending with -SHIP

Seven-letter words

AIR-SHIP	KIN-SHIP	SON-SHIP
END-SHIP	MID-SHIP	WAR-SHIP
GOD-SHIP	PAL-SHIP	WOR-SHIP
GUN-SHIP	PRE-SHIP	

Eight-letter words

AMID-SHIP	HARD-SHIP	POET-SHIP
BARD-SHIP	HEAD-SHIP	POPE-SHIP
CLAN-SHIP	HEIR-SHIP	SERF-SHIP
DEAN-SHIP	HERO-SHIP	STAR-SHIP
DUKE-SHIP	KING-SHIP	TANK-SHIP
EARL-SHIP	LADY-SHIP	TOWN-SHIP
FIRE-SHIP	LONG-SHIP	TWIN-SHIP
FLAG-SHIP	LORD-SHIP	WARD-SHIP
FORE-SHIP	MATE-SHIP	

S

Some words ending with -SKIN

Seven-letter words

CAT-SKIN	DOG-SKIN	OIL-SKIN
COW-SKIN	FOX-SKIN	PIG-SKIN
DOE-SKIN	KID-SKIN	

Eight-letter words

BEAR-SKIN	FISH-SKIN	WINE-SKIN
BUCK-SKIN	GOAT-SKIN	WOLF-SKIN
CALF-SKIN	LAMB-SKIN	WOOL-SKIN
CAPE-SKIN	MOLE-SKIN	
DEER-SKIN	SEAL-SKIN	

Some words ending with -SMAN
Seven-letter words

ART-SMAN
BAT-SMAN
DAY-SMAN
KIN-SMAN
LEN-SMAN

MAG-SMAN
MES-SMAN
MOB-SMAN
NEW-SMAN
OAR-SMAN

ODD-SMAN
PAS-SMAN
ROD-SMAN
TAP-SMAN
TOP-SMAN

Eight-letter words

BAIL-SMAN
BAND-SMAN
BANK-SMAN
BLUE-SMAN
BOAT-SMAN
BOND-SMAN
CHES-SMAN
CLAN-SMAN
CLAS-SMAN
CORP-SMAN
DOOM-SMAN
DOOR-SMAN
GAME-SMAN

GANG-SMAN
GILD-SMAN
GLAS-SMAN
GOWN-SMAN
HEAD-SMAN
HELM-SMAN
HERD-SMAN
HUNT-SMAN
ISLE-SMAN
LAND-SMAN
LINE-SMAN
LINK-SMAN
LOCK-SMAN

MARK-SMAN
PRES-SMAN
PUNT-SMAN
RAFT-SMAN
RAMP-SMAN
ROAD-SMAN
SALE-SMAN
SIDE-SMAN
SWAG-SMAN
TALI-SMAN
TIDE-SMAN
TOWN-SMAN
WOOD-SMAN

Some words ending with -SOME
Seven-letter words

AWE-SOME
FUL-SOME
IRK-SOME
LIS-SOME

NOI-SOME
TOY-SOME
TRI-SOME
TWO-SOME

WAG-SOME
WIN-SOME
WOE-SOME

S

Eight-letter words

BORE-SOME
DARK-SOME
DOLE-SOME
DUEL-SOME
FEAR-SOME
FOUR-SOME
FRET-SOME
GLAD-SOME
GLEE-SOME

GRUE-SOME
HAND-SOME
JOKE-SOME
LARK-SOME
LONE-SOME
LONG-SOME
LOTH-SOME
LOVE-SOME
MURK-SOME

PLAY-SOME
PYRO-SOME
RIBO-SOME
ROOM-SOME
TEDI-SOME
TIRE-SOME
TOIL-SOME
WORK-SOME

UNUSUAL LETTER COMBINATIONS

If you have an unusual combination of letters on your rack, or want to impress your opponent with an unusual word, a few words from World English can come in handy.

Australian words

SANGER	sandwich
SCOZZA	rowdy person
SCUNGY	miserable, sordid or dirty person
SHARPIE	a member of a teenage group with short hair and distinctive clothes
SHERANG	boss
SHYPOO	liquor of poor quality
SITELLA	small black-and-white bird
SKEG	rear fin on the underside of a surfboard
SKITE	boast
SMOKO	cigarette break
SPRUIK	speak in public
SWAGMAN	vagrant worker
SWY	a gambling game

Canadian words

SKOOKUM	strong or brave
SNYE	side channel of a river
SPLAKE	hybrid trout bred by Canadian zoologists
SWILER	seal hunter

Hindi words

SAMBAR	deer with three-tined antlers
SAMITI	polictical association
SAMOSA	triangular pastry containing spiced vegetables or meat
SARANGI	stringed instrument played with a bow
SARDAR	Sikh title
SARI	traditional dress of Indian women
SAROD	Indian stringed instrument
SWAMI	title for a Hindu saint or religious teacher

New Zealand word

SHEEPO	person who brings sheep to the catching pen for shearing

S

South African words

SCAMTO	argot of South African Blacks
SKOLLY	hooligan
SNOEK	edible marine fish
SPEK	bacon, fat or fatty pork
STEEN	variety of white grape
STOKVEL	savings pool or syndicate

Urdu words

SAHIB	title placed after a man's name
SARPANCH	head of a village council
SHALWAR	loose-fitting trousers
SHIKAR	hunting
SICE	servant who looks after horses

S

Essential info
Value: 1 point
Number in set: 6

T is one of the most common consonants in Scrabble. Four two-letter words begin with T (all scoring 2 points), but they are easy to remember as there is one for every vowel except U. Various useful three-letter words begin with T. Some that you may not know include TAI (Chinese system of callisthenics, 3 points), TAO (in Confucian philosophy, the correct course of action, 3 points) and TEF (African grass grown for its grain, 6 points). T is one of the letters of the RETAIN set and is therefore a good letter to keep if trying to get a bonus word.

Two-letter words beginning with T

TA	TI
TE	TO

Some three-letter words beginning with T

TAD	TED	TIX
TAE	TEE	TOC
TAI	TEF	TOD
TAJ	TEG	TOG
TAK	TEL	TOM
TAM	TET	TOR
TAO	TEW	TUM
TAT	TEX	TUN
TAU	THO	TUP
TAV	TIC	TUT
TAW	TID	TUX
TAY	TIG	TWP
TEC	TIL	TYE

HOOKS

Hooking requires a subtle change in a player's thought process, in that they must look at words already on the board without becoming distracted by their pronunciation. Simple hooking solutions may be overlooked by a player, but things become easier with T as it is one of the most versatile letters when it comes to combining words.

When it comes to end-hooking, players often concentrate on S, as it can be easy to convert a singular word to a plural. However, T can also be highly effective and by learning a few of the hooks below, many more options present themselves to the player.

Handy Hint: Consonantitis

If you are stuck with very few vowels in your rack but you also have a letter T, it is useful to remember that T can form several words using only consonants. These are TSK (a sound uttered in disapproval, 7 points), TWP (a Welsh word meaning stupid, 8 points), TYG (a cup with more than one handle, 7 points), NTH (of an unspecified number), 6 points, and PHT (expression of irritation), 8 points.

Some front-hooks

Two letters to three

T-AB	T-ED	T-OE
T-AD	T-EE	T-OM
T-AE	T-EF	T-ON
T-AG	T-EL	T-OO
T-AI	T-EN	T-OP
T-AM	T-ES	T-OR
T-AN	T-ET	T-OW
T-AP	T-EX	T-OY
T-AR	T-HE	T-UG
T-AS	T-HO	T-UM
T-AT	T-ID	T-UN
T-AW	T-IN	T-UP
T-AX	T-IS	T-UT
T-AY	T-IT	T-WO
T-EA	T-OD	T-YE

Three letters to four

T-ABS	T-AIL	T-ALE
T-ACT	T-AKE	T-ALL

T-APE	T-HEY	T-OWN
T-ARE	T-HIN	T-RAD
T-ART	T-HIS	T-RAM
T-ASK	T-HUG	T-RAP
T-ATE	T-ICK	T-RAY
T-EAR	T-IDE	T-RIM
T-EAT	T-ILL	T-RIP
T-ELL	T-IRE	T-ROD
T-END	T-OFF	T-ROT
T-EST	T-OIL	T-RUE
T-HAN	T-OLD	T-URN
T-HAT	T-ONE	T-WEE
T-HAW	T-OOT	T-WIG
T-HEM	T-OUR	T-WIN
T-HEN	T-OUT	T-WIT

Four letters to five

T-ABLE	T-HORN	T-REND
T-ACHE	T-HOSE	T-RIAL
T-ALKY	T-HUMP	T-RICK
T-ALLY	T-IMID	T-RIPS
T-APED	T-IRED	T-ROLL
T-APER	T-IRES	T-ROOP
T-AUNT	T-ITCH	T-ROUT
T-AWNY	T-OAST	T-RUCK
T-AXED	T-ONER	T-RUER
T-AXES	T-OUCH	T-RULY
T-EACH	T-OWED	T-RUST
T-EASE	T-OWER	T-RUTH
T-EDDY	T-RACE	T-WANG
T-EMPT	T-RACK	T-WEAK
T-EPEE	T-RADE	T-WEED
T-HANK	T-RAIL	T-WEET
T-HEFT	T-RAIN	T-WICE
T-HEIR	T-RAIT	T-WINE
T-HERE	T-RAMP	T-WINY
T-HICK	T-RASH	T-WIST
T-HIGH	T-READ	
T-HING	T-REES	

Five letters to six

T-ABBED	T-ERROR	T-OUTER
T-ABLED	T-ESTER	T-OWING
T-ABLET	T-ETHER	T-RACED
T-AILED	T-HANKS	T-RACER
T-ANGLE	T-HATCH	T-RACES
T-ANNOY	T-HAWED	T-RANCE
T-APING	T-HENCE	T-RAVEL
T-ASKED	T-HORNY	T-RIFLE
T-ASTER	T-HOUGH	T-ROUGH
T-AUGHT	T-ICKLE	T-ROWEL
T-AXING	T-INGLE	T-RUSTY
T-AXMAN	T-INNER	T-UMBLE
T-EARED	T-IRADE	T-URBAN
T-EASED	T-IRING	T-URNED
T-EASER	T-ISSUE	T-WEEDY
T-EASES	T-OASTS	T-WIGGY
T-ENDED	T-OILED	T-WINGE
T-ENDER	T-OTTER	T-WIRED
T-ENURE	T-OUTED	T-WITCH

Six letters to seven

T-ABLING	T-HEREIN	T-RIGGER
T-AILING	T-HUMPED	T-RILLED
T-ALLIED	T-INNING	T-RIMMED
T-ANGLER	T-ISSUED	T-RIPPED
T-ASKING	T-OILING	T-ROTTER
T-EARFUL	T-OUTING	T-ROUBLE
T-EASING	T-RACING	T-RUCKED
T-EDDIES	T-RACKED	T-RUFFLE
T-ENABLE	T-RAILER	T-RUSTED
T-ENDING	T-RAINED	T-UNABLE
T-ENFOLD	T-RAMPED	T-WEAKER
T-ENURED	T-RAPPER	T-WIGGED
T-ESTATE	T-RASHES	T-WINGED
T-HANKER	T-RAVELS	T-WINKLE
T-HAWING	T-REASON	T-WITCHY
T-HEREBY	T-RIFLES	T-WITTER

T

Seven letters to eight

T-ALLOWED	T-ISSUING	T-RIMMING
T-ALLYING	T-RACKING	T-RIPPING
T-ANGLING	T-RAILING	T-ROTTING
T-ANNOYED	T-RAINING	T-RUCKING
T-APELIKE	T-RAMMING	T-RUSTING
T-EARDROP	T-RAMPING	T-WEEDIER
T-ENFOLDS	T-RAPPING	T-WIGLESS
T-ENTERED	T-RASHING	T-WINGING
T-HATCHED	T-RAVELER	T-WINKLED
T-HICKIES	T-READING	T-WINNING
T-HUMPING	T-RIFLING	T-WITCHES

Some end-hooks

Two letters to three

AI-T	HA-T	OP-T
AL-T	HE-T	OR-T
AN-T	HI-T	OU-T
AR-T	HO-T	OW-T
AT-T	JO-T	PA-T
BA-T	KA-T	PE-T
BE-T	KI-T	PI-T
BI-T	LA-T	PO-T
BO-T	LI-T	RE-T
DI-T	LO-T	SI-T
DO-T	MA-T	SO-T
EA-T	ME-T	TA-T
EF-T	MO-T	TE-T
EL-T	MU-T	TI-T
ES-T	NA-T	TO-T
FA-T	NE-T	WE-T
FE-T	NO-T	WO-T
GI-T	NU-T	YE-T
GO-T	OF-T	
GU-T	OO-T	

Three letters to four

BEE-T	BOO-T	CEL-T
BEN-T	CAN-T	CHA-T
BOA-T	CAR-T	CHI-T

COL-T	KEP-T	RIF-T
COO-T	LAS-T	ROO-T
COS-T	LIN-T	RUN-T
CUR-T	LIS-T	SAL-T
DEB-T	LOS-T	SEA-T
DEF-T	LOU-T	SEN-T
DEN-T	MAL-T	SKI-T
DIE-T	MAS-T	SPA-T
DOL-T	MEL-T	SUI-T
DUE-T	MIS-T	TAR-T
EAS-T	MOA-T	TAU-T
FAS-T	MOO-T	TEN-T
FEE-T	MOS-T	TES-T
FON-T	MUS-T	TIN-T
FOR-T	NEW-T	TOO-T
GEN-T	PAC-T	UNI-T
GIF-T	PAR-T	VAS-T
GIS-T	PAS-T	VOL-T
GOA-T	PES-T	WAI-T
GUS-T	PIN-T	WAN-T
HIN-T	POS-T	WAT-T
HOO-T	RAN-T	WEN-T
HUN-T	RAP-T	WHA-T
JOL-T	REN-T	WIS-T
JUS-T	RES-T	ZOO-T

Four letters to five

AVER-T	FACE-T	OVER-T
BEAU-T	FILE-T	PLAN-T
BLUR-T	FIRS-T	PLEA-T
BOAS-T	FLEE-T	ROOS-T
BOOS-T	GRAN-T	SHIR-T
BURN-T	GUES-T	SHOO-T
CADE-T	HEAR-T	SIGH-T
CHAR-T	ISLE-T	SPUR-T
CLEF-T	JOIN-T	STAR-T
COME-T	LEAN-T	STUN-T
COVE-T	LEAP-T	TEMP-T
DEAL-T	MEAN-T	TWEE-T
EVEN-T	NIGH-T	VALE-T

T

Five letters to six

BARES-T	FORES-T	PALES-T
BASAL-T	FORGE-T	PLANE-T
BASES-T	FORGO-T	PURES-T
BLUES-T	GADGE-T	RABBI-T
BONNE-T	GAMES-T	RARES-T
BOUGH-T	HONES-T	RIPES-T
BUDGE-T	IDLES-T	SAFES-T
CACHE-T	LANCE-T	SAGES-T
CLOSE-T	LAXES-T	SHIES-T
COVER-T	LEARN-T	SONNE-T
DIVER-T	LOCUS-T	SORES-T
DRIES-T	MIDGE-T	SPOIL-T
FILLE-T	MODES-T	TURBO-T
FINES-T	MUTES-T	WEIGH-T

Six letters to seven

ARCHES-T	DEARES-T	RICHES-T
ARTIES-T	EASIES-T	ROSIES-T
BRAVES-T	FALSES-T	SINGLE-T
BROUGH-T	GRAVES-T	STALES-T
BUSIES-T	HOLIES-T	TENSES-T
CLOSES-T	INANES-T	THOUGH-T
CONSUL-T	LAZIES-T	TIDIES-T
COSIES-T	LUSHES-T	TINIES-T
COUPLE-T	NAIVES-T	TRITES-T
COZIES-T	NOBLES-T	UGLIES-T
CRUDES-T	PERCEN-T	WARRAN-T
CURRAN-T	POSIES-T	WAVIES-T

T Seven letters to eight

ANGRIES-T	DIVINES-T	GENTLES-T
BAGGIES-T	DIZZIES-T	HARDIES-T
BLONDES-T	EARLIES-T	HEAVIES-T
BULLIES-T	EMPTIES-T	INTERNE-T
CHOICES-T	FEEBLES-T	JOLLIES-T
CONTRAS-T	FLAKIES-T	LITTLES-T
CRAZIES-T	FLASHES-T	LUCKIES-T
CROSSES-T	FRESHES-T	MATURES-T
DIPLOMA-T	FUNNIES-T	MUDDIES-T

NASTIES-T	SAVAGES-T	SUNBURN-T
READIES-T	SECURES-T	SUNNIES-T
REDREAM-T	SHIPMEN-T	TALKIES-T
REGIMEN-T	SILLIES-T	TELETEX-T
REMOTES-T	SIMPLES-T	TINNIES-T
ROOMIES-T	SQUARES-T	UNLEARN-T
ROWDIES-T	STABLES-T	WEARIES-T

BLOCKERS

It is useful to know which words are blockers and can't therefore be extended before or after. You may want to play a blocker that your opponent can't extend, or you may want to avoid playing a blocker because you want to keep the board open.

Some three-letter blockers beginning with T

TAJ	TIX	TWP
THY	TUX	

Some four-letter blockers beginning with T

THAT	THUS	TOED
THEY	TIDY	TOLD
THIS	TINY	TORN

Some five-letter blockers beginning with T (except words ending in '-ED', '-J', '-S', '-X', '-Y' or '-Z')

TACIT	THIEF	TIDAL
TAKEN	THINE	TIMID
TEACH	THOSE	TRUER

Some six-letter blockers beginning with T (except words ending in '-ED', '-J', '-S', '-X', '-Y' or '-Z')

TALLER	TENSER	TINIER
TAMEST	TERGAL	TINMAN
TAPING	THRASH	TOMATO
TAUGHT	THRESH	TRENCH
TAXMAN	THRICE	TRUEST
TAXMEN	THROWN	

T

BONUS WORDS

Bonus words on your rack can be hard to spot, especially for the less experienced player. One way to help find them is by using prefixes and suffixes.

Many larger words include a common prefix or suffix – remembering these and using them where you can is a good way to discover any longer words on your rack, including any potential bonus words. The key prefix to remember beginning with T is TRI- and the key suffixes are -TION and -TIME.

Some words beginning with TRI-

Seven-letter words

TRI-ABLE	TRI-FLED	TRI-PLED
TRI-ACID	TRI-FOLD	TRI-PODS
TRI-AGED	TRI-FORM	TRI-PSIS
TRI-AGES	TRI-GAMY	TRI-SECT
TRI-ARCH	TRI-GONS	TRI-SEME
TRI-AXON	TRI-GRAM	TRI-SHAW
TRI-BADE	TRI-JETS	TRI-SOME
TRI-BLET	TRI-LITH	TRI-SOMY
TRI-BUTE	TRI-LOBE	TRI-TEST
TRI-CARS	TRI-LOGY	TRI-TIDE
TRI-CEPS	TRI-NARY	TRI-TONE
TRI-CLAD	TRI-ODES	TRI-TONS
TRI-CORN	TRI-ONES	TRI-UMPH
TRI-COTS	TRI-OSES	TRI-VETS
TRI-DARN	TRI-OXID	TRI-VIAL
TRI-DENT	TRI-PACK	TRI-ZONE
TRI-DUAN	TRI-PART	
TRI-ENES	TRI-PIER	

Eight-letter words

TRI-ACIDS	TRI-AZINE	TRI-BUTES
TRI-AGING	TRI-AZOLE	TRI-CHINA
TRI-ALIST	TRI-BALLY	TRI-CHORD
TRI-ANGLE	TRI-BASIC	TRI-CLADS
TRI-AXIAL	TRI-BLETS	TRI-COLOR
TRI-AXONS	TRI-BRACH	TRI-CORNS

TRI-CYCLE	TRI-MOTOR	TRI-POSES
TRI-DARNS	TRI-NODAL	TRI-SECTS
TRI-DENTS	TRI-OLEIN	TRI-SEMES
TRI-ETHYL	TRI-OXIDE	TRI-SHAWS
TRI-FLING	TRI-OXIDS	TRI-STATE
TRI-FOCAL	TRI-PACKS	TRI-STICH
TRI-GLYPH	TRI-PEDAL	TRI-THING
TRI-GRAMS	TRI-PHASE	TRI-TICAL
TRI-GRAPH	TRI-PHONE	TRI-TIDES
TRI-LEMMA	TRI-PLANE	TRI-TONES
TRI-LITHS	TRI-PLIED	TRI-UNITY
TRI-LOBED	TRI-PLIES	TRI-VALVE
TRI-LOBES	TRI-PLING	TRI-ZONAL
TRI-METER	TRI-PODAL	TRI-ZONES
TRI-MORPH	TRI-POLIS	

Some words ending with -TIME
Seven-letter words

AIR-TIME	DAY-TIME	RAG-TIME
ANY-TIME	LAY-TIME	SEP-TIME
BED-TIME	MIS-TIME	TEA-TIME
BIG-TIME	ONE-TIME	WAR-TIME
CEN-TIME	PAS-TIME	

Eight-letter words

CHOW-TIME	LONG-TIME	REAL-TIME
DOWN-TIME	MARI-TIME	SEED-TIME
FLEX-TIME	MEAL-TIME	SHOW-TIME
FORE-TIME	MEAN-TIME	SOME-TIME
GOOD-TIME	NOON-TIME	TERM-TIME
HALF-TIME	OVER-TIME	XENO-TIME
LIFE-TIME	PLAY-TIME	ZONE-TIME

Some words ending with -TION
Seven-letter words

ALA-TION	CAN-TION	DIC-TION
AMA-TION	CAP-TION	EDI-TION
AMO-TION	CAU-TION	ELA-TION
AUC-TION	COC-TION	ELU-TION
BAS-TION	COI-TION	EMO-TION

T

EMP-TION	MIX-TION	SEC-TION
ENA-TION	ORA-TION	STA-TION
FAC-TION	OVA-TION	SUC-TION
FIC-TION	PAC-TION	TAC-TION
LEC-TION	POR-TION	TUI-TION
MEN-TION	REC-TION	UNC-TION
MIC-TION	RUC-TION	UNI-TION

Eight-letter words

ABLA-TION	EJEC-TION	LEGA-TION
ABLU-TION	ELEC-TION	LENI-TION
ABOR-TION	EMIC-TION	LIBA-TION
ADAP-TION	ENAC-TION	LIGA-TION
ADDI-TION	EQUA-TION	LIMA-TION
ADNA-TION	EREC-TION	LOBA-TION
ADOP-TION	ERUP-TION	LOCA-TION
AERA-TION	EVEC-TION	LOCU-TION
AGNA-TION	EVIC-TION	LUNA-TION
AMBI-TION	EXAC-TION	LUXA-TION
AUDI-TION	EXER-TION	MONI-TION
AVIA-TION	FETA-TION	MUNI-TION
BIBA-TION	FIXA-TION	MUTA-TION
CIBA-TION	FLEC-TION	NATA-TION
CITA-TION	FRAC-TION	NEGA-TION
COAC-TION	FRIC-TION	NIDA-TION
CONA-TION	FRUI-TION	NIVA-TION
COOP-TION	FUNC-TION	NODA-TION
CREA-TION	GELA-TION	NOLI-TION
DELA-TION	GUMP-TION	NOTA-TION
DELE-TION	HALA-TION	NOVA-TION
DEMO-TION	HIMA-TION	NUTA-TION
DERA-TION	IDEA-TION	OBLA-TION
DEVO-TION	IGNI-TION	PACA-TION
DILA-TION	ILLA-TION	PETI-TION
DILU-TION	INAC-TION	POSI-TION
DONA-TION	INUS-TION	POTA-TION
DOTA-TION	IODA-TION	PUNI-TION
DURA-TION	JOBA-TION	PUPA-TION
EDUC-TION	JUNC-TION	QUES-TION
EGES-TION	LAVA-TION	REAC-TION

T

RELA-TION	SOLA-TION	VACA-TION
REMO-TION	SOLU-TION	VENA-TION
ROGA-TION	SORP-TION	VEXA-TION
ROTA-TION	STIC-TION	VOCA-TION
SANC-TION	SUDA-TION	VOLI-TION
SCON-TION	SWAP-TION	VOLU-TION
SEDA-TION	TAXA-TION	ZONA-TION
SEDI-TION	TRAC-TION	

UNUSUAL LETTER COMBINATIONS

If you have an unusual combination of letters on your rack, or want to impress your opponent with an unusual word, a few words from World English can come in handy.

Australian words

TOOSHIE	angry or upset
TRIELLA	three horse races nominated for a bet
TROPPO	mentally affected by a tropical climate
TRUCKIE	truck driver
TRUGO	game similar to croquet
TUAN	flying phalanger
TUART	type of eucalyptus tree

Canadian words

TILLICUM	friend
TOONIE	Canadian two-dollar coin
TULLIBEE	whitefish found in the Great Lakes
TUPEK	Inuit tent of animal skins

Hindi words

TABLA	pair of drums whose pitches can be varied
THALI	meal consisting of several small dishes
TIL	sesame
TOLA	unit of weight
TONGA	light two-wheeled vehicle
TOPEE	pith helmet

New Zealand words

TAIAHA	ceremonial fighting staff
TAIHOA	hold on!
TAKAHE	rare flightless bird

T

TANGI	Maori funeral ceremony
TANIWHA	legendary monster
TAONGA	treasure
TAPU	sacred or forbidden
TARSEAL	bitumen surface of a road
TAUIWI	non-Maori people of New Zealand
TIKANGA	Maori customs
TOETOE	type of tall grass
TOITOI	type of tall grass
TWINK	white correction fluid

Urdu words

TAHSIL	administrative division
TALOOKA	subdivision of a district
TAMASHA	show or entertainment
TANDOORI	method of cooking on a spit in a clay oven

T

Essential info
Value: 1 point
Number in set: 4

U can be a difficult tile to play effectively. In fact, there are no particularly high-scoring short words which start with U. In order to make the best of your tiles, some handy words to remember are UH (5 points), UM (4 points), UP (4 points) and UG (3 points). Also, when aiming for short words, you can save yourself some time by remembering that there are no valid three-letter words beginning with U which use Q, X or Z.

Two-letter words beginning with U

UG	UN	US
UH	UP	UT
UM	UR	

Some three-letter words beginning with U

UDO	UNI	URP
UGH	UPO	UTA
UMM	URB	UTE
UMP	URD	UTU
UMU	URE	

HOOKS

Hooking requires a subtle change in a player's thought process, in that they must look at words already on the board without becoming distracted by their pronunciation.

Some front-hooks
Two letters to three

U-DO	U-PO	U-TE
U-MM	U-RE	
U-MU	U-TA	

Three letters to four

U-DAL	U-NIS	U-SER
U-DON	U-NIT	U-TIS
U-LES	U-PAS	U-VAE
U-LEX	U-SED	U-VAS

Four letters to five

U-LAMA	U-RASE	U-RITE
U-NARY	U-RATE	U-SAGE
U-NITE	U-REAL	U-SING
U-PEND	U-REDO	U-SURE
U-PLAY	U-RENT	U-TILE
U-PLED	U-RIAL	U-VEAL
U-RARE	U-RINE	

Five letters to six

U-LEXES	U-PLEAD	U-REDIA
U-LOSES	U-PLINK	U-SABLE
U-NEATH	U-PLOOK	U-SAGER
U-NITER	U-PRATE	U-SAGES
U-NOWED	U-PREST	U-SURED
U-PASES	U-PRISE	U-SURER
U-PHANG	U-PROLL	U-SWARD
U-PLAID	U-PROSE	

Six letters to seven

U-NEARED	U-PLINKS	U-PREACH
U-NEATEN	U-PLYING	U-PRISER
U-PENDED	U-PRAISE	U-REDIAL
U-PLIGHT	U-PRATED	U-SURING

Seven letters to eight

U-PENDING	U-PRAISED	U-PRISING
U-PLAYING	U-PRAISER	U-PROLLED
U-PLINKED	U-PRATING	

Some end-hooks
Two letters to three

AM-U	EM-U	LO-U
AY-U	FE-U	ME-U
EA-U	KY-U	MO-U

U

PI-U	TA-U	UT-U
SO-U	UM-U	YO-U

Three letters to four

AIT-U	LAT-U	RAT-U
BAL-U	LEK-U	RIM-U
BAP-U	LIE-U	SUS-U
BED-U	LIT-U	TAB-U
BUB-U	MAS-U	TAP-U
EME-U	MEN-U	TAT-U
FRA-U	MOT-U	TEG-U
FUG-U	MUM-U	THO-U
GEN-U	NAM-U	TUT-U
GUR-U	PAT-U	VAT-U
HAP-U	PUD-U	WUD-U
HUH-U	PUL-U	
KOR-U	PUP-U	

Four letters to five

BANT-U	CORN-U	PARE-U
BATT-U	FOND-U	PEND-U
BITO-U	HAIK-U	PIKA-U
BUCK-U	JAMB-U	PILA-U
BUND-U	KAWA-U	QUIP-U
BUSS-U	LASS-U	TEND-U
CENT-U	MUNT-U	VERT-U

Five letters to six

CONGO-U	HALER-U	MANAT-U

Six letters to seven

MANITO-U	TAMARA-U
SUBMEN-U	TURACO-U

U

Handy Hint

UKE (7 points) is a short form of UKULELE (11 points). There are not many short high-scoring words beginning with U: UKE and UGH (a sound people make when they dislike or are disgusted by something) are the highest-scoring three-letter words at 7 points each. UMM and UMP also score 7.

BLOCKERS

It is useful to know which words are blockers and can't therefore be extended before or after. You may want to play a blocker that your opponent can't extend, or you may want to avoid playing a blocker because you want to keep the board open.

Some four-letter blockers beginning with U

UNDO	UPGO	UPSY

Some five-letter blockers beginning with U (except words ending in '-ED', '-J', '-S', '-X', '-Y' or '-Z')

UNAPT	UNHIP	UPTER
UNBID	UNMET	UREAL
UNDID	UNRID	URNAL
UNDUE	UNWET	UTERI
UNDUG	UPBYE	
UNGOT	UPLIT	

Some six-letter blockers beginning with U (except words ending in '-ED', '-J', '-S', '-X', '-Y' or '-Z')

ULTIMO	UNHURT	UNRENT
UMBRAL	UNIFIC	UNSAID
UNBENT	UNITAL	UNSAWN
UNBORE	UNJUST	UNSENT
UNCAST	UNKEPT	UNSEWN
UNCHIC	UNKIND	UNSHOD
UNCLAD	UNLAID	UNSOLD
UNCOOL	UNLASH	UNSPUN
UNCUTE	UNLOST	UNSUNG
UNDEAD	UNMADE	UNSUNK
UNDEAR	UNMEEK	UNTOLD
UNDONE	UNMEET	UNTORN
UNDREW	UNMESH	UNTROD
UNEVEN	UNMIXT	UNWELL
UNFELT	UNMOWN	UNWISH
UNFIRM	UNOPEN	UNWORN
UNFOND	UNPAID	UPBLEW
UNGAIN	UNPENT	UPDREW
UNHEWN	UNPURE	UPGONE
UNHUNG	UNREAL	UPGREW

UPGUSH	UPMOST	UPTORN
UPHAND	UPPISH	UPWENT
UPHELD	UPROSE	URETIC
UPHILD	UPRUSH	URSINE
UPHOVE	UPSENT	USABLE
UPHUNG	UPTOOK	
UPLAID	UPTORE	

BONUS WORDS

Bonus words on your rack can be hard to spot, especially for the less experienced player. One way to help find them is by using prefixes and suffixes.

Many larger words include a common prefix or suffix – remembering these and using them where you can is a good way to discover any longer words on your rack, including any potential bonus words. The key prefixes to remember beginning with U are UN- and UP- and the key suffix is -URE.

Some words beginning with UN-
Seven-letter words

UN-ACTED	UN-BOXED	UN-CORKS
UN-ADDED	UN-BURNT	UN-COUTH
UN-AGING	UN-CAGED	UN-COVER
UN-AIDED	UN-CANNY	UN-CUFFS
UN-AIMED	UN-CASED	UN-CURED
UN-AIRED	UN-CHAIN	UN-CURLS
UN-ARMED	UN-CHECK	UN-DATED
UN-AWARE	UN-CITED	UN-DEALT
UN-BAKED	UN-CIVIL	UN-DOERS
UN-BEGUN	UN-CLASP	UN-DOING
UN-BENDS	UN-CLEAN	UN-DRAWN
UN-BINDS	UN-CLEAR	UN-DRESS
UN-BLOCK	UN-CLING	UN-DRUNK
UN-BLOWN	UN-CLIPS	UN-DYING
UN-BOLTS	UN-CLOAK	UN-EAGER
UN-BONED	UN-CLOGS	UN-EARTH
UN-BOUND	UN-CODED	UN-EATEN
UN-BOWED	UN-COILS	UN-ENDED

U

UN-EQUAL	UN-LIVED	UN-SIGHT
UN-FAIRS	UN-LOADS	UN-SIZED
UN-FAKED	UN-LOCKS	UN-SLAIN
UN-FAZED	UN-LOVED	UN-SLUNG
UN-FENCE	UN-LUCKY	UN-SNAGS
UN-FILED	UN-MAKER	UN-SOLID
UN-FIRED	UN-MANLY	UN-SOUND
UN-FLUSH	UN-MASKS	UN-SPENT
UN-FOLDS	UN-MIXED	UN-SPILT
UN-FORMS	UN-MORAL	UN-SPLIT
UN-FOUND	UN-MOUNT	UN-SPOOL
UN-FROCK	UN-MOVED	UN-STACK
UN-FROZE	UN-NAMED	UN-STICK
UN-FUNNY	UN-NERVE	UN-STRAP
UN-FUSSY	UN-OILED	UN-STUCK
UN-GLUED	UN-PACKS	UN-STUNG
UN-GODLY	UN-PAVED	UN-SURER
UN-GORED	UN-PICKS	UN-TAKEN
UN-GROWN	UN-PLACE	UN-TAMED
UN-GUARD	UN-PLUGS	UN-TAXED
UN-GULAR	UN-POSED	UN-THAWS
UN-HANDS	UN-QUIET	UN-TILED
UN-HAPPY	UN-QUOTE	UN-TIMED
UN-HASTY	UN-RATED	UN-TIRED
UN-HEALS	UN-RAVEL	UN-TONED
UN-HEARD	UN-READY	UN-TRACE
UN-HELMS	UN-RESTS	UN-TRIED
UN-HINGE	UN-ROBED	UN-TRUER
UN-HITCH	UN-ROLLS	UN-TRUST
UN-HOOKS	UN-SAFER	UN-TRUTH
UN-HORSE	UN-SATED	UN-TWIST
UN-HUMAN	UN-SAVED	UN-TYING
UN-KEMPT	UN-SCARY	UN-USUAL
UN-KNOWN	UN-SCREW	UN-VEILS
UN-LACED	UN-SEATS	UN-WAGED
UN-LADED	UN-SEWED	UN-WINDS
UN-LATCH	UN-SHELL	UN-WIRED
UN-LEARN	UN-SHOED	UN-WISER
UN-LEASH	UN-SHORN	UN-WOUND
UN-LINED	UN-SHOWN	UN-WRAPS

U

Eight-letter words

UN-ABATED
UN-ACTIVE
UN-AFRAID
UN-AGEING
UN-AMUSED
UN-ARGUED
UN-ARMING
UN-AVOWED
UN-BAITED
UN-BEARED
UN-BEATEN
UN-BEGGED
UN-BELIEF
UN-BIASED
UN-BIDDEN
UN-BILLED
UN-BITTEN
UN-BOLTED
UN-BONDED
UN-BOOKED
UN-BOUGHT
UN-BOWING
UN-BRIDLE
UN-BROKEN
UN-BURDEN
UN-BURIED
UN-BUTTON
UN-CALLED
UN-CANNED
UN-CAPPED
UN-CARING
UN-CAUGHT
UN-CHOSEN
UN-CLENCH
UN-CLOTHE
UN-CLUTCH
UN-COATED
UN-COCKED

UN-COILED
UN-COMMON
UN-COOKED
UN-CORKED
UN-COUPLE
UN-CUFFED
UN-CURLED
UN-DARING
UN-DECENT
UN-DENIED
UN-DERATE
UN-DINTED
UN-DOCILE
UN-DRIVEN
UN-EARNED
UN-EASIER
UN-EASILY
UN-EDIBLE
UN-EDITED
UN-ENDING
UN-ENVIED
UN-ERRING
UN-EVENLY
UN-FALLEN
UN-FAMOUS
UN-FASTEN
UN-FENCED
UN-FILLED
UN-FILMED
UN-FOLDED
UN-FORCED
UN-FORMED
UN-FROZEN
UN-FURLED
UN-GAINLY
UN-GENTLE
UN-GIVING
UN-GUIDED

UN-HANDED
UN-HARMED
UN-HEEDED
UN-HELPED
UN-HINGED
UN-HOLIER
UN-HOOKED
UN-HORSED
UN-IRONED
UN-ISSUED
UN-JAMMED
UN-JOINED
UN-KINDER
UN-LAWFUL
UN-LEADED
UN-LEARNT
UN-LIKELY
UN-LISTED
UN-LOADED
UN-LOCKED
UN-LOVING
UN-MANNED
UN-MARKED
UN-MASKED
UN-MENDED
UN-MOVING
UN-NERVED
UN-OPENED
UN-PACKED
UN-PAIRED
UN-PLAYED
UN-PRICED
UN-PROVED
UN-QUOTED
UN-REALLY
UN-REASON
UN-RESTED
UN-RINSED

U

UN-ROLLED	UN-SOILED	UN-USABLE
UN-SAFELY	UN-SOLVED	UN-VERSED
UN-SALTED	UN-SPOILT	UN-VIABLE
UN-SAVORY	UN-SUBTLE	UN-WANTED
UN-SEATED	UN-SURELY	UN-WARILY
UN-SEEING	UN-TAPPED	UN-WASHED
UN-SEEMLY	UN-THRONE	UN-WIELDY
UN-SETTLE	UN-TIDILY	UN-WISELY
UN-SHAKEN	UN-TIEING	UN-WORTHY
UN-SHAVEN	UN-TITLED	
UN-SIGNED	UN-TOWARD	

Some words beginning with UP-

Seven-letter words

UP-BEATS	UP-HEAVE	UP-STAGE
UP-BRAID	UP-HOLDS	UP-STAIR
UP-BRING	UP-LIFTS	UP-STAND
UP-CHUCK	UP-LOADS	UP-START
UP-CLOSE	UP-LYING	UP-STATE
UP-COMES	UP-PINGS	UP-SURGE
UP-CURVE	UP-RAISE	UP-SWELL
UP-DATED	UP-RATED	UP-SWING
UP-DRAFT	UP-REACH	UP-TAKEN
UP-ENDED	UP-RIGHT	UP-TEMPO
UP-FIELD	UP-RISEN	UP-TIGHT
UP-FLUNG	UP-RIVER	UP-TOWNS
UP-FRONT	UP-ROOTS	UP-TURNS
UP-GOING	UP-SCALE	UP-WARDS
UP-GROWN	UP-SLOPE	

Eight-letter words

UP-COMING	UP-HEAPED	UP-RISING
UP-DATING	UP-HEAVED	UP-ROARED
UP-DIVING	UP-LANDER	UP-ROOTED
UP-ENDING	UP-LIFTED	UP-SCALED
UP-FLOWED	UP-LINKED	UP-SETTER
UP-FURLED	UP-LOADED	UP-SIZING
UP-GAZING	UP-LOOKED	UP-SPOKEN
UP-GRADED	UP-MARKET	UP-SPRUNG
UP-GROWTH	UP-RATING	UP-STAGED

U

| UP-STREAM | UP-SURGED | UP-THROWN |
| UP-STROKE | UP-TAKING | UP-TURNED |

Some words ending with -URE

Seven-letter words

BRAV-URE	FISS-URE	PREC-URE
CAPT-URE	FIXT-URE	PROC-URE
CENS-URE	FLEX-URE	RAPT-URE
CLOS-URE	GEST-URE	RUPT-URE
CONJ-URE	LEAS-URE	SEIS-URE
COUT-URE	LECT-URE	SEIZ-URE
CULT-URE	LEIS-URE	STAT-URE
DENT-URE	MEAS-URE	TEXT-URE
DISC-URE	MIXT-URE	TONS-URE
EPIC-URE	NURT-URE	TORT-URE
ERAS-URE	OBSC-URE	VENT-URE
FACT-URE	PAST-URE	VERD-URE
FAIL-URE	PERJ-URE	VULT-URE
FEAT-URE	PICT-URE	

Eight-letter words

ANNEX-URE	INSEC-URE	REFIG-URE
APERT-URE	JUNCT-URE	REINJ-URE
ARMAT-URE	LIGAT-URE	REINS-URE
AVENT-URE	MANIC-URE	RENAT-URE
BROCH-URE	MOIST-URE	REPOS-URE
COIFF-URE	OVERC-URE	RESEC-URE
CREAT-URE	OVERS-URE	SINEC-URE
DENAT-URE	OVERT-URE	TAINT-URE
DOUBL-URE	PEDIC-URE	TINCT-URE
EXPOS-URE	PLEAS-URE	TREAS-URE
FIXAT-URE	PRESS-URE	
FRACT-URE	PUNCT-URE	
IMMAT-URE	REASS-URE	

U

UNUSUAL LETTER COMBINATIONS

If you have an unusual combination of letters on your rack, or want to impress your opponent with an unusual word, a few words from World English can come in handy. Some beginning with U include:

Australian words

UMPIE	umpire
UNCO	awkward or clumsy
UPTA	of poor quality
UTE	utility

Hindi word

URD	bean plant

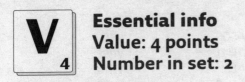

Essential info
Value: 4 points
Number in set: 2

It is important to note that there are no two-letter words with the **V** which can make it a natural blocker, preventing parallel plays. Generally it is easier to play the V with vowels but watch out for some good-scoring in combination with other high-scoring consonants such as VEX (13 points), VLY (9 points), VOW (9 points), VUM (8 points).

Three-letter words beginning with V

VAC	VAW	VLY
VAE	VEE	VOE
VAG	VID	VOR
VAR	VIM	VOX
VAS	VIN	VUG
VAV	VIS	VUM

HOOKS

Hooking requires a subtle change in a player's thought process, in that they must look at words already on the board without becoming distracted by their pronunciation.

Some front-hooks
Two letters to three

V-AE	V-EE	V-OR
V-AG	V-ET	V-OW
V-AN	V-EX	V-OX
V-AR	V-ID	V-UG
V-AS	V-IN	V-UM
V-AT	V-IS	
V-AW	V-OE	

Three letters to four

V-AIL	V-EGO	V-ILL
V-AIN	V-ELD	V-IRE
V-AIR	V-ELL	V-ITA
V-ALE	V-END	V-LEI
V-AMP	V-ERA	V-OAR
V-ANE	V-ERS	V-OLE
V-ANT	V-EST	V-ROT
V-ARE	V-ICE	V-ROW
V-ARY	V-IDE	V-UGH

Four letters to five

V-AGUE	V-ETCH	V-OARS
V-AIRY	V-EXED	V-OLES
V-ALES	V-EXES	V-OMER
V-ARIA	V-IBEX	V-OMIT
V-ARNA	V-ICED	V-OUCH
V-AUNT	V-IRED	V-OWED
V-EALE	V-IRID	V-OWER
V-EERY	V-ISIT	V-ROOM
V-ERST	V-LIES	

Five letters to six

V-AGILE	V-AWARD	V-EXING
V-AGUED	V-EALES	V-ICING
V-AILED	V-EGGED	V-IRING
V-ALINE	V-ELATE	V-IZARD
V-ALLEY	V-ENDED	V-ORANT
V-AMPED	V-ENDER	V-OTARY
V-ASTER	V-ENDUE	V-OWING
V-ATMAN	V-ENTER	
V-AUNTY	V-ERVEN	

Six letters to seven

V-ACUATE	V-ASSAIL	V-ENDING
V-ACUITY	V-AUNTER	V-ENTAIL
V-AILING	V-AUNTIE	V-ESTRAL
V-AIRIER	V-EGGING	V-OCULAR
V-ALGOID	V-ELATED	V-OUCHED
V-AMPING	V-ENATIC	V-ROOMED

V

Seven letters to eight

V-AGILITY	V-ENTAYLE	V-IRIDIAN
V-AIRIEST	V-ERISTIC	V-OTARIES
V-ALLEYED	V-ERMINED	V-OUCHING
V-ENATION	V-ICELESS	V-ROOMING
V-ENOLOGY	V-ICELIKE	

Some end-hooks

Two letters to three

DE-V	GU-V	RE-V
DI-V	LA-V	SO-V
GO-V	PA-V	TA-V

Three letters to four

CHA-V	DEE-V	MIR-V
CHI-V	ERE-V	PER-V

Four letters to five

GANE-V	OLLA-V	PARE-V

BLOCKERS

It is useful to know which words are blockers and can't therefore be extended before or after. You may want to play a blocker that your opponent can't extend, or you may want to avoid playing a blocker because you want to keep the board open.

Some three-letter blockers beginning with V

VLY	VOX

Some four-letter blockers beginning with V

VAGI	VETO	VIVO
VAIN	VEXT	VIZY
VERA	VIAE	VROT
VERD	VIBS	

Some five-letter blockers beginning with V (except words ending in '-ED', '-J', '-S', '-X', '-Y' or '-Z')

VACUA	VENAE	VIRID
VAGAL	VENAL	VITAE
VAIRE	VERRA	VIVID
VALID	VILDE	VOILA
VAPID	VILLI	VOLTA
VASAL	VINIC	VOLTI
VATIC	VIOLD	VULGO
VELUM	VIRAL	

Some six-letter blockers beginning with V (except words ending in '-ED', '-J', '-S', '-X', '-Y' or '-Z')

VACANT	VENIAL	VIRENT
VAGILE	VERIER	VIRILE
VAGROM	VERMAL	VIRING
VAGUER	VERNAL	VISCID
VAINER	VIABLE	VISIVE
VALVAL	VIBIER	VISTAL
VALVAR	VICING	VOLAGE
VANMAN	VIDUAL	VOLING
VANMEN	VILLAE	VORAGO
VARSAL	VILLAR	VORANT
VASTER	VINEAL	VORPAL
VATMAN	VINIER	VOSTRO
VATMEN	VINING	

UNUSUAL LETTER COMBINATIONS

If you have an unusual combination of letters on your rack, or want to impress your opponent with an unusual word, a few words from World English can come in handy. Here are a few examples beginning with V.

Australian words

VAG	vagrant
VEGO	vegetarian
VIGORO	women's game similar to cricket

Hindi words

VAHANA	vehicle in Indian myth
VANDA	type of orchid
VINA	stringed musical instrument

South African words

VLEI	area of marshy ground
VOEMA	vigour or energy
VROU	woman or wife

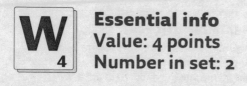

Essential info
Value: 4 points
Number in set: 2

There are only two two-letter words beginning with **W**: WE (5 points) and WO (an old-fashioned spelling of woe, also 5). There are, however, many short, common-usage words which can return good scores such as WAX (13 points), WHO (9 points) and WOK (10 points). The highest-scoring three-letter word beginning with W is WIZ (short form of wizard, 15 points).

Two-letter words beginning with W

WE	WO

Some three-letter words beginning with W

WAB	WEN	WOK
WAE	WEX	WOP
WAI	WEY	WOT
WAN	WHA	WOW
WAP	WIS	WOX
WAT	WIZ	WUS
WAW	WOF	WYE
WEM	WOG	WYN

HOOKS

Hooking requires a subtle change in a player's thought process, in that they must look at words already on the board without becoming distracted by their pronunciation.

Some front-hooks
Two letters to three

W-AB	W-AN	W-AX
W-AD	W-AR	W-AY
W-AE	W-AS	W-ED
W-AG	W-AT	W-EE
W-AI	W-AW	W-EM

W-EN   W-IS   W-OP
W-ET   W-IT   W-OS
W-EX   W-OE   W-OW
W-HA   W-OF   W-OX
W-HO   W-ON   W-US
W-IN   W-OO   W-YE

Three letters to four

W-ADD   W-AWA   W-HIT
W-AFF   W-AWE   W-HOA
W-AFT   W-AWL   W-HOM
W-AGE   W-EAN   W-HOP
W-AID   W-EAR   W-HOT
W-AIL   W-EEK   W-HOW
W-AIN   W-EEL   W-HUP
W-AIR   W-EEN   W-ICE
W-AIT   W-EFT   W-ICH
W-AKE   W-ELD   W-ICK
W-ALE   W-ELK   W-IDE
W-ALL   W-ELL   W-ILL
W-AND   W-ELT   W-IMP
W-ANE   W-END   W-INK
W-ANT   W-ERE   W-INN
W-ANY   W-EST   W-IRE
W-ARB   W-ETA   W-ISH
W-ARD   W-HAE   W-OKE
W-ARE   W-HAM   W-OLD
W-ARK   W-HAP   W-OOF
W-ARM   W-HAT   W-OON
W-ART   W-HEN   W-OOT
W-ARY   W-HET   W-ORD
W-ASH   W-HEW   W-ORE
W-ASP   W-HEY   W-ORT
W-ATE   W-HID   W-RAP
W-ATT   W-HIM   W-REN
W-AUK   W-HIN   W-RIT
W-AVE   W-HIP

Four letters to five

W-ADDY   W-AGER   W-AIDE
W-AGED   W-AGON   W-AKED

W

W-ALLY
W-ANNA
W-ARED
W-ARTY
W-ASHY
W-ATAP
W-AVER
W-AXED
W-EAVE
W-ECHT
W-EDGE
W-EDGY
W-EXED
W-EXES
W-HACK
W-HALE
W-HANG
W-HARE
W-HEAL
W-HEAR
W-HEAT
W-HEEL
W-HEFT
W-HELM

W-HELP
W-HERE
W-HIPT
W-HISH
W-HISS
W-HIST
W-HIZZ
W-HOLE
W-HOOF
W-HOOP
W-HOOT
W-HOPS
W-HORE
W-HOSE
W-HUMP
W-HUPS
W-ICKY
W-IDES
W-ILLY
W-INCH
W-IRED
W-ITCH
W-OMEN
W-OOFY

W-OOSE
W-OOZY
W-OULD
W-OVEN
W-OWED
W-OXEN
W-RACK
W-RANG
W-RAPT
W-RAST
W-RATE
W-RATH
W-REAK
W-RECK
W-REST
W-RICK
W-RING
W-RITE
W-ROKE
W-RONG
W-ROOT
W-ROTE
W-RUNG

Five letters to six

W-ACKER
W-ADDED
W-ADDER
W-ADDLE
W-AFTER
W-AGGER
W-AGING
W-AILED
W-AIRED
W-AIVER
W-AKING
W-ALLOW
W-AMBLE
W-ANGLE

W-ANION
W-ANKER
W-ANKLE
W-ANTED
W-ARKED
W-ARMED
W-ARMER
W-ARRAY
W-ASHED
W-ASHEN
W-ASHES
W-ASTER
W-AUGHT
W-AXING

W-EANED
W-EARED
W-EASEL
W-EAVED
W-EAVES
W-EBBED
W-EDGED
W-EIGHT
W-ELDER
W-ENDED
W-ESTER
W-ETHER
W-EXING
W-HALED

W-HALER
W-HAMMY
W-HEELS
W-HEEZE
W-HENCE
W-HERRY
W-HEUGH
W-HEWED
W-HILLY
W-HINGE
W-HINNY
W-HIPPY
W-HOLLY

W-HOOSH
W-ICHES
W-ICKER
W-IGGED
W-ILLER
W-IMPED
W-INDOW
W-INKED
W-INKER
W-INKLE
W-INNED
W-INNER
W-INTER

W-IRING
W-ISHES
W-ITCHY
W-ITHER
W-IZARD
W-ONNED
W-ORMER
W-OUBIT
W-OUNDY
W-OWING
W-RASSE
W-RETCH
W-RIGHT

Six letters to seven

W-ADDING
W-ADDLED
W-AILING
W-AIRING
W-AMBLED
W-ANGLED
W-ANGLER
W-ANTING
W-APPEND
W-ARKING
W-ARLING
W-ARMING
W-ARRANT
W-ARTIER
W-ASHERY
W-ASHIER
W-ASHING
W-ASPISH
W-ASSAIL
W-ATTEST
W-AXLIKE
W-EANING
W-EARING
W-EAVING
W-EBBING
W-EDGIER

W-EDGING
W-EIGHTY
W-ELDING
W-ENDING
W-HACKED
W-HACKER
W-HALING
W-HAMMED
W-HANGED
W-HAPPED
W-HEELED
W-HEELER
W-HEEZED
W-HELMED
W-HELPED
W-HEREAT
W-HEREBY
W-HEREIN
W-HEREOF
W-HEREON
W-HERETO
W-HETHER
W-HEWING
W-HIDDER
W-HINGED
W-HINGER

W-HIPPED
W-HIPPER
W-HISHED
W-HISSED
W-HISTED
W-HITHER
W-HITTER
W-HIZZED
W-HOLISM
W-HOLIST
W-HOOFED
W-HOOPED
W-HOOPER
W-HOOPLA
W-HOOTED
W-HOPPED
W-HOPPER
W-HUMPED
W-HUPPED
W-IGGING
W-ILLEST
W-IMPING
W-IMPISH
W-IMPLED
W-INCHED
W-INCHER

W

W-INCHES
W-INDIGO
W-INKING
W-INKLED
W-INNING
W-ITCHED
W-ITCHES
W-ONNING
W-OOZIER

W-OOZILY
W-RACKED
W-RANGED
W-RAPPED
W-RAPPER
W-RASSES
W-RASSLE
W-REAKED
W-RECKED

W-RESTED
W-RESTER
W-RICKED
W-RINGED
W-RINGER
W-ROOTED
W-ROUGHT

Seven letters to eight

W-ADDLING
W-AGELESS
W-ALLEYED
W-ALLOWED
W-AMBLING
W-ANGLING
W-ANTHILL
W-ARRAYED
W-ARTIEST
W-ARTLESS
W-ASHIEST
W-ASTABLE
W-EANLING
W-EASELED
W-EDGIEST
W-HACKING
W-HAMMING
W-HANGING
W-HAPPING
W-HEELING
W-HEEZING
W-HELMING

W-HELPING
W-HERRIED
W-HINGING
W-HINNIED
W-HINNIES
W-HIPLIKE
W-HIPPIER
W-HIPPING
W-HIPSTER
W-HIRLING
W-HISHING
W-HISSING
W-HISTING
W-HIZZING
W-HOOFING
W-HOOPING
W-HOOSHED
W-HOOSHES
W-HOOTING
W-HOPPING
W-HUMPING
W-HUPPING

W-INCHING
W-INDOWED
W-INKLING
W-IRELESS
W-ITCHIER
W-ITCHING
W-OOFIEST
W-OOZIEST
W-OULDEST
W-RACKFUL
W-RACKING
W-RANGING
W-RAPPING
W-RASSLED
W-REAKING
W-RECKING
W-RESTING
W-RETCHED
W-RICKING
W-RINGING
W-ROOTING

Some end-hooks

Two letters to three

BO-W
DA-W
DE-W
DO-W

FA-W
FE-W
HA-W
HE-W

HO-W
JA-W
JO-W
KA-W

KO-W
LA-W
LO-W
MA-W
ME-W
MO-W
NA-W

NE-W
NO-W
PA-W
PE-W
PO-W
RE-W
SO-W

TA-W
TE-W
TO-W
WO-W
YA-W
YE-W
YO-W

Three letters to four

ALE-W
ANE-W
ARE-W
AVO-W
BRA-W
BRO-W

CHA-W
CHE-W
ENE-W
FRO-W
PRO-W
SHA-W

SHE-W
SKA-W
SPA-W
THE-W
VIE-W
WHO-W

Four letters to five

BEDE-W
KOTO-W
NAVE-W
PAPA-W

PAWA-W
PILA-W
SINE-W
SYBO-W

THRO-W
VINE-W
VROU-W

Five letters to six

BARRO-W
BURRO-W
HALLO-W
HOLLO-W

MATLO-W
MISSA-W
MORRO-W
OUTRO-W

PURSE-W
REVIE-W
UNCLE-W

Six letters to seven

DAYGLO-W

Seven letters to eight

BUDGERO-W

RICKSHA-W

> ### Handy Hint
>
> Some of the more unusual words beginning with W are
> WAKIKI (Melanesian shell currency, 12 points), WAMBLE (move
> unsteadily, 13 points), WUXIA (genre of Chinese fiction and film,
> concerning the adventures of sword-wielding chivalrous heroes,
> 15 points) and WYVERN (heraldic beast having a serpent's tail,
> a dragon's head and a body with wings and two legs, 15 points).

W

BLOCKERS

It is useful to know which words are blockers and can't therefore be extended before or after. You may want to play a blocker that your opponent can't extend, or you may want to avoid playing a blocker because you want to keep the board open.

Three-letter blocker beginning with W

WOX

Some four-letter blockers beginning with W

WADY	WERT	WILY
WARY	WHAE	WIRY
WAVY	WHIO	WOST
WAXY	WHOA	WOWF
WENA	WHOT	WYCH
WERE	WICH	

Some five-letter blockers beginning with W (except words ending in '-ED', '-J', '-S', '-X', '-Y' or '-Z')

WANNA	WHOSE	WOWEE
WAXEN	WHOSO	WOXEN
WELCH	WIDER	WRAPT
WELSH	WILCO	WROTE
WENCH	WINCH	WROTH
WHAMO	WISER	WRUNG
WHICH	WISHT	WRYER
WHIPT	WOMEN	

Some six-letter blockers beginning with W (except words ending in '-ED', '-J', '-S', '-X', '-Y' or '-Z')

WANIER	WAXIER	WILIER
WANKLE	WHATSO	WILING
WANNER	WHILST	WIMMIN
WARIER	WHITER	WIRIER
WARING	WHOMSO	WISEST
WARMAN	WHOOSH	WISING
WARMEN	WIDEST	WITHAL
WASHEN	WIDISH	WITING
WASSUP	WIFING	WOEFUL
WAVIER	WILFUL	WORSER

W

WOWING   WRETCH   WRYEST
WRENCH   WROKEN   WRYING

BONUS WORDS

Bonus words on your rack can be hard to spot, especially for the less experienced player. One way to help find them is by using prefixes and suffixes.

Many larger words include a common prefix or suffix – remembering these and using them where you can is a good way to discover any longer words on your rack, including any potential bonus words. The key prefix to remember is WAR- and the key suffixes are -WARD, -WARDS, -WAY, -WISE, -WOOD, -WORK, -WORM and -WORT.

Some words beginning with WAR-

Seven-letter words

WAR-BLED   WAR-LOCK   WAR-SAWS
WAR-DENS   WAR-LORD   WAR-SHIP
WAR-DING   WAR-MING   WAR-SLED
WAR-DOGS   WAR-PATH   WAR-TIER
WAR-FARE   WAR-PING   WAR-TIME
WAR-HEAD   WAR-RAND   WAR-WOLF
WAR-KING   WAR-RANT   WAR-WORK
WAR-LESS   WAR-RAYS   WAR-WORN
WAR-LIKE   WAR-RENS   WAR-ZONE
WAR-LING   WAR-RING

Eight-letter words

WAR-BLING   WAR-FARER   WAR-POWER
WAR-CRAFT   WAR-HORSE   WAR-RAYED
WAR-DERED   WAR-MAKER   WAR-SLING
WAR-DRESS   WAR-MOUTH
WAR-FARED   WAR-PLANE

Some words ending with -WARD

Seven-letter words

AIR-WARD   BED-WARD   HAY-WARD
AWK-WARD   FOR-WARD   LEE-WARD

NAY-WARD
NOR-WARD
OUT-WARD
SEA-WARD

SKY-WARD
STE-WARD
SUN-WARD
VAN-WARD

WAY-WARD
WEY-WARD

Eight-letter words

BACK-WARD
BECO-WARD
CITY-WARD
DOWN-WARD
EAST-WARD
FORE-WARD
GOAL-WARD
HEAD-WARD

HELL-WARD
HIND-WARD
HIVE-WARD
HOME-WARD
KIRK-WARD
LAND-WARD
LEFT-WARD
MOON-WARD

REAR-WARD
SELF-WARD
SIDE-WARD
UNTO-WARD
WEST-WARD
WIND-WARD
WOOD-WARD
WOOL-WARD

Some words ending with -WAY

Seven-letter words

ARCH-WAY
AREA-WAY
BELT-WAY
BIKE-WAY
CART-WAY
CUTA-WAY
DOOR-WAY
FAIR-WAY
FARA-WAY
FISH-WAY
FLYA-WAY
FOLK-WAY
FOOT-WAY
FREE-WAY
GANG-WAY
GATE-WAY
GETA-WAY

HADA-WAY
HALF-WAY
HALL-WAY
HEAD-WAY
HIGH-WAY
LANE-WAY
LAYA-WAY
LIFE-WAY
PACK-WAY
PARK-WAY
PART-WAY
PATH-WAY
RACE-WAY
RAIL-WAY
RING-WAY
ROAD-WAY
RODE-WAY

ROLL-WAY
ROPE-WAY
RUNA-WAY
SHIP-WAY
SIDE-WAY
SKID-WAY
SLIP-WAY
SOME-WAY
TAXI-WAY
THRU-WAY
TIDE-WAY
TOLL-WAY
TOWA-WAY
TRAM-WAY
WALK-WAY
WIND-WAY
WIRE-WAY

Eight-letter words

AISLE-WAY
ALLEY-WAY
BROAD-WAY
CABLE-WAY
CASTA-WAY

CAUSE-WAY
CLEAR-WAY
CRAWL-WAY
CROSS-WAY
CYCLE-WAY

DRIVE-WAY
ENTRY-WAY
EVERY-WAY
FADEA-WAY
FLOOD-WAY

W

FOLDA-WAY
GIVEA-WAY
GREEN-WAY
GUIDE-WAY
HIDEA-WAY
HORSE-WAY
MOTOR-WAY
OVERS-WAY
RIDGE-WAY
RIVER-WAY
ROCKA-WAY

ROLLA-WAY
ROUTE-WAY
SLIDE-WAY
SOARA-WAY
SPEED-WAY
SPILL-WAY
STAIR-WAY
STAYA-WAY
STOWA-WAY
TAKEA-WAY
TEARA-WAY

THATA-WAY
THISA-WAY
TRACK-WAY
TRAIN-WAY
UNDER-WAY
WALKA-WAY
WASHA-WAY
WASTE-WAY
WATER-WAY

Some words ending with -WISE

Seven-letter words

AIR-WISE
ANY-WISE
END-WISE

FAN-WISE
MAN-WISE
MAP-WISE

SUN-WISE
TAX-WISE

Eight-letter words

ARCH-WISE
BEND-WISE
CRAB-WISE
DROP-WISE
EDGE-WISE
FLAT-WISE

LIKE-WISE
LONG-WISE
OVER-WISE
PAIR-WISE
RING-WISE
SIDE-WISE

SOME-WISE
STEP-WISE
SUCH-WISE
TEAM-WISE
TENT-WISE

Some words ending with -WOOD

Seven-letter words

BAR-WOOD
BAY-WOOD
BOG-WOOD
BOX-WOOD

DOG-WOOD
ELM-WOOD
INK-WOOD
LOG-WOOD

NUT-WOOD
PLY-WOOD
RED-WOOD
SAP-WOOD

Eight-letter words

BACK-WOOD
BASS-WOOD
BEAR-WOOD
BENT-WOOD
BLUE-WOOD
COLT-WOOD

CORD-WOOD
CORK-WOOD
DEAD-WOOD
FIRE-WOOD
FUEL-WOOD
HARD-WOOD

IRON-WOOD
KING-WOOD
MILK-WOOD
PEAR-WOOD
PINE-WOOD
ROSE-WOOD

| SOFT-WOOD | TEAK-WOOD | WORM-WOOD |
| SOUR-WOOD | WILD-WOOD | |

Some words ending with -WORK

Seven-letter words

ART-WORK	OUT-WORK	TOP-WORK
CUT-WORK	PIN-WORK	TUT-WORK
DAY-WORK	PRE-WORK	WAR-WORK
LEG-WORK	RAG-WORK	WAX-WORK
NET-WORK	RIB-WORK	WEB-WORK
NON-WORK	TIN-WORK	

Eight-letter words

BACK-WORK	HAND-WORK	RACK-WORK
BEAD-WORK	HEAD-WORK	ROAD-WORK
BODY-WORK	HOME-WORK	ROPE-WORK
BOOK-WORK	IRON-WORK	SEAT-WORK
BUSY-WORK	LACE-WORK	STUD-WORK
CAGE-WORK	LEAD-WORK	TASK-WORK
CASE-WORK	LIFE-WORK	TEAM-WORK
FARM-WORK	MESH-WORK	TIME-WORK
FIRE-WORK	OPEN-WORK	WIRE-WORK
FOOT-WORK	OVER-WORK	WOOD-WORK
FRET-WORK	PART-WORK	YARD-WORK
HACK-WORK	PILE-WORK	
HAIR-WORK	PIPE-WORK	

Some words ending with -WORM

Seven-letter words

BAG-WORM	EEL-WORM	SEA-WORM
BUD-WORM	LOB-WORM	WAX-WORM
CAT-WORM	LUG-WORM	WEB-WORM
CUT-WORM	PIN-WORM	
EAR-WORM	RAG-WORM	

Eight-letter words

ARMY-WORM	CORN-WORM	GLOW-WORM
BOLL-WORM	FIRE-WORM	GRUB-WORM
BOOK-WORM	FISH-WORM	HAIR-WORM
CASE-WORM	FLAT-WORM	HOOK-WORM

HORN-WORM   RING-WORM   TUBE-WORM
INCH-WORM   SAND-WORM   WHIP-WORM
LEAF-WORM   SHIP-WORM   WIRE-WORM
LUNG-WORM   SILK-WORM   WOOD-WORM
MEAL-WORM   SLOW-WORM
PILL-WORM   TAPE-WORM

Some words ending with -WORT

Seven-letter words

AWL-WORT   FEL-WORT   MUG-WORT
BLA-WORT   FIG-WORT   RAG-WORT
BUG-WORT   MAD-WORT   RIB-WORT
FAN-WORT   MUD-WORT

Eight-letter words

BELL-WORT   HORN-WORT   PILL-WORT
COLE-WORT   LEAD-WORT   PIPE-WORT
DAME-WORT   LUNG-WORT   SALT-WORT
DANE-WORT   MILK-WORT   SAND-WORT
DROP-WORT   MODI-WORT   SOAP-WORT
FLEA-WORT   MOON-WORT   STAR-WORT
GOUT-WORT   MOOR-WORT   WALL-WORT
HONE-WORT   PILE-WORT   WART-WORT

UNUSUAL LETTER COMBINATIONS

If you have an unusual combination of letters on your rack, or
want to impress your opponent with an unusual word, a few
words from World English can come in handy.

Australian words

WADDY   heavy wooden club used by native Australians
WAGGA   blanket made of sacks stitched together
WALLABY   marsupial resembling a small kangaroo
WANDOO   eucalyptus tree with white bark
WARATAH   shrub with dark green leaves and crimson flowers
WARB   dirty or insignificant person
WHARFIE   wharf labourer
WILGA   small drought-resistant tree
WIRILDA   acacia tree with edible seeds
WIRRAH   saltwater fish with bright blue spots

W

WOMBAT	burrowing marsupial
WOOMERA	spear-throwing stick
WURLEY	Aboriginal hut

Canadian words

| WAWA | speech or language |
| WENDIGO | evil spirit or cannibal |

Hindi word

| WALLAH | person in charge of a specific thing |

New Zealand words

WAI	water
WAKA	Maori canoe
WEKA	flightless bird
WERO	warrior's challenge
WETA	long-legged wingless insect
WHANAU	family
WHENAU	native land

Essential info
Value: 8 points
Number in set: 1

Two-letter words beginning with X

XI   XU

Some three-letter words using X

AXE	LUX	SIX
BOX	MAX	SOX
COX	MIX	TAX
DEX	MUX	TEX
DUX	NIX	TIX
EXO	NOX	TUX
FAX	OXO	VEX
FIX	OXY	VOX
FOX	PAX	WAX
GOX	PIX	WEX
HEX	POX	WOX
HOX	PYX	YEX
KEX	RAX	ZAX
LAX	REX	ZEX
LEX	SAX	
LOX	SEX	

Some four-letter words using X

Some useful four-letter words you may not know include BRUX (to grind one's teeth, 13 points), NIXY (a female water sprite, 14 points) and WEXE (obsolete form of wax, 14 points).

APEX	FAUX	NEXT
AXED	FIXT	NIXY
AXIS	FLAX	ONYX
AXLE	FLEX	ORYX
BOXY	FLUX	OXEN
BRUX	FOXY	OXER
COAX	GREX	OXID
CRUX	HOAX	PIXY
DEXY	IBEX	PLEX
DIXY	JAXY	POXY
DOUX	JEUX	ROUX
EAUX	JINX	SEXY
EXAM	JYNX	TAXI
EXEC	LYNX	TEXT
EXED	MAXI	VEXT
EXIT	MINX	WAXY
EXON	MIXT	WEXE
EXPO	MYXO	XYST

HOOKS

Hooking requires a subtle change in a player's thought process, in that they must look at words already on the board without becoming distracted by their pronunciation.

Some front-hooks

Two letters to three

X-IS

Four letters to five

X-ERIC   X-YLEM

Five letters to six

X-YLEMS

X

Six letters to seven

X-EROSES   X-EROTIC

Some end-hooks
Two letters to three

BO-X
DE-X
FA-X
GO-X
HE-X
HO-X
LA-X
LO-X
MA-X

MI-X
MU-X
NO-X
PA-X
PI-X
PO-X
RE-X
SI-X
SO-X

TA-X
TE-X
TI-X
WE-X
WO-X
YE-X
ZA-X

Three letters to four

APE-X
BRU-X
CRU-X
EAU-X

FLU-X
HOA-X
JEU-X
JIN-X

ONY-X
PRE-X
ULE-X

Four letters to five

BEAU-X
BORA-X
CARE-X
CHOU-X
CODE-X
FORE-X
GALA-X

LATE-X
LIMA-X
LURE-X
MALA-X
MIRE-X
MURE-X
PYRE-X

REDO-X
SILE-X
SORE-X
TELE-X
VIBE-X
VITE-X

Five letters to six

ADIEU-X
BIJOU-X

BOYAU-X
DUPLE-X

Six letters to seven

BATEAU-X
BUREAU-X
CADEAU-X
COTEAU-X

GATEAU-X
MILIEU-X
MINIMA-X
RESEAU-X

SIMPLE-X
TRIPLE-X

X

Seven letters to eight

BANDEAU-X
BATTEAU-X
BERCEAU-X
CAMAIEU-X
CHAPEAU-X
CHATEAU-X
COUTEAU-X

FABLIAU-X
JAMBEAU-X
MANTEAU-X
MORCEAU-X
NOUVEAU-X
OCTUPLE-X
PLATEAU-X

PONCEAU-X
RONDEAU-X
ROULEAU-X
TABLEAU-X
TONNEAU-X
TRUMEAU-X

BLOCKERS

It is useful to know which words are blockers and can't therefore be extended before or after. You may want to play a blocker that your opponent can't extend, or you may want to avoid playing a blocker because you want to keep the board open.

Two-letter blocker beginning with X

XU

Some five-letter blockers beginning with X (except words ending in '-ED', '-J', '-S', '-X', '-Y' or '-Z')

XERIC
XOANA

XYLIC
XYSTI

Some six-letter blockers beginning with X (except words ending in '-ED', '-J', '-S', '-X', '-Y' or '-Z')

XENIAL
XENIUM

XOANON
XYLOID

XYSTOI

Handy Hint

Power tile letters may be less common than others in the set but there are many simple and easy-to-remember words that use them. Some examples for X include: BOX (12 points), FOX (13), WAX (13), EXAM (13), NEXT (11) and TEXT (11). You could even impress your opponent with words beginning with X such as XENIA (12 points) and XERIC (14 points).

Bonus words

Seven-letter words

XANTHAM
XANTHAN
XANTHIC
XANTHIN
XENOPUS
XERAFIN
XERARCH
XERASIA
XEROMAS

XEROSES
XEROSIS
XEROTES
XEROTIC
XEROXED
XEROXES
XERUSES
XIPHOID
XYLENES

XYLENOL
XYLIDIN
XYLITOL
XYLOGEN
XYLOMAS
XYLONIC
XYLOSES
XYSTERS

Eight-letter words

XANTHAMS
XANTHANS
XANTHATE
XANTHEIN
XANTHENE
XANTHINE
XANTHINS
XANTHISM
XANTHOMA
XANTHONE
XANTHOUS

XENOGAMY
XENOGENY
XENOLITH
XENOPHYA
XENOTIME
XENURINE
XERANSES
XERANSIS
XERANTIC
XERAPHIM
XEROMATA

XEROSERE
XEROXING
XYLIDINE
XYLITOLS
XYLOCARP
XYLOIDIN
XYLOLOGY
XYLOMATA
XYLONITE
XYLOTOMY

X

Y
4

Essential info
Value: 4 points
Number in set: 2

Y is worth 4 points on its own, making it a tile with good scoring potential. There are four two-letter words beginning with Y but they use all the vowels except for I: YA, YE, YO and YU (5 points each). High-scoring three-letter words beginning with Y include YEW (9 points) and YOB (8 points). Y is also excellent for end hooking onto nouns for use as adjectives.

Two-letter words beginning with Y

YA	YO
YE	YU

Some three-letter words beginning with Y

YAD	YEA	YOK
YAE	YEH	YOM
YAG	YEP	YON
YAH	YEX	YOW
YAM	YGO	YUG
YAR	YID	YUK
YAW	YIN	YUM
YAY	YOD	YUP

HOOKS

Hooking requires a subtle change in a player's thought process, in that they must look at words already on the board without becoming distracted by their pronunciation.

Some front-hooks
Two letters to three

Y-AD	Y-AM	Y-EA
Y-AE	Y-AR	Y-EH
Y-AG	Y-AW	Y-EN
Y-AH	Y-AY	Y-ES

Y-ET
Y-EX
Y-GO
Y-ID
Y-IN
Y-OB

Y-OD
Y-OM
Y-ON
Y-OS
Y-OU
Y-OW

Y-UG
Y-UM
Y-UP
Y-US

Three letters to four

Y-AFF
Y-ALE
Y-APP
Y-ARD
Y-ARE
Y-ARK
Y-ATE
Y-AWL
Y-AWN
Y-EAN
Y-EAR

Y-EGG
Y-ELK
Y-ELL
Y-ELM
Y-EST
Y-EVE
Y-ILL
Y-IRK
Y-ODE
Y-OKE
Y-OLD

Y-OOF
Y-OOP
Y-ORE
Y-OUK
Y-OUR
Y-OWE
Y-OWL
Y-UKE
Y-ULE
Y-UMP

Four letters to five

Y-ABBA
Y-ACCA
Y-AGER
Y-AMEN
Y-ARCO
Y-AULD
Y-AWED
Y-AWNY
Y-BORE

Y-CLAD
Y-COND
Y-DRAD
Y-EARD
Y-EARN
Y-EAST
Y-EVEN
Y-EXED
Y-FERE

Y-LIKE
Y-MOLT
Y-OGEE
Y-OURN
Y-OWED
Y-ULAN
Y-UPON

Five letters to six

Y-ACKER
Y-AGGER
Y-ANKER
Y-ANTRA
Y-ARKED
Y-ARROW
Y-AWING
Y-AWNED
Y-AWNER

Y-BLENT
Y-BOUND
Y-BRENT
Y-CLEPT
Y-EANED
Y-EARDS
Y-EARLY
Y-EMMER
Y-ESSES

Y-ESTER
Y-EUKED
Y-EXING
Y-ICKER
Y-IRKED
Y-OWING
Y-OWLED
Y-OWLER
Y-PIGHT

Y

271

Y-PLAST
Y-SHEND
Y-SHENT
Y-UMPED
Y-UMPIE
Y-WROKE

Six letters to seven

Y-ARKING
Y-AWNERS
Y-AWNIER
Y-AWNING
Y-CLEPED
Y-EANING

Y-EARDED
Y-EARNED
Y-EARNER
Y-EASTED
Y-EUKING
Y-IRKING

Y-MOLTEN
Y-OWLING
Y-PLIGHT
Y-SLAKED
Y-UMPIES
Y-UMPING

Seven letters to eight

Y-ATAGHAN
Y-AWNIEST
Y-BOUNDEN
Y-CLEEPED

Y-EANLING
Y-EARDING
Y-EARLIES
Y-EARNING

Y-EASTING
Y-OURSELF

> ### Handy Hint
>
> Some useful short high-scoring words beginning with Y are YEX (Scots word for hiccup or cough, 13 points), YOK (a noisy laugh, 10 points) and YUK (a noise used to express disgust or dislike, also 10 points).

Some end-hooks
Two letters to three

AB-Y
AN-Y
AR-Y
BA-Y
BE-Y
BO-Y
DA-Y
DE-Y
DO-Y
FA-Y
FE-Y
GO-Y

GU-Y
HA-Y
HE-Y
HO-Y
JA-Y
JO-Y
KA-Y
LA-Y
LO-Y
MA-Y
MO-Y
NA-Y

NO-Y
ON-Y
OX-Y
PA-Y
SH-Y
SO-Y
ST-Y
TA-Y
TO-Y
WE-Y
YA-Y

Y

Three letters to four

ACH-Y	DOP-Y	MOB-Y
ADD-Y	DOR-Y	MOL-Y
AFF-Y	DOT-Y	MON-Y
AIR-Y	EAS-Y	MOP-Y
ALA-Y	EEL-Y	NIX-Y
ALL-Y	EGG-Y	NOS-Y
ARM-Y	ELM-Y	NOW-Y
ARS-Y	FAD-Y	OAK-Y
ART-Y	FOG-Y	OAR-Y
ASH-Y	FOX-Y	OBE-Y
AWA-Y	FRA-Y	OIL-Y
AWN-Y	FUM-Y	OKA-Y
BOD-Y	FUR-Y	OLD-Y
BOG-Y	GAB-Y	ORB-Y
BON-Y	GAM-Y	OWL-Y
BOX-Y	GAP-Y	PAC-Y
BRA-Y	GOB-Y	PAL-Y
BUR-Y	GOE-Y	PAT-Y
BUS-Y	GOR-Y	PIN-Y
CAG-Y	GUL-Y	PIP-Y
CAN-Y	HER-Y	PIT-Y
CHA-Y	HOM-Y	PIX-Y
CIT-Y	HUG-Y	POL-Y
COL-Y	ICK-Y	POS-Y
CON-Y	IFF-Y	POX-Y
COP-Y	ILL-Y	PRE-Y
COR-Y	INK-Y	PUL-Y
COS-Y	JOE-Y	PUN-Y
COW-Y	JUD-Y	QUA-Y
COX-Y	LAC-Y	RIM-Y
COZ-Y	LAD-Y	RUB-Y
DEF-Y	LEV-Y	SAG-Y
DEN-Y	LIN-Y	SHA-Y
DEW-Y	LOG-Y	SPA-Y
DEX-Y	MAN-Y	SUM-Y
DID-Y	MAR-Y	TAK-Y
DOG-Y	MAT-Y	TED-Y
DOM-Y	MIX-Y	THE-Y

273

TID-Y
TIN-Y
TOD-Y
TOE-Y
TON-Y
TOR-Y

TOW-Y
TUN-Y
TWA-Y
UPS-Y
VAR-Y
VIN-Y

WAD-Y
WAN-Y
WAR-Y
WAX-Y
WIN-Y
YUK-Y

Four letters to five

ACID-Y
AGON-Y
ANNO-Y
ANTS-Y
ARTS-Y
AUNT-Y
BALD-Y
BALM-Y
BAND-Y
BARB-Y
BARK-Y
BARM-Y
BARN-Y
BASS-Y
BATT-Y
BAWD-Y
BEAD-Y
BEAK-Y
BEAN-Y
BEEF-Y
BEER-Y
BELL-Y
BEND-Y
BIFF-Y
BILL-Y
BING-Y
BITS-Y
BLOW-Y
BLUE-Y
BONE-Y
BOOK-Y
BOOM-Y

BOOT-Y
BOSS-Y
BOTH-Y
BRIN-Y
BUFF-Y
BULK-Y
BULL-Y
BUMP-Y
BUNG-Y
BUNN-Y
BUNT-Y
BURL-Y
BURR-Y
BUSH-Y
BUSK-Y
BUST-Y
BUTT-Y
BUZZ-Y
CAGE-Y
CAKE-Y
CALM-Y
CAMP-Y
CARB-Y
CARN-Y
CARR-Y
CASK-Y
CHEW-Y
COAL-Y
COCK-Y
CONE-Y
CONK-Y
COOK-Y

COPS-Y
CORE-Y
CORK-Y
CORN-Y
COSE-Y
COVE-Y
COZE-Y
CULT-Y
CURL-Y
CURR-Y
CUSH-Y
CUTE-Y
DAFF-Y
DAIS-Y
DAMP-Y
DEAR-Y
DECO-Y
DEED-Y
DEIF-Y
DELL-Y
DICE-Y
DICK-Y
DILL-Y
DING-Y
DINK-Y
DIRT-Y
DISH-Y
DITT-Y
DITZ-Y
DOLL-Y
DOOM-Y
DOPE-Y

DORK-Y	GEEK-Y	HONK-Y
DOWD-Y	GERM-Y	HOOD-Y
DOWN-Y	GILL-Y	HOOK-Y
DUCK-Y	GIMP-Y	HORN-Y
DUMP-Y	GINN-Y	HUFF-Y
DUNG-Y	GIPS-Y	HULK-Y
DUSK-Y	GIRL-Y	HUNK-Y
DUST-Y	GLUE-Y	HUSK-Y
EARL-Y	GOLD-Y	HUSS-Y
EBON-Y	GOOD-Y	IRON-Y
EMPT-Y	GOOF-Y	ITCH-Y
EVER-Y	GOOS-Y	JAKE-Y
FAIR-Y	GOUT-Y	JAZZ-Y
FAWN-Y	GRAV-Y	JELL-Y
FELT-Y	GRIM-Y	JERK-Y
FIER-Y	GRIP-Y	JIFF-Y
FILL-Y	GULL-Y	JIVE-Y
FILM-Y	GUNG-Y	JOKE-Y
FISH-Y	GUNK-Y	JOLL-Y
FIST-Y	GUSH-Y	JOWL-Y
FIZZ-Y	GUST-Y	JUMP-Y
FLAK-Y	GUTS-Y	JUNK-Y
FLAM-Y	GYPS-Y	KELP-Y
FLAX-Y	HAIL-Y	KICK-Y
FLUE-Y	HAIR-Y	KISS-Y
FOAM-Y	HAND-Y	KOOK-Y
FOLK-Y	HANK-Y	LACE-Y
FOOD-Y	HARD-Y	LAIR-Y
FOOT-Y	HARP-Y	LARD-Y
FORA-Y	HAST-Y	LEAF-Y
FORK-Y	HEAD-Y	LEAK-Y
FORT-Y	HEFT-Y	LEER-Y
FULL-Y	HERB-Y	LEFT-Y
FUNK-Y	HILL-Y	LIME-Y
FUSS-Y	HISS-Y	LOAM-Y
FUZZ-Y	HOAR-Y	LOFT-Y
GAME-Y	HOKE-Y	LOLL-Y
GASP-Y	HOLE-Y	LOON-Y
GAUD-Y	HOME-Y	LOOP-Y
GAWK-Y	HONE-Y	LORD-Y

Y

LOUS-Y

LOVE-Y

LUCK-Y

LUMP-Y

LUST-Y

MALT-Y

MANG-Y

MASH-Y

MATE-Y

MEAL-Y

MEAN-Y

MEAT-Y

MELT-Y

MERC-Y

MESS-Y

MIFF-Y

MILK-Y

MINT-Y

MISS-Y

MIST-Y

MOLD-Y

MOOD-Y

MORA-Y

MOSS-Y

MUCK-Y

MUMM-Y

MUMS-Y

MURK-Y

MUSH-Y

MUSK-Y

NARK-Y

NEED-Y

NERD-Y

NIFF-Y

NOSE-Y

PACE-Y

PALL-Y

PALM-Y

PANS-Y

PARK-Y

PART-Y

PAST-Y

PATS-Y

PEAK-Y

PEAT-Y

PERK-Y

PHON-Y

PICK-Y

PINE-Y

PINK-Y

PITH-Y

PLUM-Y

POKE-Y

POLL-Y

PONG-Y

PORK-Y

POSE-Y

PROS-Y

PUFF-Y

PULP-Y

PUNK-Y

PUSH-Y

RAIN-Y

RANG-Y

READ-Y

REED-Y

REEK-Y

REST-Y

RICE-Y

RILE-Y

RISK-Y

RITZ-Y

ROCK-Y

ROOK-Y

ROOM-Y

ROOT-Y

ROPE-Y

RUST-Y

SALT-Y

SAME-Y

SAND-Y

SASS-Y

SCAR-Y

SEAM-Y

SEED-Y

SHAD-Y

SHIN-Y

SHOW-Y

SILK-Y

SILL-Y

SISS-Y

SLIM-Y

SLOP-Y

SNOW-Y

SOAP-Y

SOFT-Y

SONS-Y

SOOT-Y

SOUP-Y

SPIN-Y

STAG-Y

STUD-Y

SULK-Y

TACK-Y

TALK-Y

TALL-Y

TANG-Y

TATT-Y

TEAR-Y

TEEN-Y

TELL-Y

TEST-Y

TILL-Y

TIPS-Y

TOAD-Y

TOFF-Y

TOWN-Y

TWIN-Y

UNIT-Y

VAMP-Y

VEIN-Y
VIBE-Y
VIEW-Y
WACK-Y
WALL-Y
WART-Y
WAVE-Y

WEAR-Y
WEED-Y
WELL-Y
WHIN-Y
WHIT-Y
WIFE-Y
WIMP-Y

WIND-Y
WISP-Y
WOMB-Y
WOOD-Y
WOOL-Y
WORD-Y
ZEST-Y

Five letters to six

ANGST-Y
ARMOR-Y
AUGUR-Y
BAKER-Y
BARON-Y
BEACH-Y
BEARD-Y
BEAUT-Y
BEECH-Y
BLEAR-Y
BLOCK-Y
BLOKE-Y
BLOOD-Y
BLOWS-Y
BLUES-Y
BOOZE-Y
BOWER-Y
BRAIN-Y
BRAND-Y
BRASS-Y
BRAWN-Y
BRICK-Y
BROOD-Y
BROTH-Y
BROWN-Y
BRUSH-Y
CHALK-Y
CHEAP-Y
CHEEK-Y
CHEER-Y
CHILL-Y

CHIRP-Y
CHOKE-Y
CHUFF-Y
CHUNK-Y
CLASS-Y
CLOUD-Y
CLUCK-Y
CLUNK-Y
COLON-Y
COUNT-Y
CRAFT-Y
CRANK-Y
CRAWL-Y
CREAK-Y
CREAM-Y
CREEP-Y
CRISP-Y
CROAK-Y
CRUST-Y
CURVE-Y
CUTES-Y
DRAFT-Y
DRAWL-Y
DREAM-Y
DREAR-Y
DRESS-Y
DROOP-Y
DROPS-Y
EARTH-Y
EATER-Y
EIGHT-Y

FAULT-Y
FEIST-Y
FELON-Y
FILTH-Y
FINER-Y
FLAKE-Y
FLESH-Y
FLINT-Y
FLOAT-Y
FLOSS-Y
FLOUR-Y
FLUFF-Y
FLUNK-Y
FOLKS-Y
FOOTS-Y
FREAK-Y
FRIAR-Y
FRILL-Y
FRISK-Y
FRIZZ-Y
FROST-Y
FROTH-Y
FRUIT-Y
FRUMP-Y
GLASS-Y
GLITZ-Y
GLOOM-Y
GLOSS-Y
GNARL-Y
GRAIN-Y
GRASS-Y

Y

GREED-Y	SCARE-Y	STOCK-Y
GROWL-Y	SCREW-Y	STONE-Y
GRUMP-Y	SCUZZ-Y	STORE-Y
GUILT-Y	SHAND-Y	STORM-Y
HEART-Y	SHARP-Y	STRIP-Y
HERES-Y	SHELL-Y	STUFF-Y
HORSE-Y	SHIFT-Y	STUMP-Y
HOUSE-Y	SHIRT-Y	SUGAR-Y
HURRA-Y	SHORT-Y	SWAMP-Y
JAPER-Y	SHOUT-Y	SWEAT-Y
LEMON-Y	SINEW-Y	SWEET-Y
LIVER-Y	SKANK-Y	SWIRL-Y
MARSH-Y	SKIMP-Y	SYRUP-Y
MEDLE-Y	SLANG-Y	TEENS-Y
MEREL-Y	SLEEP-Y	THICK-Y
MIGHT-Y	SLINK-Y	THING-Y
MISER-Y	SLUSH-Y	THORN-Y
MOULD-Y	SMART-Y	TITCH-Y
MOUTH-Y	SMELL-Y	TOAST-Y
NIGHT-Y	SMILE-Y	TOOTH-Y
ONION-Y	SMITH-Y	TOOTS-Y
PAPER-Y	SMOKE-Y	TOUCH-Y
PARLE-Y	SNAKE-Y	TRASH-Y
PATCH-Y	SNEAK-Y	TREAT-Y
PEACH-Y	SNIFF-Y	TREND-Y
PEARL-Y	SNOOP-Y	TRICK-Y
PHONE-Y	SPACE-Y	TRUST-Y
PLUCK-Y	SPARK-Y	TWANG-Y
POINT-Y	SPEED-Y	TWEED-Y
PRICE-Y	SPICE-Y	TWEEN-Y
PRIOR-Y	SPIKE-Y	TWIRL-Y
PUNCH-Y	SPOOK-Y	TWIST-Y
QUACK-Y	SPORT-Y	VINER-Y
QUIRK-Y	STEAD-Y	WAFER-Y
RIGHT-Y	STEAM-Y	WATER-Y
ROOTS-Y	STEEL-Y	WEIRD-Y
ROUGH-Y	STICK-Y	WHIFF-Y
RUDER-Y	STING-Y	WHIMS-Y
SAVOR-Y	STINK-Y	WHINE-Y

Y

WHIRL-Y
WHIRR-Y

WHISK-Y
WHITE-Y

WIELD-Y
WORTH-Y

Six letters to seven

ALMOND-Y
ANALOG-Y
ANARCH-Y
ARCHER-Y
ARMOUR-Y
AUTUMN-Y
BALSAM-Y
BATTER-Y
BILLOW-Y
BLIGHT-Y
BLOTCH-Y
BRAVER-Y
BREATH-Y
BREWER-Y
BRIBER-Y
BURSAR-Y
BUTTER-Y
CARVER-Y
CHINTZ-Y
CHOOSE-Y
CITRUS-Y
CLIQUE-Y
CLOVER-Y
COOKER-Y
COPPER-Y
COTTON-Y
CRUNCH-Y
CURSOR-Y
CUTLER-Y
DODDER-Y
DRAPER-Y
DROUTH-Y
DYNAST-Y
EPONYM-Y
FACTOR-Y
FARMER-Y

FIBBER-Y
FIDDLE-Y
FIDGET-Y
FISHER-Y
FLAVOR-Y
FLIGHT-Y
FLOWER-Y
FORGER-Y
GADGET-Y
GINGER-Y
GLITCH-Y
GOSSIP-Y
GRAVEL-Y
GROCER-Y
GROUCH-Y
GUNNER-Y
HACKER-Y
HAUGHT-Y
HEALTH-Y
HICCUP-Y
HONEST-Y
HOSIER-Y
IMAGER-Y
JARGON-Y
JITTER-Y
JOINER-Y
KITSCH-Y
LATHER-Y
LECHER-Y
LENGTH-Y
LOTTER-Y
MARTYR-Y
MASTER-Y
MISTER-Y
MOCKER-Y
MODEST-Y

MONGER-Y
MUMMER-Y
NAUGHT-Y
NURSER-Y
ORANGE-Y
ORATOR-Y
PANICK-Y
PAUNCH-Y
PEDLAR-Y
PEPPER-Y
PHLEGM-Y
PILFER-Y
PILLOW-Y
POTTER-Y
POWDER-Y
PREACH-Y
QUIVER-Y
RAGGED-Y
RAISIN-Y
RAUNCH-Y
RECTOR-Y
RIFLER-Y
ROBBER-Y
ROCKER-Y
RUBBER-Y
SAVOUR-Y
SCRUFF-Y
SENSOR-Y
SERVER-Y
SHADOW-Y
SHIVER-Y
SHLOCK-Y
SHOWER-Y
SHRILL-Y
SILVER-Y
SKETCH-Y

Y

SLAVER-Y
SMOOTH-Y
SPIDER-Y
SPLASH-Y
SPRING-Y
SQUASH-Y
SQUEAK-Y
STARCH-Y
STREAK-Y

STRING-Y
STRIPE-Y
SURGER-Y
TANNER-Y
THIRST-Y
THRIFT-Y
TIMBER-Y
TRICKS-Y
TWITCH-Y

UNREAD-Y
VELVET-Y
VICTOR-Y
WASHER-Y
WEALTH-Y
WEASEL-Y
WEIGHT-Y
WILLOW-Y
WINTER-Y

Seven letters to eight

ADVISOR-Y
AUDITOR-Y
BISCUIT-Y
BLADDER-Y
BLOSSOM-Y
BLUSTER-Y
BOULDER-Y
BURGLAR-Y
BUTCHER-Y
CABBAGE-Y
CAJOLER-Y
CALAMAR-Y
CARTOON-Y
CHANCER-Y
CHEATER-Y
CHIFFON-Y
CHIRRUP-Y
CITATOR-Y
CLATTER-Y
COBBLER-Y
COLLIER-Y
CREAMER-Y
CRYOGEN-Y
CURATOR-Y
CUSTARD-Y
DASTARD-Y
DELIVER-Y
DRAUGHT-Y
DRUDGER-Y

ENTREAT-Y
FEATHER-Y
FLATTER-Y
FLICKER-Y
FLUSTER-Y
FRIPPER-Y
FRUITER-Y
GIMMICK-Y
GLITTER-Y
GLUTTON-Y
GREENER-Y
GRINDER-Y
GYRATOR-Y
HATCHER-Y
HEATHER-Y
HOMONYM-Y
INCISOR-Y
JEALOUS-Y
JEOPARD-Y
KNACKER-Y
LAMINAR-Y
LEATHER-Y
MILITAR-Y
MONARCH-Y
MONITOR-Y
MUSTARD-Y
NEGATOR-Y
NITPICK-Y
ORDINAR-Y

PARADOX-Y
PEDAGOG-Y
PLASTER-Y
POLYGAM-Y
POLYMER-Y
PUDDING-Y
QUIZZER-Y
RECOVER-Y
REFINER-Y
RUBBISH-Y
SADDLER-Y
SAVAGER-Y
SCHLOCK-Y
SCRATCH-Y
SCREECH-Y
SCRUNCH-Y
SEMINAR-Y
SHIMMER-Y
SHMALTZ-Y
SLIPPER-Y
SLOBBER-Y
SLUMBER-Y
SMOTHER-Y
SOLDIER-Y
SPINNER-Y
SPUTTER-Y
SQUELCH-Y
STEALTH-Y
STUDENT-Y

Y

SYNONYM-Y   TOURIST-Y   UNWORTH-Y
TABLOID-Y   TRICKER-Y   VILLAIN-Y
THUNDER-Y   TWITTER-Y   WARRANT-Y
TITULAR-Y   UNTRUST-Y   WHISKER-Y

BLOCKERS

It is useful to know which words are blockers and can't therefore be extended before or after. You may want to play a blocker that your opponent can't extend, or you may want to avoid playing a blocker because you want to keep the board open.

Some three-letter blockers beginning with Y

YAE   YEH   YEX

Four-letter blocker beginning with Y

YUTZ

Some five-letter blockers beginning with Y (except words ending in '-ED', '-J', '-S', '-X', '-Y' or '-Z')

YAULD   YOURN   YUCKO
YOGIC   YOUSE   YUMMO
YOKUL   YUCCH

Some six-letter blockers beginning with Y (except words ending in '-ED', '-J', '-S', '-X', '-Y' or '-Z')

YAKUZA   YEOMAN   YIKING
YAWING   YEOMEN   YIPPEE

BONUS WORDS

Bonus words on your rack can be hard to spot, especially for the less experienced player. One way to help find them is by using prefixes and suffixes.

Many larger words include a common prefix or suffix – remembering these and using them where you can is a good way to discover any longer words on your rack, including any potential bonus words. The key suffix to remember beginning with Y is -YARD.

Y

Some words ending with -YARD

Seven-letter words

BEE-YARD
HAL-YARD

INN-YARD
LAN-YARD

TAN-YARD

Eight-letter words

BACK-YARD
BALL-YARD
BARN-YARD
BOAT-YARD
BONE-YARD
COAL-YARD
DEER-YARD
DOCK-YARD
DOOR-YARD
FARM-YARD

FEED-YARD
FORE-YARD
HAUL-YARD
JUNK-YARD
KAIL-YARD
KALE-YARD
KIRK-YARD
MAIN-YARD
METE-YARD
RICK-YARD

SALE-YARD
SAVO-YARD
SHIP-YARD
SHOW-YARD
TILT-YARD
VINE-YARD
WHIN-YARD
WILL-YARD
WOOD-YARD

UNUSUAL LETTER COMBINATIONS

If you have an unusual combination of letters on your rack, or want to impress your opponent with an unusual word, a few words from World English can come in handy.

Australian words

YABBER   talk or jabber
YABBY   small freshwater crayfish
YACCA   grass tree
YARRAN   small hardy tree
YATE   small eucalyptus tree
YIKE   argument, squabble or fight
YUCKO   disgusting
YUMMO   delicious

South African word

YEBO   yes

Y

Z
10

Essential info
Value: 10 points
Number in set: 1

POWER TILE

Z is one of the most valuable tiles in the Scrabble set. It is easier to use than, for example, Q, as it is not so heavily reliant on another letter (as is Q on U). Various three-letter words using Z can be remembered easily as sets of two, with another fixed consonant and alternating vowels, for example ZIG, ZAG and especially ZAX, ZEX (using two power tiles and thus potentially achieving huge scores). Sets of three are also useful to keep in mind, such as CAZ, COZ, CUZ.

Two-letter words beginning with Z

ZA	ZO

Some three-letter words beginning with Z

ZAG	ZEK	ZIG
ZAX	ZEL	ZIN
ZEA	ZEP	ZIT
ZED	ZEX	ZOA
ZEE	ZHO	ZOL

Some three-letter words using Z

ADZ	DZO	POZ
AZO	FEZ	REZ
BEZ	FIZ	RIZ
CAZ	LUZ	SAZ
COZ	MIZ	SEZ
CUZ	MOZ	WIZ

Some four-letter words using Z

Some interesting four-letter words using the letter Z are AZYM (unleavened bread, 18 points) and NAZE (marshy headland, 13 points). Words beginning with Z which may be unfamiliar include ZATI (a type of macaque, 13 points) and ZOEA (larva of a crab or crustacean, 13 points). Don't forget words such as JAZY (wig, 23 points) and QUIZ (22 points) as they use more than one power tile and can return relatively high scores considering their length.

ADZE	MOZO	ZEBU
AZAN	MZEE	ZEIN
AZON	NAZE	ZERK
AZYM	NAZI	ZEST
BIZE	OOZE	ZETA
BOZO	ORZO	ZIFF
BUZZ	OYEZ	ZILA
CHEZ	PHIZ	ZILL
CHIZ	PIZE	ZIMB
COZE	PREZ	ZINC
COZY	QUIZ	ZING
CZAR	RAZE	ZIPS
FAZE	RAZZ	ZITE
FIZZ	RITZ	ZITI
FOZY	RIZA	ZOEA
FUTZ	SITZ	ZOIC
FUZZ	SWIZ	ZONA
GAZE	TIZZ	ZONE
HAZE	TOZE	ZONK
HAZY	TREZ	ZOOM
IZAR	TZAR	ZOON
JAZZ	VIZY	ZOOT
KUZU	WHIZ	ZORI
LAZO	YUTZ	ZOUK
LAZY	YUZU	ZULU
LUTZ	ZACK	ZUPA
MAZE	ZANY	ZURF
MAZY	ZARF	ZYGA
MEZE	ZATI	ZYME
MOZE	ZEAL	

HOOKS

By their nature, power tiles feature in fewer words than the other letters in the Scrabble set. As a result, examples of their use in hooking (especially end-hooking) can be few and far between. Bear in mind the prefix ZOO- as it features heavily in the longer examples.

Useful examples to remember are ZESTER (kitchen utensil used to scrape peel from citrus fruits, 15 points) and ZITHER (a stringed musical instrument, 18 points).

Z

Some front-hooks
Two letters to three

Z-AG
Z-AS
Z-AX
Z-EA
Z-ED

Z-EE
Z-EL
Z-EX
Z-HO
Z-IN

Z-IT
Z-OO
Z-OS

Three letters to four

Z-ARF
Z-ERK
Z-ETA

Z-IFF
Z-ILL
Z-OBO

Z-OON
Z-OOT
Z-OUK

Four letters to five

Z-AMIA
Z-ANTE
Z-AYIN

Z-HOMO
Z-INKY
Z-LOTE

Z-OPPO
Z-UPAS

Five letters to six

Z-ANANA
Z-ESTER

Z-INKED
Z-ITHER

Z-ONERS

Six letters to seven

Z-INCITE
Z-INKIER
Z-OOGAMY

Z-OOGENY
Z-OOIDAL
Z-OOLITE

Z-OOLITH
Z-ORBING

Seven letters to eight

Z-OOLITIC
Z-OOLOGIC

Z-OOPHYTE
Z-OOSPERM

Z-OOSPORE

> ### Handy Hint
> Power tile letters may be less common than others in the set but there are many simple and easy-to-remember words that use them. Some examples for Z include: LAZY (16 points), QUIZ (22), ZERO (13), ZAP (14), ZOOM (15) and ZONE (13).

Z

Some end-hooks
Two letters to three

AD-Z
BE-Z
BI-Z

FE-Z
MI-Z
MO-Z

PO-Z
RE-Z

Three letters to four

CHI-Z
GEE-Z
MIZ-Z

MOZ-Z
PHI-Z
POZ-Z

SIT-Z

Four letters to five

BORT-Z
CAPI-Z
CHIZ-Z

GREN-Z
MILT-Z
PLOT-Z

SPIT-Z
WARE-Z
WOOT-Z

Five letters to six

QUART-Z

SPELT-Z

SPRIT-Z

Six letters to seven

SCHNOZ-Z

BLOCKERS

It is useful to know which words are blockers and can't therefore be extended before or after. You may want to play a blocker that your opponent can't extend, or you may want to avoid playing a blocker because you want to keep the board open.

Some three-letter blockers using Z

BEZ
CAZ
FEZ
LUZ

SAZ
SEZ
ZAX
ZEX

ZOA
ZUZ

Some four-letter blockers using Z

FOZY
FUTZ
GAZY
JAZY
MAZY

MOZZ
PHIZ
PUTZ
SITZ
SIZY

TUZZ
VIZY
YUTZ
ZITE
ZIZZ

Z

BONUS WORDS

Bear in mind that the UK suffix -ISE may be substituted for the American -IZE in Scrabble. Both are acceptable and this will make the Z much easier to play when forming verb examples.

The lists are separated by prefix, and many feature the prefix ZOO- (involving animals) such as the well-known ZOOLOGY (the study of animals, 20 points) and the less-well-known ZOOLATRY (the worship of animals as divine beings, also 20 points).

Seven-letter words

ZABTIEH	ZEBROID	ZINCOID
ZACATON	ZEBRULA	ZINCOUS
ZADDICK	ZEBRULE	ZINGANI
ZAITECH	ZECCHIN	ZINGANO
ZAKUSKA	ZEDOARY	ZINGARA
ZAKUSKI	ZELATOR	ZINGARE
ZAMARRA	ZELKOVA	ZINGARI
ZAMARRO	ZEMSTVA	ZINGARO
ZAMBUCK	ZEMSTVO	ZINKIER
ZAMOUSE	ZENAIDA	ZINKIFY
ZAMPONE	ZEOLITE	ZINKING
ZAMPONI	ZESTFUL	ZITHERN
ZANELLA	ZESTIER	ZLOTYCH
ZANIEST	ZESTING	ZOARIAL
ZANJERO	ZETETIC	ZOARIUM
ZAPATEO	ZEUXITE	ZOCCOLO
ZAPPIER	ZIFFIUS	ZOECIUM
ZAPPING	ZIGANKA	ZOEFORM
ZAPTIAH	ZIKURAT	ZOISITE
ZAPTIEH	ZILLION	ZOMBIFY
ZAREEBA	ZIMOCCA	ZONALLY
ZARNICH	ZINCATE	ZONATED
ZEALANT	ZINCIER	ZONKING
ZEALFUL	ZINCIFY	ZONULAE
ZEALOUS	ZINCING	ZONULAR
ZEBRAIC	ZINCITE	ZONULES
ZEBRINA	ZINCKED	ZONULET
ZEBRINE	ZINCODE	ZOOECIA

Z

ZOOGAMY
ZOOGENY
ZOOGLEA
ZOOGONY
ZOOIDAL
ZOOLITE
ZOOLITH
ZOOLOGY
ZOONITE
ZOONOMY

ZOOPERY
ZOOTAXY
ZOOTOMY
ZOOTYPE
ZORBING
ZORGITE
ZORILLA
ZORILLE
ZORILLO
ZOYSIAS

ZUFFOLI
ZUFFOLO
ZYGOSIS
ZYGOTIC
ZYMOGEN
ZYMOSAN
ZYMOSIS
ZYMOTIC
ZYMURGY

Eight-letter words

ZABAIONE
ZABAJONE
ZADDIKIM
ZAIBATSU
ZAKOUSKA
ZAKOUSKI
ZAMBOMBA
ZAMINDAR
ZAMPOGNA
ZAMZAWED
ZAPPIEST
ZARATITE
ZARZUELA
ZASTRUGA
ZASTRUGI
ZEALLESS
ZEALOTRY
ZEBRINNY
ZECCHINE
ZECCHINI
ZECCHINO
ZELATRIX
ZEMINDAR
ZEMSTVOS
ZENITHAL
ZEOLITIC
ZEPPELIN
ZERUMBET

ZESTIEST
ZESTLESS
ZIBELINE
ZIGGURAT
ZIGZAGGY
ZIKKURAT
ZIMOCCAS
ZINCIEST
ZINCKIER
ZINCKIFY
ZINCKING
ZINCODES
ZINDABAD
ZINGIBER
ZINGIEST
ZINKIEST
ZIRCALOY
ZIRCONIA
ZIRCONIC
ZODIACAL
ZOETROPE
ZOIATRIA
ZOMBIISM
ZOMBORUK
ZONATION
ZONELESS
ZONETIME
ZOOBLAST

ZOOCHORE
ZOOCHORY
ZOOCYTIA
ZOOECIUM
ZOOGENIC
ZOOGLEAE
ZOOGLEAL
ZOOGLOEA
ZOOGRAFT
ZOOLATER
ZOOLATRY
ZOOLITIC
ZOOLOGIC
ZOOMANCY
ZOOMANIA
ZOOMETRY
ZOOMORPH
ZOONITIC
ZOONOMIA
ZOONOMIC
ZOONOSIS
ZOONOTIC
ZOOPATHY
ZOOPERAL
ZOOPHOBE
ZOOPHORI
ZOOPHYTE
ZOOSCOPY

Z

ZOOSPERM
ZOOSPORE
ZOOTHOME
ZOOTIEST
ZOOTOMIC
ZOOTOXIC
ZOOTOXIN
ZOOTROPE
ZOOTYPIC

ZOPILOTE
ZUCCHINI
ZUCHETTA
ZUCHETTO
ZWIEBACK
ZYGAENID
ZYGANTRA
ZYGODONT
ZYGOMATA

ZYGOSITY
ZYGOTENE
ZYLONITE
ZYMOGENE
ZYMOGENS
ZYMOGRAM
ZYMOLOGY
ZYMOTICS

UNUSUAL LETTER COMBINATIONS

If you have an unusual combination of letters on your rack, or want to impress your opponent with an unusual word, a few words from World English can come in handy.

Australian words

ZAMBUCK   St John ambulance attendant
ZIFF   beard

Hindi words

ZENANA   part of a house reserved for women
ZILA   administrative district in India

ZHO AND TELL

There are various alternative spellings for ZHO (a Tibetan breed of cattle, developed by crossing the yak with common cattle). These are DSO, DZO, DZHO and ZO, all of which it is worth remembering in order to form short, high-scoring words (ZHO scores 15 points and DZO is worth 13).

Z

Two- and three-letter words

Two-letter words

AA	volcanic rock
AB	abdominal muscle
AD	short form of advertisement
AE	Scots word meaning one or a single
AG	agriculture
AH	expression of pleasure, pain, or sympathy
AI	the three-toed sloth
AL	Asian shrub or tree
AM	part of the verb to be
AN	the indefinite article used before an initial vowel sound
AR	the letter R
AS	while, because, since
AT	used to indicate location or position
AW	expression of disapproval, commiseration, or appeal
AX	US spelling of axe
AY	yes
BA	the soul represented as a bird with a human head
BE	exist, live
BI	short for bisexual
BO	exclamation used to startle or surprise
BY	near to, at the side of, via; a bye
CH	obsolete form of I
DA	Burmese knife
DE	of or from
DI	plural form of deus
DO	perform, complete; a party
EA	dialect word for river
ED	education
EE	Scots word for eye
EF	the letter F
EH	exclamation of surprise or inquiry
EL	elevated railway
EM	printing meaurement
EN	printing measurement
ER	expression of hesitation
ES	the letter S
ET	past tense of eat
EX	former spouse or partner
FA	variant spelling of fah
FE	charge, fee
FY	variant spelling of fie
GI	martial arts suit
GO	to move or proceed; a turn or attempt
GU	musical instrument
HA	exclamation of derision, triumph, or surprise
HE	male person or animal
HI	hello
HM	expression of thoughtful consideration
HO	exclamation used to attract attention
ID	unconscious primitive instincts
IF	in case that; an uncertainty or condition
IN	inside, within; a way of approaching a person
IO	cry of joy or grief
IS	part of the verb to be
IT	nonhuman thing
JA	yes
JO	Scots word for a sweetheart
KA	ancient Egyptian spirit
KI	Japanese martial art
KO	Maori digging-stick
KY	Scots word for cows
LA	variant spelling of lah

LI	Chinese unit of length
LO	look!
MA	word for mother
ME	refers to the speaker or writer
MI	musical term
MM	expression of satisfaction
MO	short for moment
MU	12th Greek letter
MY	of or belonging to the speaker or writer
NA	Scots word for no
NE	not, nor
NO	expression of denial, refusal, etc
NU	13th Greek letter
NY	nigh; to approach
OB	objection
OD	hypothetical force
OE	grandchild
OF	belonging to
OH	exclamation of surprise, pain, etc
OI	exclamation used to attract attention
OM	intonation chanted as a mantra
ON	not off; the side of the field on which the batsman stands
OO	Scots word for wool
OP	short for operation
OR	conjunction used to join alternatives; gold
OS	bone
OU	South African slang for a man
OW	exclamation of pain
OX	adult castrated bull
OY	grandchild
PA	word for father
PE	17th Hebrew letter
PI	16th Greek letter
PO	chamberpot
QI	vital energy believed to circulate in the body

RE	musical term
SH	exclamation to request silence
SI	musical term
SO	variant spelling of soh
ST	exclamation to request silence
TA	thank you
TE	musical term
TI	variant spelling of te
TO	towards, in the direction of
UG	cause loathing in, hate
UH	expression of uncertainty
UM	sound of hesitation
UN	dialect variant of one
UP	in a higher place; a rise or success
UR	sound of hesitation
US	refers to the speaker or writer and another
UT	syllable used for the note C
WE	refers to the speaker or writer and another
WO	archaic spelling of woe
XI	14th Greek letter
XU	monetary unit
YA	you
YE	archaic word for you
YO	expression of greeting
YU	jade
ZA	pizza
ZO	Tibetan breed of cattle

Three-letter words

AAH	exclamation of pleasure, satisfaction, etc
AAL	Asian shrub or tree
AAS	plural form of aa
ABA	type of cloth from Syria
ABB	yarn used in weaving
ABO	offensive word for Aborigine
ABS	plural form of ab
ABY	pay the penalty for
ACE	playing card

ACH	Scots expression of surprise
ACT	something done, deed
ADD	combine
ADO	fuss, trouble
ADS	plural form of ad
ADZ	heavy hand tool
AFF	Scots word for off
AFT	at or towards the rear
AGA	Ottoman military commander
AGE	length of time
AGO	in the past
AGS	plural form of ag
AHA	exclamation of triumph, surprise, etc
AHI	the yellowfin tuna
AHS	plural form of ah
AIA	nursemaid in East
AID	assistance or support
AIL	trouble, afflict
AIM	point or direct at target
AIN	Scots word for own
AIR	the mixture of gases forming the earth's atmosphere
AIS	plural form of ai
AIT	islet, esp in a river
AKA	New Zealand vine
AKE	old spelling of ache
ALA	wing
ALB	Christian priest's robe
ALE	kind of beer
ALF	uncultivated Australian
ALL	the whole quantity of something
ALP	high mountain
ALS	plural form of al
ALT	musical term
AMA	wet nurse
AMI	male friend
AMP	ampere
AMU	atomic mass unit
ANA	in equal quantities

AND	conjunction used to express addition
ANE	Scots word for one
ANI	type of tropical American bird
ANN	payment to a parish minister's widow
ANT	small insect
ANY	one or some
APE	primate
APO	type of protein
APP	short for application program
APT	suitable, appropriate
ARB	short form of arbitrageur
ARC	part of a circle or curve
ARD	primitive plough
ARE	100 square metres
ARF	barking sound
ARK	the boat built by Noah
ARM	upper limb
ARS	plural form of ar
ART	creation of works of beauty
ARY	dialect form of any
ASH	substance left after burning
ASK	request an answer from
ASP	small poisonous snake
ASS	donkey
ATE	part of the verb to eat
ATT	old Siamese coin
AUA	the yellow-eye mullet
AUE	Maori exclamation of pain, distress, etc
AUF	old word for oaf
AUK	northern sea bird
AVA	Scots word for at all
AVE	welcome or farewell
AVO	Macao currency unit
AWA	Scots word for away
AWE	wonder and respect mixed with dread
AWL	pointed tool

AWN	bristles growing from certain grasses
AXE	tool with a sharp blade
AYE	yes
AYS	plural form of ay
AYU	small Japanese fish
AZO	chemistry term
BAA	sound of a sheep
BAC	baccalaureate
BAD	not good
BAG	flexible container
BAH	expression of contempt or disgust
BAL	balmoral, an ankle-high shoe
BAM	cheat, hoax
BAN	prohibit or forbid
BAP	large soft bread roll
BAR	length of metal, etc
BAS	plural form of ba
BAT	club used to hit the ball in sports
BAY	semicircular indentation of a shoreline
BED	piece of furniture
BEE	insect that makes honey
BEG	solicit (money, etc)
BEL	unit for comparing two power levels
BEN	mountain peak
BES	variant of beth, 2nd Hebrew letter
BET	wager
BEY	Ottoman official
BEZ	part of deer's horn
BIB	cloth worn by babies
BID	offer to buy something, esp in competition
BIG	of considerable size, number, etc
BIN	container for rubbish
BIO	short for biography
BIS	twice
BIT	small piece or portion

BIZ	short for business
BOA	large snake
BOB	move up and down repeatedly
BOD	person
BOG	wet spongy ground
BOH	exclamation used to startle or surprise
BOI	lesbian who dresses like a boy
BOK	S African antelope
BON	good
BOO	shout of disapproval
BOP	dance to pop music
BOR	neighbour
BOS	plural form of bo
BOT	larva of a botfly
BOW	lower head as sign of respect
BOX	container
BOY	male child
BRA	brassiere
BRO	family member
BRR	used to suggest shivering
BRU	South African word for friend
BUB	youngster
BUD	swelling on a plant
BUG	insect
BUM	buttocks
BUN	sweet bread roll or cake
BUR	washer fitting around the end of a rivet
BUS	large motor vehicle
BUT	except, only
BUY	acquire by paying money
BYE	goodbye
BYS	plural form of by
CAA	Scots word for call
CAB	taxi
CAD	dishonourable man
CAG	short for cagoule
CAM	device that converts a circular motion
CAN	be able to

CAP	covering for the head		CUT	divide with a sharp instrument
CAR	motor vehicle		CUZ	cousin
CAT	furry mammal		CWM	geology term
CAW	cry of a crow or raven		DAB	pat lightly
CAY	small low island		DAD	word for father
CAZ	short for casual		DAE	Scots word for do
CEE	3rd letter of the alphabet		DAG	cut daglocks from sheep
CEL	short for celluloid		DAH	term used in Morse code
CEP	another name for porcino		DAK	system of mail delivery
CHA	tea		DAL	decalitre
CHE	dialectal form of I		DAM	barrier built across a river to create a lake
CHI	22nd Greek letter		
CID	leader		DAN	judo term
CIG	short for cigarette		DAP	flyfishing with a floss silk line
CIS	chemistry term		DAS	plural form of da
CIT	town dweller		DAW	jackdaw
CLY	to steal or seize		DAY	period of 24 hours
COB	male swan		DEB	debutante
COD	large food fish		DEE	Scots word for die
COG	tooth on the rim of a gearwheel		DEF	very good
COL	high mountain pass		DEG	water (a plant, etc)
CON	deceive, swindle		DEI	plural form of deus
COO	make a soft murmuring sound		DEL	differential operator
COP	copper		DEN	home of a wild animal
COR	exclamation of surprise or admiration		DEV	Hindu god
			DEW	drops of water that form on the ground
COS	cosine		
COT	baby's bed with high sides		DEX	dextroamphetamine
COW	mature female bovine animal		DEY	commanders of the Janissaries of Algiers
COX	coxswain		
COY	affectedly shy or modest		DIB	fish with a bobbing bait
COZ	archaic word for cousin		DID	part of the verb to do
CRU	vineyard		DIE	cease living
CRY	shed tears		DIF	short for difference
CUB	the young of some animals		DIG	cut into earth, esp with a spade
CUD	partially digested food		DIM	badly lit
CUE	signal to an actor or musician to begin		DIN	loud unpleasant noise
			DIP	plunge briefly into liquid
CUM	with		DIS	treat someone with contempt
CUP	drinking vessel		DIT	term used in Morse code
CUR	mongrel dog		DIV	stupid or foolish person

DOB	(as in dob in) inform against	ECU	French coin
DOC	doctor	EDH	character of the runic alphabet
DOD	cut the hair of	EDS	plural form of ed
DOE	female deer	EEK	expression indicating shock
DOF	South African word for stupid	EEL	snakelike fish
DOG	domesticated four-legged mammal	EEN	Scots form of eye
DOH	musical term	EFF	say the word 'fuck'
DOL	unit of pain intensity	EFS	plural form of ef
DOM	title given to monks	EFT	newt
DON	put on (clothing)	EGG	oval or round object laid by female birds
DOO	Scots word for dove	EGO	conscious mind of an individual
DOP	tot of alcoholic drink	EHS	plural form of eh
DOR	European dung beetle	EIK	Scots form of eke
DOS	plural form of do	EKE	increase, enlarge, or lengthen
DOT	small round mark	ELD	old age
DOW	Arab vessel	ELF	small mischievous fairy
DOY	beloved person	ELK	large deer of N Europe and Asia
DRY	lacking moisture	ELL	unit of length equal to approximately 45 inches
DSO	Tibetan breed of cattle		
DUB	give (a person or place) a name	ELM	tree with serrated leaves
DUD	ineffectual person	ELS	plural form of el
DUE	something owed	ELT	young female pig
DUG	part of the verb to dig	EME	uncle
DUH	response implying that the speaker is stupid	EMO	type of music
		EMS	plural form of em
DUI	plural form of duo	EMU	large flightless bird
DUN	brownish-grey	END	come to a finish
DUO	duet	ENE	variant of even
DUP	open	ENG	phonetics symbol
DUX	the top pupil in a class or school	ENS	existence in the most general abstract sense
DYE	colouring substance		
DZO	Tibetan breed of cattle	EON	long period of time
EAN	give birth	ERA	period of time
EAR	organ of hearing	ERE	before
EAS	plural form of ea	ERF	plot of land for building purposes
EAT	chew and swallow food		
EAU	drainage channel	ERG	unit of work or energy
EBB	(of tide water) flow back	ERK	aircraftman
ECH	Shakespearean word for eke out	ERN	archaic variant of earn
ECO	short for ecology	ERR	make a mistake

ERS	bitter vetch	FEY	whimsically strange
ESS	the letter S	FEZ	brimless tasselled cap
EST	treatment that helps people achieve psychological growth	FIB	trivial lie
		FID	spike for separating strands of rope
ETA	7th Greek letter		
ETH	character of the runic alphabet	FIE	exclamation of disapproval
EUK	itch	FIG	soft pear-shaped fruit
EVE	evening or day before an event	FIL	Shakespearean word for the shaft of a vehicle
EVO	evening		
EWE	female sheep	FIN	the organs of locomotion in fish
EWK	itch	FIR	tree
EWT	archaic form of newt	FIT	be appropriate for
EXO	excellent	FIX	make or become firm, stable, or secure
EYE	organ of sight		
FAA	Scots word for fall	FIZ	make a hissing sound
FAB	excellent	FLU	viral infection
FAD	short-lived fashion	FLY	move through the air on wings
FAE	Scots word for from	FOB	short watch chain
FAG	slang word for cigarette	FOE	enemy, opponent
FAH	musical term	FOG	mass of condensed water vapour in the air
FAN	object used to create a current of air		
		FOH	expression of disgust
FAP	drunk	FON	fool
FAR	at, to, or from a great distance	FOP	man excessively concerned with fashion
FAS	plural form of fa		
FAT	having excess flesh on the body	FOR	in the place of, in favour of
FAW	gypsy	FOU	Scots word for full
FAX	electronic system for sending documents	FOX	reddish-brown bushy-tailed animal
		FOY	loyalty
FAY	fairy or sprite	FRA	brother: a title given to an Italian monk or friar
FED	FBI agent		
FEE	charge	FRO	back or from
FEG	segment from an orange	FRY	cook in fat or oil
FEH	Hebrew coin	FUB	put off, fob
FEM	feminine	FUD	rabbit's tail
FEN	flat marshy land	FUG	hot stale atmosphere
FER	same as far	FUM	mythological phoenix
FES	plural form of fe	FUN	enjoyment or amusement
FET	fetch	FUR	soft hair of a mammal
FEU	right of use of land	GAB	talk or chatter
FEW	not many		

GAD	go about in search of pleasure	GOO	sticky substance
GAE	Scots word for go	GOR	God!
GAG	choke or retch	GOS	plural form of go
GA	girl	GOT	part of the verb to get
GAM	school of whales	GOV	short for governor
GAN	archaic word for begin	GOX	gaseous oxygen
GAP	break or opening	GOY	Jewish word for a non-Jew
GAR	pike-like fish	GUB	white man
GAS	airlike substance that is not liquid or solid	GUE	musical instrument
		GUL	oriental carpet design
GAT	pistol or revolver	GUM	flesh in which the teeth are set
GAU	district set up by the Nazi Party	GUN	weapon
GAY	homosexual	GUP	gossip
GED	Scots word for pike	GUR	unrefined cane sugar
GEE	mild exclamation of surprise	GUS	plural form of gu
GEL	jelly-like substance	GUT	intestine
GEM	precious stone or jewel	GUV	short for governor
GEN	information	GUY	man or boy
GEO	small fjord or gully	GYM	gymnasium
GET	obtain or receive	GYP	swindle
GEY	intensifier	HAD	part of the verb to have
GHI	clarified butter	HAE	Scots form of have
GIB	metal wedge	HAG	ugly old woman
GID	disease of sheep	HAH	exclamation of derision, triumph, or surprise
GIE	Scots word for give		
GIF	obsolete word for if	HAJ	Muslim pilgrimage
GIG	single performance by musicians	HAM	meat from a pig's thigh
		HAN	archaic form of have
GIN	spirit flavoured with juniper berries	HAO	monetary unit
		HAP	luck, chance
GIO	gully, creek	HAS	part of the verb to have
GIP	pain, torture	HAT	covering for the head
GIS	plural form of gi	HAW	hawthorn berry
GIT	contemptible person	HAY	grass cut and dried as fodder
GJU	musical instrument	HEH	exclamation of surprise
GNU	ox-like antelope	HEM	bottom edge of a garment
GOA	Tibetan gazelle	HEN	female domestic fowl
GOB	lump of a soft substance	HEP	fruit of the dog rose
GOD	worshipped spirit	HER	refers to a female person or animal
GOE	Spenserian word for go		
GON	geometrical grade	HES	plural form of he

HET	short for heterosexual	HUM	low continuous vibrating sound
HEW	cut with an axe	HUN	member of Asiatic nomadic peoples
HEX	evil spell		
HEY	expression of surprise or for catching attention	HUP	cry to make a horse turn
		HUT	small house, shelter, or shed
HIC	sound of a hiccup	HYE	hurry
HID	part of the verb to hide	HYP	hypotenuse
HIE	hurry	ICE	water in its solid state
HIM	refers to a male person or animal	ICH	dialect form of I
		ICK	expression of disgust
HIN	Hebrew unit of capacity	ICY	very cold
HIP	part of the body between pelvis and thigh	IDE	silver fish
		IDS	plural form of id
HIS	belonging to him	IFF	conjunction used in logic
HIT	strike, touch forcefully	IFS	plural form of if
HMM	expression of thoughtful consideration	IGG	ignore, snub
		ILK	type
HOA	exclamation to attract attention	ILL	not in good health
HOB	flat top part of a cooker	IMP	mischievous small creature
HOC	Latin for this	INK	coloured liquid used for writing or printing
HOD	open wooden box attached to a pole		
		INN	pub or small hotel
HOE	long-handled tool	INS	plural form of in
HOG	castrated male pig	ION	atom
HOH	exclamation to attract attention	IOS	plural form of io
HOI	cry used to attract attention	IRE	anger
HOM	sacred plant	IRK	irritate, annoy
HON	short for honey	ISH	issue, expiry
HOO	expression of boisterous emotion	ISM	doctrine, system, or practice
		ISO	short segment of film
HOP	jump on one foot	ITA	type of palm
HOS	plural form of ho	ITS	belonging to it
HOT	having a high temperature	IVY	evergreen climbing plant
HOW	in what way	IWI	Maori tribe
HOX	hamstring	JAB	poke sharply
HOY	cry used to attract attention	JAG	cut unevenly
HUB	centre of a wheel	JAI	victory (to)
HUE	colour	JAK	South and South East Asian tree
HUG	clasp tightly in the arms	JAM	pack tightly into a place
HUH	exclamation of derision	JAP	splash, spatter
HUI	meeting of Maori people	JAR	wide-mouthed container

JAW	bone in which the teeth are set	KEG	small metal beer barrel
JAY	bird	KEN	know
JEE	move a horse faster	KEP	catch
JET	aircraft	KET	Scots word for carrion
JEU	game	KEX	type of plant
JEW	obsolete offensive word meaning haggle	KEY	device for operating a lock
		KHI	letter of the Greek alphabet
JIB	triangular sail	KID	child
JIG	type of lively dance	KIF	marijuana
JIN	Chinese unit of weight	KIN	person's relatives collectively
JIZ	wig	KIP	sleep
JOB	occupation	KIR	alcoholic drink
JOE	Scots word for a sweetheart	KIS	plural form of ki
JOG	run at a gentle pace	KIT	outfit or equipment
JOL	party	KOA	Hawaiian tree
JOR	movement in Indian music	KOB	antelope
JOT	write briefly	KOI	type of carp
JOW	ring (a bell)	KON	Spenserian word for know
JOY	feeling of great delight	KOP	African hill
JUD	large block of coal	KOR	ancient Hebrew unit of capacity
JUG	container for liquids	KOS	Indian unit of distance
JUN	monetary unit	KOW	branch, bunch of twigs
JUS	right, power, or authority	KUE	the letter Q
JUT	project or stick out	KYE	Scots word for cows
KAB	ancient Hebrew measure	KYU	judo term
KAE	jackdaw	LAB	laboratory
KAF	letter of the Hebrew alphabet	LAC	(in India and Pakistan) 100,000 rupees
KAI	New Zealand word for food		
KAK	S African offensive word for faeces	LAD	boy or young man
		LAG	go too slowly
KAM	Shakespearean word for crooked	LAH	musical term
KAS	plural form of ka	LAM	thrash, beat
KAT	shrub whose leaves have narcotic properties	LAP	part between the waist and knees
KAW	cry of a crow	LAR	boy or young man
KAY	the letter K	LAS	plural form of la
KEA	large parrot	LAT	former coin of Latvia
KEB	Scots word meaning miscarry a lamb	LAV	short for lavatory
		LAW	rule binding on a community
KED	(as in sheep ked) sheep tick	LAX	not strict
KEF	marijuana	LAY	part of the verb to lie

LEA	meadow
LED	part of the verb to lead
LEE	sheltered side
LEG	limb
LEI	(in Hawaii) garland of flowers
LEK	monetary unit
LEP	Spenserian word for leap
LES	offensive short form of lesbian
LET	allow, permit
LEU	monetary unit
LEV	monetary unit
LEW	tepid
LEX	system or body of laws
LEY	land temporarily under grass
LEZ	offensive short form of lesbian
LIB	short for liberation
LID	movable cover
LIE	make a deliberately false statement
LIG	function with free refreshments
LIN	cease
LIP	fleshy folds at the mouth
LIS	fleur-de-lis
LIT	part of the verb to light
LOB	ball struck or thrown in a high arc
LOD	type of logarithm
LOG	portion of a felled tree
LOO	word for lavatory
LOP	cut away (twigs and branches)
LOR	exclamation of surprise or dismay
LOS	approval, praise
LOT	great number
LOU	Scots word for love
LOW	not tall or high
LOX	smoked salmon
LOY	narrow spade with a single footrest
LUD	lord
LUG	carry or drag with great effort

LUM	chimney
LUR	musical horn
LUV	love
LUX	unit of illumination
LUZ	supposedly indestructible bone
LYE	caustic solution
LYM	bloodhound
MAA	bleat
MAC	short for macintosh
MAD	mentally deranged
MAE	(as in mae west) inflatable life jacket
MAG	short for magazine
MAK	Scots word for make
MAL	illness, pain
MAM	word for mother
MAN	adult male
MAP	representation of the earth's surface
MAR	spoil or impair
MAS	plural form of ma
MAT	piece of fabric
MAW	animal's mouth
MAX	the full extent
MAY	used to express possibility
MED	doctor
MEE	Malaysian noodle dish
MEG	short for megabyte
MEL	pure form of honey
MEM	13th letter in the Hebrew alphabet
MEN	plural form of man
MES	plural form of me
MET	part of the verb to meet
MEU	the plant spignel
MEW	cry of a cat
MHO	former name for siemens
MIB	marble used in games
MIC	short for microphone
MID	intermediate
MIG	marble used in games

MIL	unit of length	NAP	short sleep
MIM	prim	NAS	has not or was not
MIR	Russian peasant commune	NAT	supporter of nationalism
MIS	plural form of mi	NAW	no
MIX	combine or blend	NAY	no
MIZ	shortened form of misery	NEB	beak of a bird
MNA	Greek weight	NED	derogatory Scots word for a young working-class male
MOA	large extinct flightless bird		
MOB	disorderly crowd	NEE	born
MOC	short for moccasin	NEF	church nave
MOD	sixties youth group	NEG	photographic negative
MOE	more	NEK	mountain pass
MOG	short for moggy	NEP	catmint
MOI	me	NET	meshed fabric
MOL	SI unit mole	NEW	recently made
MOM	word for mother	NIB	writing point of a pen
MON	dialect variant of man	NID	pheasant's nest
MOO	cry of a cow	NIE	archaic spelling of nigh
MOP	cleaning device	NIL	nothing
MOR	layer of acidic humus	NIM	game with matchsticks
MOS	plural form of mo	NIP	pinch
MOT	girl or young woman	NIS	friendly goblin
MOU	Scots word for mouth	NIT	egg or larva of a louse
MOW	to cut grass or crops	NIX	be careful!
MOY	coin	NOB	person of social standing
MOZ	hex	NOD	lower and raise (one's head)
MUD	wet soft earth	NOG	alcoholic drink
MUG	large drinking cup	NOH	drama of Japan
MUM	word for mother	NOM	name
MUN	dialect word for must	NON	not
MUS	plural form of mu	NOO	a Scots word for now
MUT	printing measurement	NOR	and not
MUX	spoil	NOS	plural form of no
MYC	oncogene	NOT	expressing negation
NAB	arrest (someone)	NOW	at or for the present time
NAE	Scots word for no	NOX	nitrogen oxide
NAG	scold constantly	NOY	harass
NAH	no	NTH	of an unspecified number
NAM	distraint	NUB	point or gist
NAN	word for grandmother	NUN	female member of a religious order

NUR	knot of wood	OOH	exclamation of surprise
NUS	plural form of nu	OOM	title of respect
NUT	fruit	OON	Scots word for oven
NYE	flock of pheasants	OOP	Scots word meaning to bind
NYS	plural form of ny	OOR	Scots word for our
OAF	stupid person	OOS	plural form of oo
OAK	tree	OOT	Scots word for out
OAR	pole with a broad blade	OPE	archaic word for open
OAT	grass grown for its edible seed	OPS	plural form of op
OBA	Yoruba chief or ruler	OPT	show a preference
OBE	ancient village	ORA	plural form of os
OBI	Japanese sash	ORB	decorated sphere
OBO	ship carrying oil and ore	ORC	whale
OBS	plural form of ob	ORD	point of a weapon
OCA	South American herbaceous plant	ORE	mineral
		ORF	disease of sheep
OCH	expression of surprise	ORS	plural form of or
ODA	room in a harem	ORT	fragment
ODD	unusual, peculiar	OSE	long winding ridge of gravel, sand, etc
ODE	lyric poem		
ODS	plural form of od	OUD	musical instrument
OES	plural form of oe	OUK	Scots word for week
OFF	not on; away	OUP	Scots word meaning to bind
OFT	often	OUR	belonging to us
OHM	unit of electrical resistance	OUS	plural form of ou
OHO	exclamation of surprise or derision	OUT	outside
OHS	plural form of oh	OVA	plural of ovum
OIK	person regarded as inferior	OWE	be obliged to pay money
OIL	viscous liquid	OWL	bird of prey
OKA	unit of weight	OWN	used to indicate possession
OKE	unit of weight	OWT	dialect word for anything
OLD	having lived for a long time	OXO	(as in oxo acid) acid that contains oxygen
OLE	exclamation of approval		
OLM	salamander	OXY	oxygen
OMS	plural form of om	OYE	grandchild
ONE	single	OYS	plural form of oy
ONO	Hawaiian fish	PAC	soft shoe
ONS	plural form of on	PAD	material for protection
ONY	Scots word for any	PAH	exclamation of disgust, disbelief, etc
OOF	money		
		PAL	friend

PAM	knave of clubs	POD	seed case of peas
PAN	metal container for cooking	POH	exclamation expressing contempt
PAP	soft food, mash	POI	ball of woven flax
PAR	usual or average condition	POL	short for politician
PAS	dance step	POM	short for pommy
PAT	tap lightly	POO	defecate
PAV	short for pavlova	POP	make a small explosive sound
PAW	animal's foot	POS	plural form of po
PAX	kiss of peace	POT	round deep container
PAY	give money for goods	POW	sound imitative of a collision, explosion, etc
PEA	plant, vegetable	POX	disease
PEC	pectoral muscle	POZ	short for positive
PED	pannier	PRE	before
PEE	urinate	PRO	in favour of
PEG	pin or clip	PRY	make an impertinent inquiry
PEH	letter in the Hebrew alphabet	PSI	23rd letter of the Greek alphabet
PEN	instrument for writing in ink	PST	sound to attract attention
PEP	high spirits	PUB	building with a licensed bar
PER	for each	PUD	short for pudding
PES	technical name for foot	PUG	small snub-nosed dog
PET	animal kept for companionship	PUH	exclamation expressing contempt
PEW	seat in a church	PUL	Afghan monetary unit
PHI	21st letter in the Greek alphabet	PUN	play on words
PHO	noodle soup	PUP	young dog
PHT	expression of irritation or reluctance	PUR	obsolete form of purr
PIA	pious	PUS	yellowish fluid
PIC	photograph, picture	PUT	place in a position
PIE	pastry dish	PUY	small volcanic cone
PIG	animal	PYA	monetary unit of Myanmar
PIN	piece of stiff wire for fastening	PYE	book for finding Church services
PIP	small seed in a fruit	PYX	receptacle for the Eucharistic Host
PIR	Sufi master	QAT	shrub whose leaves have narcotic properties
PIS	plural form of pi	QIS	plural form of qi
PIT	hole in the ground	QUA	in the capacity of
PIU	musical term meaning more	RAD	former unit of radiation
PIX	photographs	RAG	fragment of cloth
PLU	beaver skin used as a unit of value		
PLY	work at (a job or trade)		
POA	type of grass		

RAH	US word for cheer	RIT	Scots word for cut or slit
RAI	type of Algerian pop music	RIZ	dialectal past form of rise
RAJ	(in India) government	ROB	steal from
RAM	male sheep	ROC	mythological bird
RAN	part of the verb to run	ROD	slender straight bar
RAP	hit with a sharp quick blow	ROE	mass of eggs in a fish
RAS	headland	ROK	mythological bird
RAT	long-tailed rodent	ROM	male gypsy
RAW	uncooked	ROO	kangaroo
RAX	stretch or extend	ROT	decompose or decay
RAY	single line of light	ROW	straight line of people or things
REB	soldier in the American Civil War	RUB	apply pressure and friction
REC	short for recreation ground	RUC	mythological bird
RED	colour	RUD	redness, flush
REE	Scots word for walled enclosure	RUE	feel regret for
REF	short for referee	RUG	small carpet
REG	short for registration number	RUM	alcoholic drink
REH	(in India) surface crust on the soil	RUN	move quickly
REI	former Portuguese coin	RUT	furrow made by wheels
REM	dose of ionizing radiation	RYA	Scandinavian rug
REN	archaic variant of run	RYE	grain
REO	language	SAB	short for saboteur
REP	short for representative	SAC	pouchlike structure in an animal
RES	residence	SAD	sorrowful, unhappy
RET	moisten or soak flax	SAE	Scots word for so
REV	revolution (of an engine)	SAG	sink in the middle
REW	archaic spelling of rue	SAI	capuchin monkey
REX	king	SAL	salt
REZ	reservation	SAM	collect, gather up
RHO	17th letter in the Greek alphabet	SAN	short for sanatorium
RHY	archaic spelling of rye	SAP	fluid that circulates in plants
RIA	long narrow inlet of the seacoast	SAR	marine fish
RIB	bone	SAT	part of the verb to sit
RID	clear or relieve (of)	SAU	archaic past form of see
RIF	discharge from military service	SAV	saveloy
RIG	arrange in a dishonest way	SAW	hand tool
RIM	edge or border	SAX	saxophone
RIN	Scots variant of run	SAY	speak or utter
RIP	tear violently	SAZ	musical instrument
		SEA	mass of salt water

304

SEC	short for second	SOH	musical term
SED	old spelling of said	SOL	liquid colloidal solution
SEE	perceive with the eyes or mind	SOM	monetary unit
SEG	metal stud on shoe sole	SON	male offspring
SEI	type of whale	SOP	concession to pacify someone
SEL	Scots word for self	SOS	plural form of so
SEN	monetary unit	SOT	habitual drunkard
SER	unit of weight	SOU	former French coin
SET	put in a specified position or state	SOV	sovereign
		SOW	scatter or plant
SEW	join with thread	SOX	informal spelling of socks
SEX	state of being male or female	SOY	(as in soy sauce) salty dark brown sauce
SEY	Scots word for part of cow		
SEZ	informal spelling of says	SPA	resort with a mineral-water spring
SHA	be quiet		
SHE	female person or animal	SPY	obtain secret information
SHH	sound made to ask for silence	SRI	title of respect
SHY	not at ease in company	STY	pigpen
SIB	blood relative	SUB	short for subeditor
SIC	so or thus	SUD	singular form of suds
SIF	South African slang for disgusting	SUE	start legal proceedings against
		SUI	of himself, herself, itself
SIK	Australian slang for excellent	SUK	open-air marketplace
SIM	simulation game on a computer	SUM	result of addition, total
SIN	offence or transgression	SUN	star around which the earth revolves
SIP	drink in small mouthfuls		
SIR	polite term of address for a man	SUP	swallow liquid
SIS	short for sister	SUQ	open-air marketplace
SIT	rest one's body on the buttocks and thighs	SUR	above
		SUS	become aware of
SIX	one more than five	SWY	gambling game
SKA	type of West Indian pop music	SYE	strain something
SKI	snow sport	SYN	Scots word for since
SKY	upper atmosphere	TAB	small flap or projecting label
SLY	crafty	TAD	small bit or piece
SMA	Scots word for small	TAE	Scots word for to
SNY	side channel of a river	TAG	label bearing information
SOB	weep with convulsive gasps	TAI	(as in tai chi chuan) Chinese system of callisthenics
SOC	feudal right to hold court		
SOD	(piece of) turf	TAJ	tall conical cap
SOG	soak	TAK	Scots word for take

TAM	short for tam-o'-shanter	TOC	communication code for T
TAN	coloration of the skin	TOD	unit of weight
TAO	philosophical term	TOE	digit of the foot
TAP	knock lightly	TOG	unit of thermal resistance
TAR	thick black liquid	TOM	male cat
TAS	cup, goblet, or glass	TON	unit of weight
TAT	tatty or tasteless article(s)	TOO	also, as well
TAU	19th letter in the Greek alphabet	TOP	highest point or part
TAV	22nd letter in the Hebrew alphabet	TOR	high rocky hill
		TOT	small child
TAW	convert skins into leather	TOW	drag, esp by means of a rope
TAX	compulsory payment levied	TOY	something designed to be played with
TAY	Irish dialect word for tea		
TEA	drink	TRY	make an effort or attempt
TEC	short for detective	TSK	expression of disapproval
TED	dry hay	TUB	open round container
TEE	small peg for golf	TUG	pull hard
TEF	grass grown for its grain	TUI	New Zealand bird
TEG	two-year-old sheep	TUM	stomach
TEL	large mound formed from accumulated rubbish	TUN	large beer cask
		TUP	male sheep
TEN	one more than nine	TUT	sound of mild reprimand
TES	plural form of te	TUX	short for tuxedo
TET	9th letter of the Hebrew alphabet	TWA	two
		TWO	one more than one
TEW	toil	TWP	stupid
TEX	unit of weight	TYE	trough used in mining
THE	definite article	TYG	cup with two handles
THO	short for though	UDO	perennial plant
THY	of or associated with you (thou)	UDS	'God's' or 'God save'
TIC	spasmodic muscular twitch	UEY	u-turn
TID	girl	UFO	flying saucer
TIE	fasten with string	UGH	exclamation of disgust
TIG	children's game	UGS	plural form of ug
TIL	another name for sesame	UKE	short for ukulele
TIN	soft metallic element	ULE	rubber tree
TIP	narrow or pointed end of anything	ULU	type of knife
		UMM	sound of hesitation
TIS	plural form of ti	UMP	short for umpire
TIT	small songbird	UMU	type of oven
TIX	tickets		

UNI	short for university	VOE	bay or narrow creek
UNS	plural form of un	VOL	short for volume
UPO	upon	VOR	(in dialect) warn
UPS	plural form of up	VOW	solemn and binding promise
URB	urban area	VOX	voice or sound
URD	type of plant with edible seeds	VUG	small cavity in a rock or vein
URE	extinct wild ox	VUM	swear, vow
URN	container for the ashes of the dead	WAB	Scots word for web
		WAD	small mass of soft material
URP	dialect word for vomit	WAE	old form of woe
USE	put into service or action	WAG	move rapidly from side to side
UTA	type of lizard	WAI	in New Zealand, water
UTE	utility vehicle	WAN	pale and sickly-looking
UTS	plural form of ut	WAP	strike
UTU	reward	WAR	fighting between nations
UVA	grape or berry	WAS	part of the verb to be
VAC	short for vacation	WAT	Thai Buddhist monastery or temple
VAE	bay or narrow creek		
VAG	vagrant	WAW	sixth letter of the Hebrew alphabet
VAN	motor vehicle for transporting goods		
		WAX	solid shiny fatty or oily substance
VAR	unit of reactive power		
VAS	vessel or tube that carries a fluid	WAY	manner or method
VAT	large container for liquids	WEB	net spun by a spider
VAU	sixth letter of the Hebrew alphabet	WED	marry
		WEE	small or short
VAV	sixth letter of the Hebrew alphabet	WEM	womb or belly
		WEN	cyst on the scalp
VAW	Hebrew letter	WET	covered or soaked with water
VEE	the letter V	WEX	wax
VEG	short for vegetable	WEY	measurement of weight
VET	check the suitability of	WHA	Scots word for who
VEX	frustrate, annoy	WHO	which person
VIA	by way of	WHY	for what reason
VID	video	WIG	artificial head of hair
VIE	compete (with someone)	WIN	come first in a competition
VIG	interest on a loan	WIS	know or suppose
VIM	force, energy	WIT	clever humour
VIN	French wine	WIZ	accomplished person, whizz
VIS	power, force, or strength	WOE	grief
VLY	low marshy ground	WOF	fool

WOG	Australian word meaning influenza
WOK	bowl-shaped Chinese cooking pan
WON	monetary unit
WOO	seek the love or affection of
WOP	strike or beat
WOS	plural form of wo
WOT	wit, to know
WOW	exclamation of astonishment
WOX	obsolete form of the verb to wax
WRY	drily humorous
WUD	Scots word for wood
WUS	casual term of address
WYE	the letter Y
WYN	rune equivalent to English W
XIS	plural form of xi
YAD	pointer used for reading the Torah
YAE	Scots word meaning one or a single
YAG	artificial crystal
YAH	exclamation of derision or disgust
YAK	Tibetan ox with long shaggy hair
YAM	tropical root vegetable
YAP	bark with a high-pitched sound
YAR	nimble
YAW	turn from side to side while moving
YAY	exclamation of approval
YEA	yes
YEH	yes
YEN	monetary unit of Japan
YEP	affirmative statement
YES	expresses consent
YET	up until then or now
YEW	evergreen tree
YEX	hiccup, belch
YGO	archaic form of the verb to go
YID	offensive word for a Jew
YIN	Scots word for one
YIP	emit a high-pitched bark
YOB	bad-mannered aggressive youth
YOD	10th letter in the Hebrew alphabet
YOK	chuckle
YOM	day
YON	that or those over there
YOS	plural form of yo
YOU	person or people addressed
YOW	variant of ewe
YUG	one of the four ages of mankind
YUK	expression of dislike or disgust
YUM	expression of delight
YUP	informal affirmative statement
YUS	plural form of yu
ZAG	change direction sharply
ZAP	kill (by shooting)
ZAS	plural form of za
ZAX	small axe for cutting slates
ZEA	type of grass
ZED	the letter Z
ZEE	the letter Z
ZEK	Soviet prisoner
ZEL	Turkish cymbal
ZEP	type of long sandwich
ZEX	tool for cutting roofing slate
ZHO	Tibetan breed of cattle
ZIG	change direction sharply
ZIN	short form of zinfandel
ZIP	fastener with two rows of teeth
ZIT	spot or pimple
ZIZ	short sleep
ZOA	plural form of zoon
ZOL	South African slang for a cannabis cigarette
ZOO	place where live animals are kept
ZOS	plural form of zo
ZUZ	silver coin of ancient Palestine
ZZZ	informal word for sleep